THE QUALITY JOURNEY

THE QUALITY

JOSEPH H. BOYETT
STEPHEN SCHWARTZ
LAURENCE OSTERWISE
AND ROY BAUER

JOURNEY

*How Winning the
Baldrige Sparked
the Remaking of
IBM*

Contains the Complete Text of IBM Rochester's
Winning Application for the
Malcolm Baldrige National Quality Award

A DUTTON BOOK

DUTTON
Published by the Penguin Group
Penguin Books USA Inc., 375 Hudson Street,
New York, New York 10014, U.S.A.
Penguin Books Ltd, 27 Wrights Lane, London W8 5TZ, England
Penguin Books Australia Ltd, Ringwood, Victoria, Australia
Penguin Books Canada Ltd, 10 Alcorn Avenue, Toronto, Ontario, Canada M4V 3B2
Penguin Books (N.Z.) Ltd, 182–190 Wairau Road, Auckland 10, New Zealand

Penguin Books Ltd, Registered Offices:
Harmondsworth, Middlesex, England

First published by Dutton, an imprint of Dutton Signet,
a division of Penguin Books USA Inc.
Distributed in Canada by McClelland & Stewart Inc.

First Printing, October, 1993
10 9 8 7 6 5 4 3 2 1

REGISTERED TRADEMARK—MARCA REGISTRADA

LIBRARY OF CONGRESS CATALOGING-IN-PUBLICATION DATA:
Boyett, Joseph H.
    The quality journey : how winning the Baldrige sparked the remaking of IBM / Joseph
H. Boyett; Stephen Schwartz, Laurence Osterwise, and Roy Bauer.
    p. cm.
Includes index.
ISBN 0-525-93659-9
1. International Business Machines Corporation. 2. Computer industry—United
States—Quality control. 3. Computer industry—United States—Management. 4.
Malcolm Baldrige National Quality Award. I. Schwartz, Stephen B. II. Title.
HD9696.C64I48316—1993
338.7'61004'0973—dc20   93-15203
                                                                      CIP

Printed in the United States of America
Set in Electra and Serifa
Designed by Eve L. Kirch

To the people of Rochester, who, individually and collectively, rose to a remarkable level of teamwork and excellence. In doing so, they became a guiding light for the transformation of IBM.

To the leaders of IBM, whose vision, wisdom, courage, and commitment made the Market-Driven Quality transformation of IBM possible.

Finally, to our families and friends, especially our wives and children, who always expected the best from us and would accept nothing less.

CONTENTS

Appendices

ACKNOWLEDGMENTS

This story of the transformation of IBM draws heavily upon the experiences of three of the four coauthors, Stephen B. Schwartz, Laurence L. Osterwise, and Roy A. Bauer, who were intimately involved in the events documented in this book. As such, this book is a personal reflection on the events at IBM during the last half of the 1980s and the first few years of the 1990s. To supplement these personal recollections and gather additional documentation, coauthor Joseph Boyett and principal researcher for this project Jimmie Towns Boyett conducted extensive interviews with IBM executives, managers, employees, business partners, and customers. We would like to express our sincere appreciation to all of those inside and outside IBM whose willingness to share their personal insights and experiences made this book possible. In particular, we are indebted to the following individuals whose input greatly enriched the story contained in these pages:

The IBM Senior Management Committee:

> John F. Akers, chairman of the board, IBM Corporation
> Jack D. Kuehler, vice chairman of the board, IBM
> Corporation

Terry R. Lautenbach, IBM senior vice president, retired
Frank A. Metz, Jr., IBM senior vice president, retired

Other IBM Executives, Managers, and Employees:

Kevin Anderson, manager of advanced systems, System
Management, IBM Rochester
Gerald J. Balm, senior quality engineer, IBM Corporate
Market-Driven Quality
Jim Buchanan, site education manager, IBM Rochester,
IBM Skill Dynamics
Tom Burcak, program manager, MDQ assessment, IBM
Corporate Market-Driven Quality, retired
Donald B. Butler, director of employee relations, Special
Programs, IBM
William J. Colucci, president, IBM Workforce Solutions
Raul Cosio, director of supply, manufacturing &
distribution, IBM Latin America
Heinz K. Fridrich, IBM vice president, Manufacturing
Thomas E. Furey, Jr., assistant general manager, IBM
Programming Systems; site general manager of Santa
Teresa Laboratory
Victor J. Goldberg, IBM vice president, Management Systems
Jim Grace, program manager, IBM Corporate Market-
Driven Quality
Robert J. Griffin, director AS/400 brand management,
Application Business Systems
Mike Jacobson, solutions offerings, Industrial Sector
Division, IBM
Lori Kirkland, program manager, MDQ Assessment, IBM
North America
Robert J. Labant, IBM senior vice president, general
manager, IBM U.S.
Mark E. Langman, process management director, IBM
Richard J. Martino, director of personnel programs, IBM
Asia Pacific Group
Dar Moen, administrative assistant to the site general
manager, IBM Rochester
George W. Moore, director of OEM Operations, IBM PC
Company

Ron Olness, manager of employee relations, IBM
Rochester, retired
Lazlo J. Papay, director of Market-Driven Quality Assessment,
IBM Corporate MDQ
Deb Pesch, Speak-up coordinator, IBM Rochester
Carl E. Ruoff, director of Market-Driven Quality—
Manufacturing and Development, IBM Corporate MDQ
Peter R. Schneider, IBM vice president, Development
Karl D. Shurson, production facility manager, IBM
Rochester, IBM ADSTAR
Leslie D. Simon, IBM director of public affairs
Robert F. Talbot, vice president and assistant general manager
services, Management Services, IBM Credit Corporation
Philip S. Thompson, director of development strategy,
Application Solutions Line of Business
Robert C. Timpson, vice president and area general manager,
Northeastern Area, IBM North America
Patrick A. Toole, IBM senior vice president,
Manufacturing and Development
Dick Ulland, staff communications specialist, IBM Rochester
Gus A. Vassiliades, IBM director, Manufacturing
Products and Processes
Earl F. Wheeler, IBM senior vice president and general
manager, Programming Systems

We would also like to express our gratitude to Jimmie Towns
Boyett. In addition to conducting much of the research for this
book, she helped develop questions for and participated in all of
the interviews that were conducted, wrote major sections of this
book, edited the numerous drafts of the manuscript, and oversaw
most of the administrative details associated with making this
book a reality. However this book might ultimately be judged, it
benefited greatly from her involvement.

For their help in compiling documentation and generally as-
sisting us with research for this book, we would like to thank
Bev Hermes, librarian, Olmsted County, Minnesota Historical
Society; and Jackie Daniels, research librarian, Dekalb County,
Georgia Public Library.

We also express our appreciation to Dr. Curt Reimann, director, Malcolm Baldrige National Quality Award, National Institute

of Standards and Technology; and Dr. Ruth Haines, director, Federal Quality Institute, for their assistance in helping us clarify the history of the Baldrige award.

Finally, we would like to thank our agent, Maria Carvainis, and editor, Hilary Ross, for their continuing interest in and support for this book. Their belief in the significance of the story we had to tell was a continuing source of inspiration.

All of the above deserve credit for what is right about this book. Any errors or omissions are ours alone.

Joseph H. Boyett
Stephen Schwartz
Laurence Osterwise
Roy Bauer
December 1992

INTRODUCTION

The Quality Journey is the inside story of how a leading American company tried to reinvent itself for the 1990s. On a more personal level, this book is about winning and losing and the efforts of well-intentioned men and women to learn both from success and from failure. The story of what happened to them and their company is told in their own words.

The Quality Journey is also about a three-part solid crystal stele, standing fourteen inches tall and containing an eighteen-karat gold-plated medal, the Malcolm Baldrige National Quality Award, that has become, in the words of *Fortune* magazine, the business equivalent of "the Grand Slam, the Academy Award, and the Pulitzer" all rolled into one.

Since 1987, the Malcolm Baldrige National Quality Award has captured the imagination of executives not just at IBM but at thousands of other American companies, both large and small. By 1992, practically every large American company and many smaller ones were assessing themselves against Baldrige criteria. Although only a few American companies had ever won the award, and the chances of any company's winning were very slim, hundreds of American companies had applied for the award and thousands were preparing to apply. Damned by some quality experts, the award was praised by many more. Yet there is little doubt that the award has a powerful impact on any American business that pursues it. It is clear that the Baldrige award criteria represent the best diagnostic tool available to companies today to help them reinvent themselves to meet the competition of the 1990s and beyond, if for no other reason than that the application asks the tough questions most American managers have never had to address. In doing so, the award forces managers to rethink how they run their businesses and to redesign them for the better.

The Quality Journey is the story of IBM's quest for the Baldrige award and the role the Baldrige award has played, and continues to play, in the company's transformation. But first and foremost, this book is about people. Specifically, it is the story of what happened to eight thousand people who work at IBM's Rochester, Minnesota, manufacturing and development site and who, in the mid-1980s, began a journey to total quality that continues today. Along the way, the people at Rochester developed one of the most successful products in IBM's history and won the Malcolm Baldrige National Quality Award. In the process, they became a model for the transformation of IBM that is even now impacting the lives of some 300,000 IBM employees around the world.

The pages that follow explain how the people at IBM Rochester, and at IBM in general, came to realize that they needed to change the way they ran their business, how they developed a vision for a new and better IBM, and how the Baldrige award helped them begin to realize that vision. Their story, as we said, is very much a human story. As such, it is filled with twists and turns, with triumphs and failures. It is also filled with the process of learning. How does a company like IBM reinvent itself? How can the pursuit of the Baldrige award help? Is the Baldrige just another award, or does the pursuit of the level of excellence framed by the Baldrige criteria really make a difference in how a company is run? More important, is the pursuit of the Baldrige worth the effort and expenditure? Does it really lead to lasting results? The pages that follow detail the sometimes painful path and long, long journey IBM took to answer those questions. Like so many human stories, this one begins with triumph followed by disaster.

1

From Dominance to Decline

In 1987, when the legislation creating the Malcolm Baldrige National Quality Award was passed, IBM was a colossus of American business, albeit a colossus in trouble. No one in IBM in 1987 expected the Baldrige award to play a pivotal role in IBM's future. But then, just a few years earlier, no one inside or outside IBM had expected the company to find itself in trouble. After all, the history of IBM was one of salesmanship, growth and a string of successes, not lingering troubles.

Everyone familiar with the history of the company was shocked at its troubles. What had happened to the icon of American business that had first built, then dominated the market for punch-card accounting equipment in the twenties, thirties and forties and then repeated that performance with computers in the fifties, sixties and seventies? Of course, as there always are, there were telltale signs of trouble long before the mid-1980s. But in the early to mid-1980s, few people inside or outside of IBM were noticing what was going wrong with IBM simply because so much was going right.

1

The Boom Years: 1981–1984

The early 1980s had been boom years for IBM. Between 1980 and 1984, IBM posted an average annual growth in data processing revenues of almost 20 percent. Its 1984 total revenues of $46 billion were $40 billion larger than its nearest competitor, Digital Equipment Corporation (DEC), and its annual *growth* in revenue actually exceeded DEC's *total* annual revenues four out of the five years of the early 1980s.

Table 1.1
DP Revenue Growth and Totals
IBM vs. DEC: 1980–1984

Year	IBM's DP Revenue*	IBM's Growth in DP Revenue*	DEC's DP Revenue*
1980	21,367	3,029	2,743
1981	26,340	4,973	3,587
1982	31,500	5,160	4,019
1983	35,603	4,103	4,827
1984	44,292	8,689	6,230

*In billions of dollars.
Source: *Datamation 100,* June 1981–1985 (annual reports).

According to published reports, IBM's stated goal in 1984 was to reach $185 billion in revenues by 1994, a compounded growth rate of 15 percent annually, which would likely put $100 billion between it and the next largest computer company.

Commenting on the period of the mid-1980s in a 1992 interview, a senior executive at IBM noted:

In the early to mid-1980s, IBM and the computer industry enjoyed some of the greatest growth years the industry had ever seen. There were the years in the '60s with the System/360 [mainframe computer]. There were some years in the '70s with minicomputers, but we had seen nothing like the early to mid-'80s before. Technology coalesced in large computers. The personal computer came on the scene and was a major success. And IBM's midrange computers enjoyed a great deal of success. During the first half of the '80s, the marketplace was absorbing enormous amounts of technology, so much that we could and did just sit back and take orders.

It was the "best of times" for IBM. In its May 1985 issue, *The Economist*, reflecting upon IBM's outstanding performance for 1984, noted that IBM was "on top of the world" with profitability that almost defied gravity. It made 70 percent of the profits of the computer industry, had 70 percent of the market for mainframes, and controlled 40 percent of the market for personal computers, up from 0 percent just three years previously. Its dominance in mainframes, where profit margins reached 75 percent, was so complete that the mere announcement of a new computer model by IBM could effectively freeze the market as customers refused to buy any other company's product between the time of the IBM announcement and the first shipment of new IBM machines, which could be months away. IBM seemed invincible and it exuded confidence. Yet there were disturbing signs that trouble might lie ahead.

IBM's venture into the home computer market, with its PCjr, had been an embarrassing failure. In spite of aggressive attacks on its competitors that had led to antitrust suits in the 1970s, plenty of competitors remained to give IBM headaches. There was dawning recognition that the 50 to 60 percent annual increase in demand for mainframe processing power necessary for IBM to achieve its ambitious growth plan might not occur as customers scaled back their acquisitions and moved more processing to smaller midrange and/or microcomputers. Finally, and most ominously, there was a dip in IBM's 1985 first-quarter earnings, the first in three years. And second-quarter 1985 earnings looked disappointing. Never mind, said IBM, the sales of new computers and a lower dollar will lift revenues in the remaining two quarters. But they didn't.

Table 1.2
Revenue Growth 1981–1987
IBM vs. the Datamation U.S. 100

Year	IBM's Total DP Revenue (in millions)	IBM's Percent DP Revenue Growth	Percent DP Revenue Growth—Remaining Datamation Top U.S. 100
1981	$26,340	23.3	21.1
1982	31,500	19.6	15.5
1983	35,603	13.0	17.3
1984	44,292	24.4	12.7
1985	48,554	9.6	11.1
1986	49,591	2.1	12.5
1987	50,486	1.8	14.7

Source: *Datamation 100,* 1982–1988 (annual reports).

The Bust

At first, there wasn't a lot of concern. Nineteen eighty-five had been a bad year for the industry in general, and one could always blame the "uncertain North American economy, currency fluctuations, [and] sluggish capital spending," as *Datamation* reported in its June 15, 1986, issue. In November 1985, *Forbes* noted, "Fundamentally, the computer slump is a major market correction, the kind that refreshes a major trend and gets it ready to resume its upward course." It did, but not for IBM.

In March 1986, *Business Week* asked the question on everyone's mind, "What's Wrong at IBM?" The computer industry had shown signs of an upturn, but IBM was reporting weak first-quarter earnings and its stock had dropped ten points. The market for mainframes, which were so critical to IBM, *Business Week* noted, had slowed markedly, and IBM's newest large system, the 3090 series, wasn't selling as well as expected. Its personal computer was becoming less profitable because of price cutting forced on IBM by cheaper, knockoff clones, and sales were also disappointing for IBM in midrange computers, such as its System/36.

Problems in the Midrange

IBM's problems with its midrange computers were, in many respects, typical of the problems the company as a whole was experiencing. IBM had gotten into a new series of midrange computers in 1969 when it released its System/3 computer. The System/3 was designed to address the needs of smaller businesses that wanted easy-to-operate computers with a wide range of ready-to-use software which performed such tasks as planning, scheduling, office administration, and so on. It was followed in 1975 by the introduction of the System/32, the first in the line of System/3X products which would offer customers "upward compatibility." When the System/34 was announced in 1977, customers were able to move from one machine to the next newest and not have to rewrite software or make major changes to their operations. Then in 1978, IBM announced a much more powerful midrange machine that was to become the darling of sophisticated users and "techies"—the System/38. In power and technical capabilities, the System/38 was like a supercharged race car, compared with the "family sedan" System/3 series, but it was incompatible with the System/3 computers.

In addition to the System/3 series and the System/38, IBM had three other midrange computers—the 8100, the Series/1, and the 4300. Each was developed as a stand-alone unit by different IBM development labs and couldn't share software or data with each other or with other IBM computers. This incompatibility presented IBM with a serious problem.

With the proliferation of computers of all sizes in the late 1970s and early 1980s, customers were demanding that their different size machines—mainframes, midrange departmental machines, and personal computers, which were just beginning to explode into the business world—be able to "talk" to each other and share information. Midrange users, primarily departments and small businesses, were demanding the ability to upgrade and expand their equipment without having to undergo costly, time-consuming, and risky conversions of application programs and data files.

IBM was losing out on both counts. Its various midrange machines were incompatible, so business applications like inventory or billing that ran on one model wouldn't run on another. And some of its machines, such as the System/36, which had been introduced in 1983 as an ongoing solution, were rapidly running out of horsepower. They simply wouldn't be able to continue to handle the processing needs of their users.

IBM's compatibility and horsepower problems in its midrange line were golden opportunities for their competition. Hewlett-Packard, Wang, Data General, Tandem, NCR, Olivetti, Nixdorf, Fujitsu, and DEC in particular were grabbing customers and taking market share from IBM.

The Failure of the Fort Knox Project

In an attempt to resolve these problems and regain market share, IBM launched a project, code-named Fort Knox, in 1982. Fort Knox was supposed to find a single replacement for the five separate and incompatible midrange systems IBM had at the time. Roy Bauer, Emilio Collar and Victor Tang describe the purpose and challenge of the Fort Knox project in their 1992 book *The Silverlake Project* as follows:

> The idea behind Fort Knox was straightforward. It was to serve as the single successor to IBM's diverse midrange machines. Customers who owned different machines would be able to move their data and software onto a Fort Knox. While that sounds simple enough, making Fort Knox compatible with all those other machines posed a mind-boggling undertaking. If IBM made cars instead of computers, Fort Knox would have been tantamount to combining the features of a sports car, a station wagon, a compact, a luxury car, and a pickup truck into a single all-appealing vehicle.

The Fort Knox project involved over four thousand IBM employees at four development labs and followed IBM's traditional process for product development. It didn't work. There were many reasons why Fort Knox failed, but it failed mainly because, while perhaps technically feasible, the problems of merging five separate machines were daunting. Perhaps more importantly, the programmers and engineers working on the project in the four separate labs hung tenaciously on to the features and functions they wanted, regardless of what IBM's customers wanted or needed, and could never reach consensus. Eventually, Fort Knox became a "five-hump camel" and had to be put out of its misery. It was an example of the kind of failure to listen to customers and respond rapidly and effectively to market demands that would create problems for IBM in the coming years.

Yet, in spite of such failures, IBM executives continued to maintain that the company's sluggish performance was merely temporary and largely due to matters beyond their control. But, for analysts and other IBM watchers, the explanations from IBM management were beginning to raise even more questions than they answered.

Revolution in the Industry

It wasn't that IBM didn't attempt to respond to the slump. By the end of 1986, IBM reduced its inflated work force by five thousand and had announced that it would eliminate an additional twelve thousand positions in 1987, mainly through retirement and attrition. In the midrange field, IBM had started delivering its 9370 computer, a S/370-based solution to the midrange problem, hoping that it would fill a hole in its midrange computer family. And the company had announced a new generation of personal computers to enthusiastic response by analysts. Yet the entire computer industry had fundamentally changed. It was simultaneously undergoing a revolution in customer expectations, competition and technology. The "phenomena" of customer demands for compatibility and ease of use was not limited to the midrange consumer. The traditional IBM customer, the MIS directors who faithfully bought IBM mainframes, had been joined by those who bought microcomputers for home and office use, as well as by the minicomputer customer. IBM customers, from micros to mainframes, demanded the same capabilities. "I want my personal computer to 'talk' to my mainframe." "I want my Series/1 to run my System/38 software." "I want to buy a larger computer, and I want my old software to run on it."

Worst of all, these same customers were asking IBM, "Fujitsu can do it, so why can't you?" IBM still had to worry about their historic competitors like DEC, Amdahl, Hewlett-Packard, Honeywell and Burroughs, but names like Hitachi, NEC, Nixdorf and Siemens were joining the list. The competition for market share in the computer industry had become truly international by the early 1980s, and IBM was, like many other U.S. companies, still trying to figure out how to function in this new global market.

In the midst of this revolution, industry growth was diminishing, and IBM was having trouble adapting to the new realities. A group of angry customers made that point to IBM executives, in no uncertain terms, in the fall of 1986.

Showdown at Purchase

Since the early 1970s, IBM had made a practice of holding strategic planning conferences in the spring and fall of each year. Attended by senior IBM executives, these conferences focused on subjects that would become the foundation for major changes in the company. For example, a conference in 1977 had resulted in preparations that ultimately led to the creation of the IBM personal computer.

For the fall 1986 conference, John Akers, IBM's chairman and CEO, asked his director of market research and manager of market information and analysis to come up with something a little different. They brought back a proposal to invite senior executives from IBM customer companies to participate in the conference and react to the presentations IBM executives would be making. These customers then would be asked to present their views on IBM. Customers had *never* been invited to such conferences before, so the idea was totally foreign to IBM's culture. When presented with the idea, Akers didn't respond for a few minutes. Then he said, "Okay, let's try it." It was to become a watershed decision.

The conference began shortly after 1:00 P.M. on Tuesday, November 4, 1986, in a conference room at IBM's offices in Purchase, New York. Eighteen of IBM's top executives and six customers were seated around a horseshoe-shaped conference table. The guest customer executives included Richard Bourgerie, vice president and group executive of Allied-Signal; Hiroyuki Yoshino, director and board member of Honda Motor Company; Arthur Ryan, vice chairman of Chase Manhattan Bank; Yoshio (Terry) Terasawa, executive vice president of Nomura Securities Company; Sydney (Bud) McMorran, executive vice president of Toronto-Dominion Bank; and Heinrich Steinmann, executive vice president of Union Bank of Switzerland.

Akers opened the meeting by introducing the guest executives. Then he said, "We are not here to make final decisions. We are here to discuss and debate." Skeptical about whether Akers really wanted to hear their opinions, the customer executives sat back and waited as Akers turned over the meeting to Bill Filip, IBM's director of business plans, for what was to be a two-hour presentation on the long-range business outlook.

Filip began his presentation. The information industry will have a slower growth rate over the next ten years than previously forecast, he stated. Instead of 19 percent a year, Filip's projection showed 12 percent. Revenues that were currently split 42 percent software and services and 58 percent hardware, he said, would move to a 50/50 split by 1994. Then Filip put up a chart showing the world economy in a state of tentative equilibrium. There are positives and negatives, he said, and he began to discuss the two. At that point, Terry Terasawa of Nomura Securities broke in. "I don't know about this chart," he said. "I think the U.S. dollar is getting stronger again. Japan's discount rate is lowering. I think the U.S. dollar may regain strength against the Japanese yen."

Arthur Ryan of Chase Manhattan then spoke up. He agreed with Terasawa. "The deficit outlook is poor at best. The economy is going to hobble along, but we have a much more pessimistic outlook."

With that, the dam broke and the customer executives became full-fledged participants in what had once been the most private of IBM meetings. The customer comments rapidly turned from the state of the world economy to what they thought of IBM, and a lot of what they had to say wasn't very flattering. For example:

In a lot of cases, you look too much at problems the way you see them, not the way we see them.

We need better communication. You need to tell us what you're planning.

We're committed to reducing our development cycle time. We want you to do the same. Everything you do is too slow.

You don't provide consistent worldwide service for our multinational operations.

You have to listen to the customer thoroughly and carefully before designing a product or providing a service.

You're dealing with new kinds of customers. Once you sold almost exclusively to the information systems people, the computer specialists. Now, as computers become pervasive in all aspects of business, you must be able to sell to everyone.

You have to get rid of some of the acronyms and talk in real words that I and other executives can understand.

We need IBM's help in planning, developing and implementing solutions if we are to meet the many new competitive challenges we face in the evolving international marketplace.

There's a lot of talk about products, but there have to be some shifts in IBM's thinking. My problem is solutions, not what products do I buy. It's how do I deliver a service to my customers? How do I get an edge?

We have to understand what it is IBM is doing and, more importantly, what IBM would like to do for us. IBM has to talk to us.

We now make software decisions, not hardware decisions. In the past, we might have bought IBM and then built the software. Today we buy the software and run it on the equipment it was designed to run on. It's not a question of looking for you to give us the latest and greatest technology.

For the next two days, the customers went on with their complaints and concerns, venting their frustration with IBM. John

Akers sat back, listened, took notes and made assignments on the spot for IBM executives to fix the things customers were telling him were wrong. The other IBM executives who were present expressed their dismay and frustration and promised to make changes.

At the conclusion of the three-day conference, Akers summarized what he had heard:

> We have learned from this experience that our customers need a clear statement of our product and technology directions—a statement that is repeatable and understandable. We also recognize that we have to get our products to market faster. In fact, we have to do everything in IBM faster than we've ever done it before.
>
> On the technical side, this conference has reiterated the importance of software in selling hardware and that packaged solutions and systems integration—putting it all together—are fundamental to our success.
>
> Our guests have pointed out to us that the global market is not just rhetoric. We need to be more consistent in our offerings to them and ensure continuous availability of our systems. We should enhance our partnerships with our customers and nurture and develop their trust with more two-way communications.
>
> Our customers have also told us that IBM is in a unique position to help, and my message to our customers is: We hear you, and we will meet those challenges with excellence.

The Need for Fundamental Change

IBM's 1986 Purchase conference became a turning point in the history of the company. If nothing else, it brought home to John Akers and his closest advisors the fact that the answer to the question *Business Week* had posed—"What's Wrong at IBM?"—was simple: *plenty*. And it wasn't getting any better.

IBM ended 1986 with virtually no increase in revenues, its worst showing in forty years. Profits were down for the second year in a row. Still, IBM earned close to $5 billion in 1986, more than any other company in the world, and had a 14 percent return on equity. Such performance wasn't *bad* by normal company standards, but IBM wasn't a normal company in the eyes of the world. "The world does not expect mere competence from IBM," said *Fortune* in a January 1987 story, "it expects heroics." The world just wasn't getting what it expected from IBM and questioned whether it ever would again. Was something fundamentally wrong with the company that had become, in the words of *Fortune* magazine, a "near-icon," "national asset," and "symbol of managerial and technological excellence"? Would there ever again be a powerful, invincible, hugely profitable Big Blue? No one knew and it didn't seem very likely—*not without some fundamental changes.*

It was a lesson IBM as a corporation was just beginning to learn, and that lesson was the starting point for their transformation. But, it was a lesson IBM's midrange manufacturing and development site at Rochester, Minnesota, nicknamed "Fortress Rochester," had already learned. For the next few years, what happened at IBM Rochester would eerily foreshadow what was to happen to IBM as a corporation.

2

Fortress Rochester

In her book *The Doctors Mayo*, Helen Clapesattle describes Rochester, Minnesota, in this way:

If you take a bus from Minneapolis to Rochester, Minnesota, you ride southward for ninety miles through a rolling countryside that in summer is a patchwork quilt in the greens of corn, small grains, clover, and alfalfa. The black and white of grazing cattle and the recurring pattern of a hip-roofed barn flanked by the tall pillar of a silo tell you that this is a dairy land.

The towns that interrupt at every ten or fifteen miles are small, some of them just a few stores and houses grouped around a filling station at a crossroads, others large enough to boast a bank, a hotel above one of the cafes, perhaps a cheese factory or a cannery, and a furniture store that is also the undertaker's establishment. They might all be called, as one of them is, Farmington, for they exist solely as service stations for the farmers.

And then suddenly from the crest of a hill you see the metropolitan skyline of Rochester. Among the dairy farms and market villages you have come upon a city of great hospitals and crowded hotels; a city with hundreds of acres of parks and playgrounds, with fine stores and specialty shops; a city that is a crossroads of airlines, railroads, and national highways.

Here in the rural calm of southern Minnesota, without a scenic wonder or historic shrine in sight, is a city of thirty thousand inhabitants [approximately seventy thousand in 1990] that has an annual transient population of ten times that number. For here, in this "little town on the edge of nowhere," is one of the world's greatest medical centers, to which men come from the ends of the earth for treatment and instruction.

This is the paradox of Rochester.

Of course, Clapesattle is speaking of the Mayo Clinic and its associated hospitals when she refers to the "world's greatest medical centers." What she doesn't mention in her description is that located just a few miles north of the famous Mayo Clinic is the IBM Rochester development and manufacturing site.

Housed in a sprawling main complex of two-story interlocking blue buildings which are large enough to hold seventy football fields, this "nice little business in the corn fields," as it is called by those who work there, is the second largest employer in Rochester and, if it were not a division of the IBM corporation, would be the second largest computer company in the world, second only to IBM itself.

There have been three highly significant events in the history of the city of Rochester, Minnesota. The first was a devastating tornado that swept through the town on a sweltering hot summer day in 1883 killing twenty-four people, seriously injuring forty others, and all but destroying one-third of the town. The second was the creation of what became the world-famous Mayo Clinic shortly after the 1883 tornado. The third significant event was IBM's decision in 1956 to locate a plant in Rochester.

IBM's decision to locate in Rochester resulted from the company's nationwide search for new manufacturing sites, coupled with the determined courting by a group of two hundred Rochester business, professional, labor and civic leaders. Local legend adds the fortunate circumstance that an old World War II buddy of Thomas Watson, Jr., son and successor to IBM's founder, Thomas Watson, Sr., happened to live there.

Regardless of which factor had the greatest influence, IBM did locate in Rochester and built an $8 million, 550,000 square-foot manufacturing plant that, after construction, was expected to employ fifteen hundred people by 1958. For the first ten years of its existence, Rochester was primarily involved in manufacturing components for computers, particularly devices to read, collate and prepare punch cards that were the staple for processing computer data at the time. In the 1960s, the Rochester plant grew in size and employment and expanded from pure manufacturing into development with its own core of engineers and programmers. By 1969, the site was manufacturing the first totally Rochester-developed midrange computer, the System/3. In later years, it would develop and manufacture the System/32, System/34, System/38, and finally in 1983 the System/36, all in the midrange family. Since Rochester produced midrange computers, it became a key participant in the Fort Knox project when it was launched in 1982 and was severely impacted by the cancellation of the project a few years later.

The Crisis

If the failure of the Fort Knox effort was a problem for IBM—and it was a major problem—canceling the Fort Knox project was devastating to IBM Rochester, although many Rochester employees didn't yet realize the seriousness of the situation. By the summer of 1985, both the System/36 and the System/38 were rapidly becoming senior products by industry standards. Compared to the faster and more sophisticated machines available from, or under development by, the competition, they would soon represent old technology.

With the forty-to-sixty-month traditional timeframe for developing a new line of computers in IBM and the loss of several years of precious development time because of the failure of the Fort Knox project, IBM Rochester was facing the prospect of being without a product line in a very few years. Many at Rochester were comfortable with the continuing revenue stream the System/36 and System/38 were generating at the time and didn't yet fully recognize the seriousness of the problem they were facing. But they *were* facing a problem. In a few short years, the System/36 and System/38 no longer would be competitive. IBM Rochester would become a site without a mission, and, in IBM, a site without a mission tended to dry up and blow away or fragment into a bunch of little missions. Either way, it wasn't a fun outlook or prospect. Rochester was facing a genuine crisis, and key IBM executives were worried about what might happen to the site. They could see nothing good coming from the cancellation of Fort Knox, but they were wrong. While it certainly didn't seem so at the time, the cancellation of Fort Knox would prove to be one of the best things that could have happened to Rochester and to IBM, since it left Rochester's management with no alternative but to change the way they ran their business. The old ways of doing things were no longer enough. If it hoped to create a new product line in time to save itself, Rochester would be forced to fundamentally and radically change its approach to product development. In the process, it would significantly improve its product quality and its relationship with its customers, as well as set an example for the rest of IBM. But first, some breakthrough thinking was required.

The Breakthrough Idea

The breakthrough idea was a brainchild of Rochester engineer and programmer Pete Hanson. A "gear head" who drove hot rods and snowmobiles in his spare time, Hanson had been a blunt and outspoken critic of the Fort Knox project from the beginning. He was totally convinced that it would never work and wasn't at all reluctant to voice his disagreement with the approach.

By early 1985, months before Hanson was proved right and Fort Knox was canceled, he had gone to the head of Rochester's programming development, Dave Schleicher, and sought permission to recruit a five-person team to investigate the possibility of creating a single machine by combining the System/36 and System/38. Given the okay to proceed, Hanson assembled a mix of talents to work with him: Larry Whitley, a System/36 engineer and hardware designer; Tom Konakowitz, a product planner; Wayne Richards, a technologist; and Erik Thorpe, a former IBM salesman.

Hanson and his team originally named their project "Passport" and then renamed it "Silverlake" after the famous local power plant reservoir Silver Lake. The reservoir had gained local notoriety because it never froze, even during the coldest winter, as a result of the constant inflow of heated water from the power plant. Consequently, it attracted thousands of Canadian geese who made the lake their winter home, and it served as a kind of tourist attraction and therapy for Mayo Clinic patients and their families.

Hanson's proposal to create a single machine out of the System/36 and System/38 wasn't new. Efforts to create a single follow-on product for the two machines had been tried before, but all previous efforts had failed. Yet Hanson and his Silverlake crew succeeded. They did so with the kind of breakthrough thinking that is usually necessary for fundamental change.

Previous efforts to build a single machine to replace the System/36 and System/38 had begun with one inviolate assumption which had been accepted as a given by nearly everyone at IBM. The new machine would have to be built off the System/36. There were two reasons for this. First, there were ten times more System/36 users than System/38 users, and that large a customer base couldn't be abandoned. Second, a System/38 unit cost $1 million, versus $10,000 for the System/36. Thus, a new computer based upon the System/38 would undoubtedly be too expensive as a replacement product for System/36 customers. But the System/38 had advanced features like integrated relational data bases, security and communications, as well as some advanced programming concepts, all of which were important features for future development. The problem was that every time anyone tried to take System/38 applications and run them on a System/36 in emulation mode (i.e., making the System/36 operate like a System/38), the System/36 slowed to a crawl and then died.

Hanson and his crew succeeded by ignoring the previous "inviolate" assumptions and turning things upside-down. "Why not," they reasoned, "try running System/36 applications in emulation mode on a much more powerful System/38?" They did just that and succeeded. Not only did the System/38 run the System/36 applications, but it actually hummed. In a spring 1985 demonstration to Rochester management, the Silverlake team proved that their concept of building a System/38-based follow-on product was at least technically feasible. Of course, the system they had built didn't work perfectly, and it was a far cry from something IBM could sell. But they proved that their concept would work in principle.

By the fall of 1985, the Silverlake team had further refined their concept. Yet they were still far from having something they wanted to show to IBM senior management, particularly their new division head, Stephen Schwartz. They hadn't counted on Schwartz's curiosity about new ideas.

Enter Steve Schwartz

Steve Schwartz, a native of Chicago, had joined IBM in 1957 after graduating from Northwestern University with a degree in industrial engineering. Schwartz had held a variety of positions in IBM in sales, development, and general management. In 1985, after spending three years in Japan as vice president of IBM's Asia Staff Operations, he was tapped to head IBM's newly created Systems Products Division, of which IBM Rochester was a part.

Schwartz made the first trip to Rochester in his new capacity in late November 1985. He quickly discovered that with the cancellation of Fort Knox, most of the development focus at Rochester had turned to pumping a little more life into the System/36 and System/38. However, as he toured the facility, Schwartz began to hear rumors about the Silverlake team. Always interested in a new idea, Schwartz was anxious to see what this project was all about, since he was worried about the future of the Rochester site and was eager to see anything that might provide a solution. The Silverlake team resisted. But Schwartz insisted on seeing something, so the Silverlake team finally agreed to a demonstration in January 1986. Only later did Schwartz realize what he had been asking the team to do:

> They committed to give a live demo of this concept the second week in January. The thing I should have realized, because I didn't know the Rochester people then, was that they would work around the clock from that point on—through Thanksgiving, through Christmas, weekends, nights—to produce something they felt they could show me. In January, as they had promised, they came in and were able to demonstrate exactly what they said they would demonstrate. It was a prototype and it was a feasibility study and there was a lot of work between that and something you could deliver to the marketplace, but they proved the feasibility with the prototype.

What they actually demonstrated was a fairly sophisticated manufacturing application package running on both systems.

Schwartz was impressed. Maybe this was a way out of Rochester's bind and IBM's bind, he thought. He just needed to know two things—how much it would cost and how long it would take. The Rochester team didn't know how much it would cost. For time, they gave him the standard IBM answer—probably fifty or sixty months.

"That's terrific," replied Schwartz, "but irrelevant. If it takes you fifty or sixty months, we won't still be in the business." Schwartz had already had several meetings on this with all the people in Rochester. Everyone agreed that if they didn't deliver a replacement midrange computer by the summer of 1988, all of the discussions would be academic. So he gave them the marching orders: "Go back and give me a plan to get there by the summer of 1988 and tell me what the odds are on making it."

The Thousand-to-One Shot

A few weeks later, the Rochester team returned with their graphs, charts and estimates, and Schwartz went before IBM's senior management with his proposal. He described Silverlake and what the Rochester people hoped to accomplish. The whole idea was feasible, he told them, but expensive and a long shot. The price tag would be nearly $1 billion. Then Schwartz held up a huge chart showing what had to be done and the time line to get there.

"Here we are now," he said, "and here is the product introduction date in 1988. Here are five key checkpoints, each shown in red. Today our odds of making it are a thousand to one." Schwartz pointed to the third checkpoint. "If we get to here and are successful," he said, "our odds improve to five hundred to one. Here at the next checkpoint, they get better. I can't promise you we'll succeed, but we've got a shot at making something happen. The only thing we can promise you is that we will know what our odds are along the way, and we will keep you informed."

At that point Schwartz paused and drew a breath. This was

the senior management committee at IBM. Like the top executive team at any company, it was not a group you wanted to irri-
tate. But the stakes were too high for Schwartz, Rochester and
IBM for him to pull his punches now. "There is only one thing,"
he said. "If we are going to have any chance at all, we've got to
run this project like our own business. We make our own decisions. We don't spend a lot of time interacting with the bureaucracy. If you'll agree to that, we've got a chance. If not, we
shouldn't even try."

John Akers gave him the nod, and the others agreed. They really had no alternative.

The Small Company Environment

From then on, Rochester began operating as a small company.
They did their own planning, created their own development and
manufacturing approaches, developed their own profit and loss
statements, did their own costing, established their own terms
and conditions, and did their own direct reporting to IBM's senior management committee.

The executive level of IBM accepted Rochester's unique inde-
pendence because they had seen the Silverlake presentation, and
they knew the terms and conditions of the "thousand-to-one"
shot. They also knew Rochester and its excellent reputation for
performance. If any site could pull this off, it was Rochester.

For the next two and a half years, Schwartz constantly ran in-
terference for Rochester. Akers backed him every time and supported a direct communication channel to his office so Schwartz
and/or Rochester could reach him in minutes or hours, not in
the normal days and weeks, if they needed him. Furthermore,
Akers backed away from the day-to-day and week-to-week reviews. He asked for a report on how they were doing only once
a year, a reporting schedule unheard of in IBM. Commenting on
the importance of the "small company" environment, Schwartz
said in a 1992 interview:

> I don't think we would have been able to make the fundamental
> changes we had to make if John had not agreed to allow us to op-
> erate as our own business. The only way we had a chance of making

it work was if everyone left us alone. So we were allowed to run Rochester like an independent business and make our own decisions, and we didn't have to spend a lot of time interacting with the bureaucracy. That also allowed us to say, "We have no one to blame but ourselves if we can't make it happen." Akers turned us loose to succeed or fail. It was up to us.

Enter Tom Furey

No sooner had Schwartz sold the senior management committee of IBM on a "thousand-to-one" shot than he faced a critical problem. The head of Rochester's development lab, Tony Mondello, left Rochester to take another position in IBM. Just at the start of what was perhaps the most critical development effort in Schwartz's career, he was left without a manager to head the development effort. He needed to get someone to Rochester quickly. And he needed someone good. He turned to Tom Furey.

Furey, who held a degree in mathematics from the University of Massachusetts, had joined IBM in 1963 as a systems engineer. Later he had held several management positions at IBM's Kingston, New York, lab, where he had worked on mainframe computer operating systems and telecommunications products. Schwartz had worked with Furey on several occasions in the past and had grown to like his management style, which, among other things, involved relying heavily on reaching consensus with his people for major decisions. At the time Schwartz asked him to go to Rochester, Furey was the director of IBM's telecommunications strategy. After several discussions, Schwartz convinced Furey to go to Rochester. It was only later, after he had been there a few days, that Furey began to realize that Schwartz had not fully explained the challenges Furey would be facing.

Furey arrived in Rochester in late February 1986. He described his first impressions as follows:

When I got there, I discovered that very little work had been done on the proposal Schwartz had presented to the management committee. Worse, Schwartz had neglected to mention to me that they still had seven models of the System/36 and System/38 to get out before they could even get to work on this new project. I took one look at Rochester and felt like I had bought a pig in a poke.

If Furey wasn't too pleased with Rochester, the Rochester people weren't too excited about Furey either. To them Furey was an outsider, an East Coast "smoothie," and an "executive type." It wasn't love at first sight, by a long shot. They couldn't understand why Schwartz would pick this guy. Later, they came to appreciate Schwartz's choice.

The Warring Tribes

Furey's first impression of Rochester was that very little had been done to move the Silverlake project along since Akers had given them the go-ahead. He soon found out why. The System/36 and System/38 developers were barely speaking to each other. Furey immediately put in a call to Schwartz:

Steve, listen, the System/36 and System/38 people down here, they're like warring tribes. They spend more time competing with each other than they do competing with the real competition. Unless we can somehow get them together, I think our odds here are going to be a lot worse than a thousand to one.

Schwartz's response was disconcerting, to say the least. "Umh," said Schwartz. "I was afraid that might be the case."

Furey, wondering what else Schwartz might be afraid was the case but had not told him, said, "Give me an opportunity to see if I can get the team focused on the challenge they are facing. I'll call you back in ninety days and tell you if I think this thing is still feasible."

For the next few weeks, Furey held a series of roundtable discussions with his people, listening to what they had to say and trying to get into their psyche. What would motivate them to complete this project within the time frame they had? It didn't take him long to understand the rivalry between the two groups.

While the System/36 and System/38 people agreed that precious time had been wasted on the Fort Knox effort, they agreed about little else. The System/36 had been the most successful of the two computer systems, but the System/38 was a technically more advanced product. The System/36 people saw the Silverlake proposal, with its idea of basing the new system on the System/38, as just as misguided as the Fort Knox project had been. They could just see the "System/38 bigots" taking over, the whole thing becoming a horror show and its never working. Plus, the System/36 people were worried about their own future. They knew they couldn't work on a System/38 machine. The difference between the two machines was like the difference between a Romance language and a Slavic language. It wasn't like moving from French to Italian, where you might be able to fake your way through it. This was a totally different thing. They would need a lot of training to work on a System/38-type machine. So what was going to happen to them? They couldn't program a System/38. They couldn't design circuits for it. But they were in the majority, and they knew one thing. It was going to be a disaster.

Instead of getting depressed at what he heard, the more Furey talked to his people, the more he began to see a way out. Furey knew that IBM employed a significant number of the local work force and was as important to the local economy as the Mayo Clinic. In fact, shortly after arriving at Rochester he heard a local joke, derived from a combination of civic pride and the anxiety that the city had because it was largely dependent on two employers. The joke went, "There's only one business in Rochester—keeping the Mayo Clinic and IBM content."

Fortress Rochester

Over the years, Rochester had kept IBM happy. The city provided the company with a dependable, productive, inventive but frequently stubborn and anxiety-prone work force which was strongly independent and usually distrustful of anyone or anything from "back east." Since few IBMers wanted to be transferred to the frigid Midwest, IBM Rochester recruited, for the most part, native midwesterners to meet its needs. It ended up with a solid core of small-town farmers' sons and daughters from states like Minnesota, Iowa, Nebraska, Wisconsin and North Dakota. With a strongly ingrained work ethic, they were fiercely loyal to IBM Rochester, if not necessarily to IBM. They loved their lifestyle, their city and their jobs. They didn't want to leave Rochester but knew they might have to if, one day, IBM decided they couldn't produce anymore and "pulled the plug." They were protective of their site and suspicious of the rest of IBM. Consequently, within IBM they were given the nickname of "Fortress Rochester."

Furey concluded that if he could play off this "fortress" mentality and off the anger and frustration that both groups felt about the Fort Knox failure, then he might be able to bring them together. Plus, both groups felt underappreciated for their accomplishments and technical prowess. If he could play up the things that they did well and get them to focus on the real competition, rather than fighting with each other, then maybe the project could be completed on schedule. He decided to call Schwartz back and give him the good news.

"This thing might work," he told Schwartz. "We might not be able to finish this project as early in 1988 as you want, but I think if we get them working together, we can do it by sometime in '88." Schwartz gave him the go-ahead.

With Schwartz's approval, Furey had to get two things done right away if he was going to get the development team on track. First, he needed a different organizational structure, one that would get the System/36 and System/38 people working with each other rather than against each other. Second, he had to convince them that this crisis was real. He would spend the next three or four months concentrating on those two things.

Restructuring to Focus on the Competition

Furey already had some ideas about the structure he wanted. First, he felt he needed part of the organization focused on the challenge of delivering the new models of the System/36 and System/38 that would be necessary to keep the business alive and satisfy current customers until the Silverlake project could be finished sometime in 1988. That was what he considered the immediate, "Today" problem. Second, Furey needed to bring together engineers and programmers from the System/36 and System/38 groups and focus them on one product and one schedule for completing Silverlake. It was critical, Furey felt, for this group to be under one set of decision makers. This second group would deal with the "Tomorrow" problem—getting the new computer designed and developed.

The final piece of the structure, in Furey's view, should deal with broader issues that went beyond just taking care of customers today with new versions of the System/36 and System/38 or developing a replacement product. Furey was concerned that Rochester's people were too inwardly focused and too tactical in their thinking. He felt he needed a group that would focus on strategy and look beyond the System/36/38 "Today" and the Silverlake "Tomorrow" to the future—five or more years beyond the '88 Silverlake announcement. This group would be key to keeping Rochester from ever again facing a crisis such as the one they faced in 1986. In short, Furey had decided that he wanted to create an organization that could manage in three time frames at once—today, tomorrow and beyond. Most importantly, Furey wanted to create an organization that totally eliminated the "warring tribes" and focused Rochester on the real enemy—the competition. This would require building the teams with members from every segment of the organization and getting them to begin functioning for the good of the site as a whole. Once they reached that level of understanding, Furey knew that the teams could operate independently and without conflict. After all, they would all have the same goals.

After talking to his people, Furey had the organization model pretty well worked out in his mind. He knew he could simply draw the new structure on a chart and announce it but decided not to. Instead, Furey chose to let his people come up with the organization themselves, with, of course, a little help.

He put together a task force of ten people drawn from different parts of the organization. He briefed them on his idea concerning managing in three time frames—today, tomorrow, and beyond. He told them to take nothing for granted, to start with a clean slate and only the basic assumptions about the multiple time frames he had given them. Then he sent them off to create a new structure and bring back their proposals.

Over the next three months, the group struggled with what to do. They would come back with proposals. Furey would review them. "No, that was a good effort but not quite right," he would say. They kept reworking their proposal. Furey kept rejecting it and gradually shaping it.

Eventually the group fashioned something Furey could accept. It was a structure with four distinct groups:

- The first group would focus on "Today"—getting out the new versions of the System/36 and System/38.

- The second group would focus on Silverlake and bring together people from both the System/36 and System/38 sides of Rochester in one coordinated effort.

- The third group would be a kind of "think tank" responsible for market planning and developing strategies. They would focus on the future beyond Silverlake.

- Finally, there would be a group that would focus on human relations in the lab and managing day-to-day operations. This group would be responsible for finding ways to boost morale, shore up employees' skills, and generally make sure that the other three groups worked together smoothly and had the resources they needed to perform.

By late spring, Furey had the structure he needed in place. But he still needed the hearts and minds of the people, not just in the lab but across the site, if Silverlake was going to be successful.

Communicating the Need to Change

Furey and a number of others understood how critical Silverlake was for IBM and for Rochester. But their view wasn't shared by the vast majority at Rochester. To many of them, things were fine. Rochester was making money. The System/36 and System/38 were still selling well. People were too comfortable. Schwartz and Furey set out to make them feel a little *un*comfortable, with the support of the site general manager, Larry Osterwise.

Osterwise had joined IBM in 1969 and moved through the ranks in a variety of technical and managerial assignments. He came to Rochester as site operations manager in October 1983, then moved in rapid succession to systems plant manager and site general manager in 1984 and 1985, respectively. Osterwise had spent the last two years attempting to communicate a message to Rochester's employees that was similar to and compatible with Schwartz and Furey's message. Osterwise had acknowledged Rochester's good track record, but he tried to get them to understand that they couldn't afford to just sit on their accomplishments. They had to get better to survive. As Will Rogers put it, "Even if you are on the right track, you will get run over if you just sit there." So Osterwise was ready and willing to join Schwartz and Furey in their campaign.

Over the next few months, Furey, Schwartz and Osterwise launched a massive communications effort across the site. Steve Schwartz later reflected on the importance of this communication effort:

> As I look back, one of the things we did right was spend a lot of time in the first half [of 1986] making sure that all eight thousand employees in Rochester understood the problem. We shared all of the business numbers, the revenue flows, the profits with them—all of the things you normally don't share with employees. In big meetings and small roundtables, we spent the first half of that year in massive communications. So I think what really happened is we energized employees at all levels with a common understanding of the problem, and that's where all the creativity started.

The message was always the same and they repeated it over and over. It went much like this:

> These are the numbers. In a few years the System/36 and System/38 will be history unless we do something. A site that doesn't have a revenue flow and has nothing in its development stream can't remain alive and vital.
>
> Sure, this is a great place to work. But if we don't change, we can't even maintain the status quo. There is no such thing as standing still in this world. We must go forward or go away.
>
> Speed is increasing. It's absolutely required that we pick up the pace. The '88 deadline for Silverlake isn't arbitrary. It is a reality.

You don't believe we have a crisis now? That doesn't really matter. What matters is whether you believe we will have a crisis someday if we don't do something about it. Do you believe the auto industry or the textile industry believed they had a crisis or would have one? Look what happened to them. If you don't believe we have a crisis, that's okay. In fact, it's better. If you think the crisis is a little way off, then we have time to do something about it. It's up to you.

It took a while, but the message finally began to sink in. Gradually, more and more people at Rochester began to see themselves on a ship sailing toward an iceberg. The iceberg might not be on the horizon yet, but it was there waiting for them. They could take action now, change course, sail off into a different direction, maybe miss the iceberg and save themselves. Or they could sit and wait for their ship to hit the iceberg. Then it would be too late. Gradually, they did begin to believe that they needed to change. They needed a course correction. But what should it be?

3

Becoming Market-Driven: The Silverlake Project

In 1986 IBM's Rochester, Minnesota, manufacturing and development site, like most of IBM, was "product-driven," not "market-driven." Rochester designed and developed their products in virtual isolation. There was very little input from customers. Certainly, what input there was came piecemeal and erratically. Osterwise reflected, "Our view back then was that if we built a better mousetrap customers would beat their way to our door. We just developed what we liked and unleashed it on the market." Schwartz, Osterwise and Furey understood that approach to product development had to stop. Furey had an idea of just the person who might put facts into their strategy. His name was Victor Tang.

Furey had worked with Vic Tang previously at IBM's Kingston lab, where Tang, as manager of strategic planning, had helped develop a niche strategy critical to the success of a large computer screen venture. Tang, Furey knew, was a mathematician, an engineer who spoke four languages, and a true "global thinker." So Furey called Tang and asked him to come to Rochester.

"Vic," Furey had pleaded, "we have a product-driven organization here. We don't have a good idea of the customers and markets we are trying to serve. I need you to help me figure out the markets we want to serve and the strategies we have to bring to the table."

It took some persuading. Tang wasn't sure he wanted to go to Rochester, but finally agreed on one condition. In addition to being responsible for developing strategy, Tang wanted a strong technology component. He wanted Furey's okay to look at the possibility of adding a little technical "wizardry" to Silverlake.

Furey agreed to the condition. He had to. He needed Tang.

Understanding the Market

Tang arrived in Rochester in July 1986. He found the situation as bad as Furey had told him it was. Several years later, Tang described his first impressions:

> It was like Tom had told me. They concentrated completely on trying to build better technology. They were used to doing all things for all people, not focusing on a particular customer, but treating every customer as if he or she were like every other customer. They were used to doing planning, what little they did, by anecdote—the most recent customer story, or "rear-view mirror" of what they had done before. I had to upgrade their planning skills and get them focused.

Tang started out by asking a simple question over and over, "Who are the customers we want to serve?" "Let's figure out the market we want to serve," he said, "and then let's segment the market into groups of customers that have different needs and wants who are likely to respond in a similar way to our offerings. Then, let's pick the most meaningful segments and position products against those most meaningful and attractive segments."

There was nothing new about what Tang was proposing. It was just basic marketing, the kind of thing any student might learn in any graduate business school marketing class. The only thing new about it was that the concepts were new to Rochester.

It took time and bringing in professors from some of America's top business schools to lecture and instruct, but eventually Tang got his ideas across. They had to segment the market by size, geography, industry or some other criteria to break the market down into reasonable, coherent groups. Once they had done that, they needed to target particular segments of the market where Rochester had a good chance of being successful and meeting its revenue and profit goals. Finally, they would have to position their products in that marketplace by stressing the features, functions and benefits most attractive to their target customers. It sounded simple. But it took months to do. In the process, Rochester learned several crucial things:

1. Large customers, those with over five thousand employees, who had been the traditional focus of Rochester's design and development efforts, constituted, in reality, only a small percentage of midrange system purchasers. The vast majority of buyers were small businesses with five thousand or fewer employees.

2. These small businesses didn't buy computers. They bought applications software and whatever computer the software ran on. They were more interested in solutions to business problems than in technology or hardware.

3. While Rochester had many competitors in the midrange computer field, some 250 in total, not all competitors were equal. Most had less than 2 percent of the market. Only six had more than 4 percent. Rochester didn't have to compete against all 250 competitors. It could focus its efforts on a subset.

Eventually, Tang and his crew settled on seventeen major industrial segments where they felt Rochester should and could compete. These included insurance, product and service distribution, health care, manufacturing, engineering, and state and local government. To reach these markets, they would position their product by offering five attractive benefits to these customers:

1. Simplicity of use;
2. Lots of application software;
3. The ability to create software quickly with few programmers;
4. A range of models so that a business could start with a small, inexpensive system and move easily to more ad-

vanced and sophisticated systems as its needs expanded; and, finally,

5. Plenty of support, including an "Electronic Classroom" built into the computer to teach customers how to use it and "Electronic Customer Support" to allow updating of software and diagnosis and repair of the computer via telephone.

Reducing the Cycle Time

When Schwartz pitched the Silverlake project to IBM's executives, he held up a chart showing a series of checkpoints. By passing each checkpoint, Rochester improved its odds of making the 1988 deadline. It was now the fall of 1986. The first checkpoint had arrived. It involved breaking in a new processor microchip for the system's main processor. If the chip worked perfectly, Rochester's odds of success improved by half—from 1,000 to 1 to just 500 to 1. If the chip failed—if it wasn't flawless—Rochester would automatically be off-schedule by nine months, and those were nine months that would be almost impossible to recapture.

Typically, chip design was a kind of trial and error process. Roy Bauer, who was manager of laboratory operations and process development at the time, explained the process as follows:

> The way you got assembly defects out of the process was by debugging. You'd send your tapes out east to the chip plants, and you would get chips made from your engineering design. Then you would get them back and put them together, and your engineers would sit at an oscilloscope and start tracing circuits to see what you missed when you assembled all the things together. The old process was build chips, debug them, assemble the system, then debug again. Once you identified the system problems, you would make design changes and go through a second pass. Finally, you would get something you could give to the programmers so they could start testing code. In a typical system, you would have two hundred or three hundred overflow wires you had added because there were problems with the way the chips and the circuit assemblies worked together. The circuit board on the back of the computer would look

like spaghetti with all the overflow wires on it. Depending upon the complexity of the machine, this whole debug process could take six to twelve months.

Rochester didn't have six to twelve months, not if they were going to meet their first checkpoint. They had to do something different. So they broke with past practice.

In the past, IBM engineers and scientists had used single chip simulation to test their engineering designs. Using huge programs that might run for days, they could create possible events and simulate how a single chip might perform. They could then adjust their designs without having to go through the time-consuming process of actually building a chip and testing it to see what was wrong. But that was testing one chip at time. The different chips still had to work together to make the entire computer work. No one had tried to simulate the entire system before, not until Silverlake.

Under the leadership of Jim Flynn, a hard-driving, chain-smoking, "old salt" of an engineer, the Rochester hardware engineering team took simulation to the system level. Using a powerful supercomputer called EVE, for Engineering Verification Engine, they simulated and tested the performance of not just one chip at a time, but the entire "brain" of the computer itself. Instead of the usual months, they were able to bring up a prototype machine in weeks, and instead of having two to three hundred overflow wires per circuit board, the system had only six when they finished.

Rochester cut months off the development cycle and met its first checkpoint. The odds of Silverlake's failing dropped, and their confidence soared. Rochester programmers and engineers also learned something. Doing things in parallel was much better than doing them in sequence. They could apply this "parallel development concept" to the entire Silverlake project. But to do that they would have to involve customers and business partners a lot earlier than normal. They would have to break another IBM rule.

Making the Customer the Final Arbiter

Traditionally, IBM had been secretive in its product development activities. No one outside of a lab was allowed to know what was being done, not even IBM's own sales and support organization. Once a project was near completion, IBM might turn to a few customers and ask for their help in running new machines and sorting out the final bugs. But, by then, the basic functions of the machine and how it operated were pretty well set. There was customer involvement, but it was limited and late. By the time customers got involved in any significant way, IBM was already committed to a machine that might or might not meet customers' needs.

For Rochester and the Silverlake project, such secrecy just wouldn't work. Rochester couldn't afford to produce a machine that was a failure. And Rochester wouldn't have months or years to fix what customers didn't like about Silverlake once it was released. They had to do what the customers wanted from the first. That meant bringing in customers earlier than ever before and not just customers. Rochester also had to be concerned about involving its business partners—all those independent application software developers and marketers who created the "software solutions" to customers' problems and through which Rochester sold a vast majority of its machines.

Throughout the Silverlake project, Rochester involved its customers and business partners in ways IBM had never done before. Customer councils were convened on a regular basis, where representatives from System/36 and System/38 user companies, such as Farm Fresh Dairies, Merck Pharmaceuticals, Gannett Publishing, Bally's Casinos, and Caterpillar Tractor, among many others, came in for two days to hear about development plans, discuss features and functions and provide their feedback to Rochester's programmers and engineers. Business partners who would have to develop or modify software to run on the new machine were invited to Rochester to spend from a few days to as much as several weeks working on prototype machines to convert their software applications. Eventually, Rochester was involving customers and business partners, as Osterwise liked to say, "all the way from the twinkle in the developer's eyes to installation and support after the sale." It was a level of early and sustained involvement and sharing of information with non-IBMers unheard of in the company. It was also a level of openness that many tradition-bound IBMers didn't like. When they complained, Schwartz told them to go away. Rochester had a job to do and was doing it. That is until November of 1987. Then, as Furey later recalled, "everything went to hell in a handbasket."

Responding to Problems

It wasn't that no one expected trouble. It was just that their confidence was so high. After making their first checkpoint in the fall of 1986, they continued to meet checkpoint after checkpoint. The odds of success kept improving. As the odds improved, spirits improved. Then trouble came.

The first problem was less serious than it appeared on the surface. In the middle of November 1987, Dave Schleicher, Furey's head of programming, came into Furey's office. Schleicher looked totally dejected. He had bad news. "Tom," he said, barely able to look Furey in the face, "we can't make the schedule I committed to you."

"What's the problem?" asked Furey.

"We just can't process as much code as we thought we could," explained Schleicher. "We're behind and getting further behind each day."

At the beginning of the project, estimates were that Silverlake would require three thousand person-years of programming. It was an impossibly fast processing rate which required an innovative approach to software development, as Roy Bauer, Emilio Collar, and Victor Tang explained in their book *The Silverlake Project*:

> The programming we were doing was for the operating system, along with several programming tools and "utilities" used for basic housecleaning functions. The operating system is the "traffic cop" from which all other software operates. Silverlake's operating system had to be unusually large because it had to be able to run applications created for both the incompatible System/36 and System/38. Plus we were integrating into the basic operating system functions that customers would normally have to purchase separately. These

functions allowed the Silverlake to communicate with other computers over telephone lines, protect data against unauthorized access, and create databases from any and all of the information on
it. . . .

Dave Schleicher and his programmers broke the entire task into
what they called "milestones." Each milestone consisted of one of
Silverlake's major functions. Each milestone was to be a freestand-
ing, completely functional part of the whole. . . .

This approach to the programming work was like building a jet-
liner out on the runway. First, we built the landing gear. Then we
constructed a fuselage as we pushed it up and down the tarmac. We
added engines so that it could taxi itself. We put on a cockpit with
the pilots inside to drive it toward a takeoff slot. We tacked on wings
as it was about to go airborne. And, we added everything else while
the jet was in the air, knowing that when we installed seats we could
safely make a transatlantic flight filled with passengers.

In spite of their innovative approach to software development,
when Schleicher and his team had given Furey their original estimates of the time required to complete the programming, Furey
had not been as confident of their ability to meet the estimates
as they had been. As a consequence, he had gone back to
Schwartz early in 1986 with a request for a three-month extension. So when Schleicher came in with his "bad news," Furey was
not totally surprised.

As Schleicher continued his confession, "We can only do a
million lines every *eight days,* not every five as we planned," Furey
could only think, "This is the kind of problem that you love to
manage. Given the impossible task that they had set for themselves, even a million lines of code every *eight* days is fantastic."

Furey told Schleicher to take his eight-day rate, go back and
recalculate a new estimate of when they could finish. Doing
some quick calculation in his own head, Furey decided June
might be just right.

A few days later, Schleicher came back with his new estimate.
They thought they could make it by the next November!

"How predictable," thought Furey. "As soon as they got released from their original commitment, the schedule went marching to the west eight months instead of what I estimated should
just be two or three." It just wasn't good enough, so Furey insisted that Schleicher and his crew try again. This time they got

it right—the answer was June. Furey nodded and said, "I can live with that."

The second problem was more serious. While much of the Silverlake project was under Rochester's control, a planned, new tape drive was being developed for Silverlake by another lab halfway across the country. But the other lab had fallen behind its schedule. By November it became obvious that the new tape drive would never be ready in time. To save itself, Rochester had to revert to using old tape drives like those used with the System/36 and System/38. It was an enormous task. The complete tape drive program for the system had to be redone. And it had to be redone in just 120 days if they were going to meet the announcement schedule. There was nothing else to do. Rochester went on an exhausting, seven-day-a-week schedule to find a solution.

Ironically, System/36 and System/38 customers hadn't *wanted* a new tape drive. Tape drives cost as much as fifty thousand dollars each, and customers simply wanted to move their old tape drives over to the new system, not buy new ones. In this instance, Rochester failed to listen to its customers. As a result, it created a development crisis and risked damaging the new customer relationship. Fortunately, Rochester's customers got their wish, but only because IBM wasn't able to do something that it had insisted on doing in spite of customer opposition.

Executing with Excellence

After the November problems, Furey remained nervous. In early January, he polled his people on where they stood. They reported that everything looked like it was progressing on schedule once again, but Furey still wasn't satisfied. Maybe he was missing something. He called Schwartz. "Steve," he said, "I must be crazy. I now think we might just be able to make this thing."

"So? That's good, isn't it?" asked Schwartz.

"Yeah, but," said Furey, "I'm afraid I'm getting too close to it. Look, this thing is the largest program ever done. I've now convinced myself we can do it. It makes me nervous that I may be losing my perspective. I'd feel better if you sent some guys out here. Let them spend a couple of weeks auditing both engineering and programming. Then let them come back and tell me what *they* think."

Schwartz agreed, hand-picked a team of experienced development managers from other sites, and sent them to Rochester. For two weeks they checked the project out. Then they went to Furey with their findings. "Well," they told him, "it's big all right. It's the biggest thing we have ever seen. And did you know, you've got over 60,000 open software problems, but your tracking system only tracks up to 9,999, so you can't even put most of them [the problems] on your system. And most people can't turn around a million lines of code in months, much less in eight working days like you are doing. So you've got one big project! But," they went on, "in spite of all of that, we don't know of anything that you could look at differently to tell you how you are doing. So, if you think you are on schedule, then you must be on schedule."

Furey didn't know *what* to think.

By February, the software problems were still growing. Furey and Schwartz tracked them on a regular basis on their charts, and they were looking for the charts to change. They hadn't yet. And it was getting close, real close, to the time when they should see their charts take a nosedive if they were to meet their deadline.

Schwartz and Furey were looking at graphic displays of a defect model constructed by Rochester early in the development process. Based upon historical data, the model predicted, for both hardware and software, a pattern for problem identification and resolution. Early in the project, there would be few defects. Then as the project progressed, more problems would be found, and they would start resolving them. But, for a time, the number of outstanding problems would continue to increase as more were found than resolved. At some time, however, the pattern should reverse itself. They should start coming down the other side of the defect curve. As fewer problems were found than resolved, the total number of outstanding problems would begin to drop. Given their speed of problem resolution, the model predicted when the turnaround had to occur if Silverlake was to meet its announcement date. Through the fall of 1987 and into the winter of 1988, Rochester had been climbing the defect curve almost exactly as the model had predicted. The model predicted a turnaround sometime in mid-February. It didn't happen.

By mid-February, defects had still not hit their peak. When would they turn the corner? Furey didn't know. Yet somehow, in spite of what the model was saying, he felt that they *had* turned the corner. Or was it just that Furey had been right when he worried that he really was too close to the situation to see the reality of what was happening? He waited. Schwartz waited. And the number of defects just kept climbing.

Then, in late February, just a few days after the model had predicted they would, the number of outstanding problems started dropping, and they kept dropping. The model had been unbelievably accurate, but recalled Furey, "It was scarier than hell."

Orchestrating the New Product Announcement

IBM planned one of its biggest announcements ever for Silverlake, which had by now been renamed the AS/400 (Application System/400). IBM would unveil its new midrange computer in a worldwide, simultaneous announcement. To plan for the great unveiling, IBM had assembled an announcement council of senior marketing, service, manufacturing and development executives a year in advance. The committee met monthly, reviewed issues and tried to get ahead of the "hype" already appearing in the industry media. Still, there was a lot of speculation based on the information that was already out about the AS/400. It was all very open—too open for many in IBM who relished the days of secrecy.

Schwartz wasn't as worried about the openness as he was about the expectations the media had raised. "Were expectations going to get ahead of us?" he wondered. "Were people going to expect more than we would be able to deliver?" It wasn't a comforting thought.

June 21, 1988, was announcement day. More than two thousand members of the press and guests assembled at IBM's Manhattan headquarters to see and to hear about the machine, but John Akers was nowhere to be found.

For the first time in IBM's history, the CEO celebrated the announcement of a new product with the people who had developed and manufactured it. The morning of the announcement, John Akers was in Rochester, Minnesota. Addressing a sea of white shirts, IBM-style, Akers told the audience that the announcement of the AS/400 was coming at dinner in Tokyo, lunch in Frankfurt, brunch in New York and breakfast in Rochester, and might cause a bit of indigestion to IBM's competitors in the industry.

Over 100,000 customers and prospective customers watched the worldwide, simultaneous announcement over the largest closed-circuit telecast in IBM history. There were additional remarks, then, in a puff of smoke and to the strains of the theme from *2001: A Space Odyssey*, the AS/400—all six models—rose slowly and majestically from the stage floor. The AS/400 was a reality.

Not only was the AS/400 a reality, it became a roaring success almost immediately. In August, Rochester started shipping its new computer. By the end of the year, they had sold and shipped nearly thirty thousand units to customers—a better record than IBM had with their highly successful personal computer. From the start, the AS/400 was a phenomenal success for IBM. But that is not to say that there weren't some problems, including one major problem, that could have been the death knell for IBM's new product line.

Responding to Customer Feedback

Schwartz had been concerned about the preannouncement hype. So had Furey, Osterwise, and nearly everyone else associated with the AS/400. They felt the machine was good, but they had to be certain. They wanted immediate feedback from customers. Were they satisfied with their new machine or not?

Rochester was doing customer surveys and marketing surveys quarterly. But still that seemed too late. If there was going to be a problem with the AS/400, Schwartz, Furey and Osterwise didn't want to wait to find out from a quarterly survey or the trade press. They wanted to know right away, so they started looking for ways to get more current information. Schwartz suggested that they use their telemarketing center to gather this information.

Rochester's telemarketing center had been created by Jim Kelly, a member of Osterwise's staff who had a marketing background, in early 1986. Concerned about how Rochester could help sales of the System/36 and System/38, Kelly's team came up with the idea of placing "800" numbers in ads, extolling the benefits of the machines and suggesting that potential customers call for more information. Rochester employees would then take the calls, qualify the leads, and pass them along to IBM marketing reps, who would follow up and make the sale. The idea worked well.

With the announcement of the AS/400, Schwartz, Furey and Osterwise decided to use Kelly's "outbound telemarketing" capability. Rochester's telemarketing center started making calls to new AS/400 customers to get early feedback. They manned the center with engineers, programmers, retired IBM Rochester employees and others from various parts of the site. They were shocked at the customer reaction.

A typical call would go something like this:

CUSTOMER: Where did you say you are calling from?

ROCHESTER: IBM at Rochester, Minnesota. We just wanted to thank you for your business and find out how things were going.

CUSTOMER: You're from Rochester, Minnesota, and you're calling me in California, and you want to do what? Is this the computer company? Is this IBM? You're calling to thank me? I don't believe it.

The conversation would go on like that for three to five minutes. Customers were genuinely shocked. IBM cared enough to call. Somehow they just couldn't believe it.

Eventually, the call would get around to the customer's experiences with the new AS/400. Most liked the machine. Some, however, had little glitches: "I've been trying to get this thing up and running and . . ." Often it was a simple problem. With engineers, programmers and manufacturing people on the line, the customer got an answer right away. Then there were times when the customer would need to be called back. The important thing was that Rochester was not only getting information, but also resolving customer problems before they showed up in any survey. Then one big problem surfaced.

Through its follow-up calls and other channels, Rochester started to get wind of a problem with the smaller AS/400, often referred to as the low-end machine. In standard configuration, the machine was sold with four megabytes of memory, which was sufficient, customers were told, to run their applications. For some applications, however, that wasn't the case. Customers began to complain that their software wouldn't run or, if it did run, ran too slowly. And it wasn't just a few customers complaining. A pattern had emerged and the problem was real. It was also serious.

The problem became clear to Schwartz and Furey on a Tuesday in mid-October. The following Monday, Schwartz and Furey were scheduled to appear before COMMON, the AS/400 users group, at a regularly scheduled meeting. They were concerned that the question about the low-end machine would come up, and they would need an answer. Schwartz and Furey had a series of hurry-up meetings. It soon became obvious to them what they needed to do. If the machines couldn't run effectively in four megabytes of memory, then IBM would just have to give each customer an additional four megabytes of memory, at least until the problem could be fixed. Loaning or giving away that much memory could cost IBM $15 to $20 million. But what choice did the company have compared to ruining the AS/400's reputation and risking a projected $12 billion a year in sales?

On Sunday, Schwartz met with the board of directors of COMMON and shocked them when he told them of the decision. Furey then went before the full users group on Monday. He gave his presentation and then took questions from the audience. He expected questions about the memory problem on the low-end machine, but he got none. Then he said, "I'm going to answer a question you haven't even asked. The question is: 'How well do System/36 applications run in four megabytes on the AS/400?' Well, the answer is 'Not well.' But the good news is that we are going to loan an additional four megabytes of memory to all of you who have this problem until we can get it fixed." Osterwise later recalled the press reaction to Furey's announcement: "The next day, they ran stories saying, 'The new IBM! It admits it had a problem, takes it on itself to fix the problem, and even finds the problem before the customers find it.' " The whole issue had been completely defused.

The decision Schwartz and Furey made to loan the four megabytes of memory to customers who were having a problem wasn't unusual for IBM. It was the kind of decision IBM normally would have made, but only after weeks or months of deliberation at the top level. The decision might have been made in time to stop the bad publicity, but probably not. What was unique about the situation with the AS/400 memory problem was that Schwartz and Furey made the decision themselves within a few days or hours and got executive approval without going through layers of bureaucracy. It was just another example of operating in the "small company environment"—the kind of environment that Schwartz had demanded from the beginning. And it was an example of how good Rochester had become at responding to the market.

Market-Driven Rochester

The development of the AS/400 totally broke with IBM tradition. Facing a crisis and few choices, IBM Rochester undertook fundamental change—the kind of change necessary for any company or organization hoping ever to become world-class in quality. Yet Rochester wasn't so much pursuing quality as it was pursuing survival. Without the crisis, Rochester most likely never would have attempted so much change so fast.

To survive, Rochester had to do the impossible. It had to develop a new product in half the normal time. Pursuing that one critical goal, Rochester was allowed and began to do things that would have been impossible for it to do at another, less traumatic time, but all of which were key ingredients of world-class quality:

- It was freed from the bureaucracy and allowed to operate as a small, entrepreneurial-type enterprise.

- It was forced into restructuring its development staff to focus their energies and efforts on the competition, rather than infighting.

- Rochester leaders were forced to open up and share information with their employees; to empower employees to create change; and to develop a much better and more in-depth understanding of their target customer and his/her needs and expectations.

- Their need for speed forced them into parallel development and into a level of customer involvement IBM had not allowed before.

- Finally, their fear of failure forced them to seek ways to get better feedback from customers and to be more responsive to customer problems.

Rochester didn't make any of these changes in order to pursue world-class quality. Rochester changed to survive. In the process, and somewhat to their surprise, they became market-driven, and the quality of their products and services became very good. With the success of the AS/400, they thought they were great. They weren't. Becoming great would take another few years. But the path to greatness was already being laid, and it was coming from an unlikely source.

4

Stumbling Upon the Path to Greatness

In the late spring of 1987, when Rochester was still over a year away from launching the AS/400, Bob Talbot, who was the chief financial officer of the IBM Information Systems and Product Group, was called to George Conrades's office in Armonk, New York. Conrades was the chief executive officer of this group. At that meeting, Talbot was informed that he was being offered the job as chief quality officer for IBM to replace Bill Eggleston, who was retiring. He recalled sitting in one of those upholstered chairs in Armonk, dumbfounded at this offer.

Talbot, who was in his early forties at the time, was an unlikely candidate to be a director of quality for a company like IBM, or for any major company for that matter. Having joined IBM right out of Iona College in 1966, Talbot had been a division controller, division vice president, and financial planning director, and by 1987 he was group director of finance for IBM's Information Systems and Products Group, which made midrange system printers, typewriters and banking systems. All of his experience had been on the financial side of the business, not manufacturing, development or operations, where he might have learned something about quality.

Talbot had been working his way up the ranks of financial

management in IBM. In the process, he had gotten a reputation as an executive who could be very determined and could get things through the IBM bureaucracy. His tactics had gotten results, but they hardly made him a shining example of quality practice. The two previous quality executives in IBM were much older and more senior-line executives. This made sense because the role of the chief quality officer required one to be judgmental of others, and it helped to have a track record of having "walked the talk." In some business areas in IBM, as well as other companies, an executive was put into the quality job when he or she was "at the end of the line." "Why me, George?" asked Talbot. "This job is the kiss of death for somebody like me. I know we've had our problems in our group, but certainly I can't be blamed for all of them."

Conrades listened patiently and tried to persuade Talbot that this really was a good opportunity. Finally, Conrades's patience ran out and he said, "If you won't take my word for it that this is something the company wants you to do, I suggest you talk to Akers."

John Akers, a former navy carrier pilot, had joined IBM in 1960 as a sales trainee in San Francisco. Following several marketing assignments, he had become president of the Data Processing Division in 1974. Then, in rapid succession, he moved through the positions of vice president, assistant group executive, group executive, senior vice president, and IBM president. Finally in 1985 and 1986, respectively, he became chief executive officer and chairman of the board.

For two years, Akers had been trying to fix what was wrong. He had not had much success. He knew that IBM had to strengthen customer partnerships, improve product competitiveness, and restructure and reduce its head count. As Talbot waited outside Akers's office to be summoned to their meeting, Akers was still looking for an effective means to address the problems facing IBM. He knew IBM's product quality was at least part of the problem.

IBM's Quality Efforts

It wasn't that IBM hadn't tried to improve its quality. It had, and there were some notable successes. In the 1960s, long before many other U.S. companies, IBM had experimented with process improvement, zero defects, quality circles and a host of other quality programs that were to become popular in the 1980s. In 1967, IBM issued Corporate Instruction 105 requiring that "the quality of a new product at general availability must be superior to that currently available in the industry." By the late 1970s, companies like Milliken and Xerox, later Baldrige Award winners, were coming to IBM to learn about the pilot quality improvement projects IBM had under way, such as the highly successful effort to improve reliability and availability of display terminals that IBM launched in 1979.

Then in the early 1980s, IBM started bringing in quality gurus like W. Edwards Deming and Joseph Juran, who were credited with much of Japan's success, and Phil Crosby, the former ITT director of quality who had written the 1979 best-seller *Quality Is Free*. Between 1980 and 1983, IBM sent hundreds of executives to Phil Crosby's Quality College in Florida to learn about making zero-defect products and about the importance of measuring the cost of quality. IBM would adopt the cost-of-quality idea with a vengeance.

The Cost of Quality

The ideas that IBM managers heard about at Crosby's Quality College weren't new. The concept of "zero defects" had its origin in the Martin Company in the early 1960s, and Joseph Juran had suggested calculating the cost of achieving a given level of quality as early as 1951 in the first edition of his classic *Quality Control Handbook*. What Crosby did was to popularize these concepts by packaging them. Crosby said he had identified what he called "five erroneous assumptions" most managers made about quality. Two of these "erroneous assumptions," in particular, hit home with IBM managers.

First, Crosby said, managers assumed that quality meant goodness, or luxury, or shininess, or weight, or some dreamy thing that no one could precisely define. "Wrong," said Crosby. Quality was "conformance to requirements." Requirements for any product or service could, and should, be clearly stated, and, once stated, they could be understood and managed.

Second, Crosby said, it was erroneous to assume that quality was an intangible and therefore immeasurable. Quality, he argued, could be measured precisely by the oldest and most respected measure managers had—hard, cold cash. The true measure of quality was the cost of quality, or more precisely, the cost of non-conformance to requirements—the cost of doing things wrong. Just track and add up the cost of scrap, rework, warranty costs, service (except regular maintenance), inspection labor, engineering changes, purchase order changes, software correction, consumer affairs, audits, quality control labor, test labor, acceptance equipment costs, and other costs of doing things wrong and you had the cost of quality. If the figure you arrived at exceeded 2.5 percent of your sales dollars, said Crosby, you had a direct opportunity to increase your return on sales by the exact amount you reduced your quality costs. That could be significant, argued Crosby, since, by his estimate, the cost of quality in the typical American business wasn't just 2.5 percent. Rather, it represented 20 percent or more of sales in manufacturing businesses and 35 percent of operating costs in service companies. If he was right in his estimates, and he felt he was, then the potential savings from reducing the cost of quality were enormous. By calculating and reporting the cost of quality, argued Crosby, you would turn your people on to the whole concept of quality. Crosby explained:

> The cost of quality is the catalyst that brings the quality improvement team and other management people to full awareness of what is happening. Before that, often they are only going through the motions of the program just to give the right impression. . . . The cost of quality takes the business of quality out of the abstract and brings it sharply into focus as cold, hard cash. Suddenly the potential for achievement is there. Suddenly, it really is a profit maker instead of a negative thought.

Two things happened as a result of the IBM trips to the Quality College. First, IBMers began to speak a common quality language. That helped since people finally began to understand each other a little better when they talked about quality. However, the second thing that happened *didn't* help.

IBM became obsessed with calculating, tracking and reporting quality costs. Every month, cost-of-quality results rolled up the chain of command in reams of printout. Quality-costs charts were posted for all to see and updated regularly. Everyone knew what poor quality was costing IBM. There was just one problem. No one was doing much about it. By 1983 or 1984, the cost-of-quality program had failed to produce significant results and was collapsing under its own bureaucratic weight. IBM management was ready to move on. This time they decided to try process management with a corporate-wide program called Quality Focus on the Business Process, or QFBP.

Quality *Focus* on the *Business Process*

The idea behind QFBP was to identify key business processes such as billing, order entry, manufacturing, and the like; assign process owners; flowchart the processes; and look for ways to improve. While the concept of process management had been tried before in IBM and elsewhere, mostly in manufacturing, the QFBP program was different in that it extended the concept to nonmanufacturing areas such as planning, distribution and human resources.

Throughout 1984 and 1985, thousands of IBMers were trained in process management. Process owners were appointed, meetings were held, and walls began to fill with process flowcharts. There were some notable successes. For example, IBM's Rochester, Minnesota, manufacturing and development site was able to take its throughput time for card assembly and test, its largest dollar-inventory item, from twenty-five days down to about two days. Yet many other locations were frustrated with QFBP and never got beyond the learning phase to tackle real problems. By the spring of 1987, IBM management was again looking for something new—another, more successful quality program. Akers thought Bob Talbot might be the guy to help him find that "something new."

The New Quality Director

In a 1992 interview, Talbot recalled sitting in Akers's office on the third floor of IBM's Armonk headquarters, listening as Akers laid out what he had in mind. Talbot had worked with Akers in the early 1980s as a charter member of the Information and Communications Group that Akers headed very successfully for four years. Akers mobilized this group to move quickly, building a track record of increased market share and profitability. It was proving more difficult to duplicate the same track record on a corporate level. He told Talbot that he wasn't even sure he needed a quality director at this time. He was getting advice from some people who said that quality was now in the fabric of the business and that he could eliminate the position. He wasn't sure if this was true, but he wanted to take a new approach.

Akers was convinced that IBM had to be lighter on its feet and that it had far too many employees. He acknowledged Talbot's good reputation in the financial community for being a hard-nosed financial person and one who knew how to "hot-wire" the system to get things done. It was a bit like hiring a thief to catch a thief. Anyone who knew how to "hot-wire" the system probably could find a way to improve it.

Akers wanted to start right away by identifying all the work in the corporation that could be eliminated because it wasn't directly related to meeting customer needs. He called the top IBM team together and told them that Talbot had been asked to tackle this problem and could count on Akers's full support to make this happen.

Akers's advised Talbot to educate himself on what successful companies around the world were doing to systematically improve market share and profitability over a sustained period of time. He also wanted Talbot to inspect all of the major IBM plants, labs, marketing areas and operations in other countries. After this fact gathering, Akers requested that Talbot come back to the Corporate Management Committee, the committee that assisted Akers in the management of IBM, with a series of recommendations on what to do.

One of the first things that Talbot learned in his new capacity was that the IBM director of quality receives an enormous number of requests for speaking engagements. Early in his new assignment, Talbot honored some of these requests. But in retrospect, Talbot admitted that his early speeches must have shown that he had an embarrassing lack of background in the quality arena.

One fateful day, Talbot's lack of knowledge and the seriousness of the quality problems IBM was facing were brought home to him in direct and fearful terms. It happened in a meeting between Talbot and the quality directors from a number of IBM laboratory and manufacturing sites.

Talbot's "Fateful Day"

The meeting had been orchestrated by Gabe Pall. Pall was the director of IBM's Quality Institute and had been fighting a rearguard action for years to preserve what was left of IBM's quality organization and its hard-won knowledge base about quality and quality improvement. Pall's struggle wasn't an easy one. He faced determined opposition from some IBM executives who argued that *quality is in the fabric of the business* and thus the responsibility of line personnel, not corporate executives. They had already succeeded in cutting the corporate quality training group from eighteen people who dispensed roughly six thousand person-years of training per year down to six people and two thousand person-years. Yet Pall had hung on. Later, Talbot would compare Pall's role in keeping the faith and preserving what was left of the corporate quality organization to that of the whiskey priest in Graham Greene's novel *The Power and the Glory:*

> In the story there is this whiskey priest who was constantly dodging bullets and escaping from the government forces that didn't want the church in their country. Toward the end of the book, the government troops are going to catch him, and the priest thinks he has wasted his life. Then, this villager says, "Oh, Father you kept us alive. Just knowing you were there and that they couldn't catch you caused us to keep the faith." That was Gabe's role. He kept the faith.

The meeting started with Talbot talking about the work plan for the Work Elimination Project that Akers requested. One could sense that he was not clicking with the audience. Finally, Chris Behr, who led the quality effort in IBM's Burlington, Vermont, plant and who had worked with Talbot in the late 1960s in Burlington, spoke up. Talbot later recalled Behr's comments:

> Talbot, this company is losings its way on quality. We used to be a leader in quality techniques in the nation, and we are quickly losing our edge. I haven't had a senior quality review in ages. Everybody assumes it's *in the fabric of the business,* but without that constant attention, the quality is just going to continue to suffer. The *coup de grace* that proves that the company isn't taking quality seriously is that they put a *clown like you* in this position.

Initially, the audience was shocked by what Behr said but began to laugh as they realized that Talbot and Behr had the kind of relationship that allowed such comments. As the meeting continued, others began expressing their anger and frustration over the fact that the very proud IBM reputation was on the verge of being tarnished because of this mistaken belief that *quality is in the fabric of the business.* Talbot later recalled that it was the most hostile environment he ever survived but one that proved to be very helpful for the future of IBM.

The Call from Sandy McDonnell

About the time Talbot was being introduced to the more unpleasant aspects of his new job, John Akers was being introduced to the Malcolm Baldrige National Quality Award in the form of a telephone call from Sandy McDonnell, the chairman of McDonnell-Douglas. McDonnell was trying to raise money to support the Baldrige award. He wanted IBM to contribute fifty thousand dollars, and he wanted Akers to help with the fund-raising efforts and to agree to serve on the Baldrige Board of Overseers.

Although Akers didn't know much about the Baldrige award at the time, the existence of the award wasn't really new to him. IBM had, in fact, lent its support to efforts to create the award. Bill Eggleston had testified before Congress in its support.

Akers knew that the idea for a national award to recognize

business achievement in productivity and quality had been proposed by President Reagan's White House Conference on Productivity in 1983. After that, a number of groups, particularly the American Productivity Center and a group led by Florida Power and Light Company's chairman, John Hudiburg, had been working to create a national quality award patterned after Japan's Deming Prize. After years of work and several abortive attempts at getting legislation through a less-than-enthusiastic Congress or getting White House approval to create an award, the Hudiburg group succeeded. Public law 100-107 was passed by Congress and signed by the president in August 1987. It had been named in honor of Reagan's good friend and secretary of commerce, Malcolm Baldrige, who had died unexpectedly in a rodeo accident the month before. The act creating the award stated that a national quality award would help improve quality and productivity by

1. Helping to stimulate American companies to improve quality for the pride of recognition while obtaining a competitive edge through increased profits;
2. Recognizing the achievement of those companies that improve the quality of their goods and services and providing an example to others;
3. Establishing guidelines and criteria that can be used by business, industrial, governmental, and other organizations in evaluating their own quality improvement efforts; and
4. Providing specific guidance for other American organizations that wish to learn how to manage for high quality by making available detailed information on how winning organizations were able to change their cultures and achieve eminence.

Talbot later recalled a helicopter trip during which Akers recounted his conversation with Sandy McDonnell. "What do you think, Bob? Should we get into this?" Talbot remembered Akers asking. In response, Talbot explained:

Well, Bill Eggleston and I talked about that before. He said although he had worked on the award he wasn't sure how much we should support it. He and some others are worried about it becoming political or some kind of standards bureaucracy. So he's not sure we should be involved. But, Curt Reimann [director, Malcolm Baldrige National Quality Award, National Institute of Standards and Technology] is in charge of administering the award, and we know Reimann. He's got impeccable integrity. So it's a gamble, but I think we can work with them. I think we should go ahead.

"Well, then," Akers said, "that's what we will do. Now I've got to go out and raise some money." Talbot then offered, "I'll talk to Milliken." Of course, Talbot was referring to Milliken and Company. IBM and Milliken had been sharing ideas about quality for a number of years, and Talbot was already scheduled to speak to Milliken's top executives at a conference Milliken was planning for February 1988.

The Milliken Challenge

Before Talbot could call Milliken, he received a call from Dr. Tom Malone, Milliken's chief operating officer. It was obvious from the conversation that Milliken and Company had also been contacted by the Baldrige fund-raisers. "Bob," Talbot recalls Malone saying, "Roger [Milliken, chairman of Milliken and Company] and I talked this Baldrige thing over, and we feel that it's a fifty-thousand-dollar investment that is well worth making. If IBM is in, so is Milliken."

"That's great, Tom," said Talbot. "When I am at your conference in February, I intend to hurl a challenge at your people."

On February 4, 1988, at Callaway Gardens, Georgia, Talbot did as he promised and issued his challenge. IBM and Milliken would be the best quality practitioners in the nation, and *IBM would win the Baldrige award before Milliken.*

The Fly Off

Having committed themselves to help fund the award and having made a we'll-win-before-you-do challenge to Milliken, Akers and Talbot decided to have IBM apply for the award. They knew IBM, as a whole, probably couldn't win. But they were certain that some sites in IBM could win, and a single site could apply under the eligibility guidelines. The question was which site should go for it? Neither Akers nor Talbot realized that they had stumbled upon their "different approach" with this decision. At the time, all they were interested in doing was improving IBM operations and, perhaps, winning an award. They decided to have a "fly off" and let the sites compete for the honor of representing IBM.

In 1988, IBM U.S. was divided into seven lines of business:

- Application Business Systems
- Application Solutions
- Communications Systems
- Enterprise Systems
- Personal Systems
- Programming Systems
- Technology Products

Within each of these lines of business, IBM had multiple sites. The "fly off" Akers and Talbot had planned would involve a competition between the lines of business to select a site to compete for the Malcolm Baldrige National Quality Award on behalf of IBM. Each line of business would nominate one of its sites as its best quality practitioner. After being given some training on the Baldrige award and a few weeks to prepare, the nominated sites would then be visited by a corporate quality team that would evaluate the site documentation and make a recommendation for a site to go for the award. The selection of a site had to be made soon to give them time to prepare their application. A seventy-five-page written application was due at the National Bureau of Standards by May 20.

Talbot already had a mental list of the sites that would come out on top because of their reputations for quality and customer satisfaction. He was sure that Application Business Systems's candidate would be "Fortress Rochester," particularly with all the innovative things they had been doing during the development of the AS/400. So he decided to call Larry Osterwise. His timing could not have been worse. It was February 1988, and Rochester still had not turned the defect curve on the AS/400.

Osterwise's first response to Talbot was an unequivocal "No! I don't want to do that. We've got our hands full out here. Plus," Osterwise complained, "the last thing I need is another set of auditors coming in and telling me that I don't do enough of statistical process control or something. We just don't need that. Anyway, I hate auditors."

Talbot wasn't terribly surprised by Osterwise's response. He had known Larry for years and knew that he could bring him around in time. All he had to do was get Osterwise hooked on the award. Talbot dropped into his best negotiating posture and urged Osterwise at least to look at the Baldrige criteria. Osterwise recalled the conversation as going something like this:

I'll send you some copies of the guidelines. Just read them. Get a couple of your people in Rochester to look them over and see what you think. Get them to put together something my guys can look at, will you?

Osterwise reluctantly agreed. Talbot had hooked his winner. Look out, Milliken!

Rochester's 1988 Baldrige Assessment

A few days after Osterwise got copies of the award application from Talbot, he called a meeting with his key managers to discuss who should lead the effort to assess the Rochester site against the new award criteria. Several people were suggested, but the team kept coming back to one manager who, as it happened, was out of town at the time. His name was Roy Bauer.

Bauer first worked at Rochester in 1967, then returned to the site both after a tour of duty in the army and after an assignment at corporate headquarters. He had begun as a manufacturing engineer, progressed through various assignments in manufacturing, served as the site operations manager, and in 1986 became the manager of laboratory operations for the AS/400 development project. Bauer's choice to lead the assessment effort seemed a logical one. First, he had broad general management experience, and second, he had been doing a lot of work in Rochester's development laboratories on process management and on the introduction of the AS/400. Third, and perhaps more importantly, Bauer was known to have a talent for condensing reams of data into simple but meaningful visual presentations. Since the application for the award would have to be written in just seventy-five pages, according to the application guidelines, the selection team felt certain that the ability to tell a succinct but credible story to examiners, who for all they knew would not even understand the midrange computer business, would be critical. Bauer, it was agreed, had that ability if anyone did.

Bauer was assigned to review the award criteria and determine if Rochester had a chance to win. "Most importantly," Bauer was told, "do it fast." Talbot's corporate quality team would visit the plant in just three weeks to see the results of his efforts. By then they would want to see evidence that Rochester had the documentation, not only to support writing an application, but, more importantly, to win the award.

Bauer assembled a team of twelve people from different areas of the site to help him with the assessment. None were senior managers. Their first step was just to read the award criteria Talbot had sent them. They had no idea how the criteria had been developed and certainly no sense of how important the criteria would become to IBM and to Rochester. They were just trying to understand what information the criteria was seeking so that they could assemble it for the corporate review.

How the Baldrige Criteria Were Developed

The criteria Bauer and his team were reading covered forty-one pages and had been developed by the National Bureau of Standards (NBS) of the United States Department of Commerce (now the National Institute of Standards and Technology [NIST]) under the leadership of Curt Reimann. Reimann was an NBS scientist, with only a limited exposure to quality improvement techniques, who had gotten the assignment because, as he said in a 1992 interview, he was "the highest ranking official in NBS at that time with an interest in the subject." Reimann had also developed at least a handshaking acquaintance with some of the leaders in the quality field through his involvement with quality associations such as the American Society for Quality Control in his role as deputy director of the National Measurement Laboratory.

Since Reimann was by no means a quality professional, he had begun his efforts to develop the award criteria in the early fall of 1987 by reviewing existing quality awards, such as the Deming Award in Japan and NASA's quality award. He also reviewed the draft criteria for a productivity/quality award which had been prepared by a group of quality professionals from America's major companies who were working with the American Productivity and Quality Center (then the American Productivity Center) in Houston, Texas.

Reimann was not totally satisfied with any of the existing award criteria and recognized that he needed the support of the quality community if the Baldrige award was to succeed. He started calling people he already knew to ask them who in the United States knew something about quality. Based on these calls, Reimann began compiling a list of people with a good reputation in the quality field and talking to them.

Between September and December of 1987, Reimann spent most of his time on the telephone or in meetings with quality professionals who represented every segment of the quality community in the United States. Many were disciples of one or more of the "Quality Gurus" such as W. Edwards Deming, Joseph Juran, Phil Crosby and Armand Feigenbaum in the United States and/or Genchi Taguchi or Kaoru Ishikawa in Japan. Some were part of the "soft school" of quality that emphasized quality improvement through the use of quality circles and teams. Others were more interested in statistical tools such as statistical process control (SPC) or design of experiments (DOE). Most of the people Reimann contacted weren't quality consultants or academicians. Rather, they were, for the most part, quality directors and other quality professionals working in large and small U.S. companies. They were the kind of people Bob Talbot had encountered on his "fateful day" when he had been told that he didn't know anything about quality. They were practitioners, and they held strong opinions. They often disagreed with each other, but they had one thing in common. They felt passionately about the need for American business to improve the quality of its products and services, and they wanted to see America's new quality award succeed.

Reimann listened to what these quality professionals had to say, mediated disputes, and, over the course of just six months, forged a consensus within the U.S. quality community. The document Reimann's team at NBS created was not perfect by any means. None of the quality professionals agreed with every statement in the criteria. Most disagreed with minor points. But most agreed that what did emerge was the best thinking the United States had to offer in the late 1980s about what a company had to do to achieve total quality and total customer satisfaction.

The criteria that emerged from the debate and discussion were all-encompassing. Yet they were also nonprescriptive. They provided general guidelines of what companies needed to do, but they didn't insist upon specific quality tools or techniques or a specific approach. For example, the criteria asked for examples of "sustained and visible executive involvement in the development of an effective corporate quality culture" but didn't specify what that involvement had to be.

The 1988 Baldrige Criteria

The 1988 Baldrige criteria that had emerged from Reimann's networking with U.S. quality professionals and that Bauer and his Rochester team were poring over during February of 1988 had seven categories of examination items.

Category 1.0—Leadership
Category 2.0—Information and Analysis
Category 3.0—Strategic Quality Planning
Category 4.0—Human Resource Utilization
Category 5.0—Quality Assurance of Products and Services
Category 6.0—Results from Quality Assurance of Products
                and Services
Category 7.0—Customer Satisfaction

The first five categories, said the award application instructions and guidelines, were intended to examine the processes that made up the applicant's overall quality system, the measures established by the applicant for assessing quality improvement, and the results obtained using the measures. The remaining two categories focused primarily upon quality improvement gains achieved for products and services and improvements in customer satisfaction. Each category was assigned points, and the total points of the seven categories came to 1,000.

As Bauer and his IBM Rochester team reviewed the criteria, they quickly saw that each of the seven major categories had been broken down into four to ten subcategories, and each subcategory had been broken down further into one to four examination items. In total there were seven categories, forty-two subcategories and sixty-two examination items.

Category 1.0 dealt with leadership and was worth 150 points. It was broken down into six subcategories and dealt with such matters as how the organization's key executives demonstrated sustained and visible leadership in developing a quality culture; how they developed their quality policy or philosophy and communicated the policy to all employees; what type of management system they had put in place to improve quality; how they allocated resources for quality improvement; and how they supported quality improvement activities outside their company through, for example, participation in professional societies.

Category 2.0, which was worth 75 points, dealt with information and analysis. Here the criteria asked how the organization collected, analyzed, and used data on product/service performance trends for quality improvement and quality control.

Category 3.0 covered strategic quality planning and was worth 75 points. It asked how quality considerations were taken into account during the organization's planning process and asked for a list of the organization's operational (one-to-two-year) and strategic (three-to-five-year) quality improvement goals.

Category 4.0 dealt with human resource utilization and was worth 150 points. It dealt with such areas as how quality goals were communicated to employees; how employees were involved in quality improvement efforts; what type of training employees had been given in quality improvement techniques; how the organization recognized and rewarded employees for quality improvement; and generally how the organization's personnel policies and practices supported quality improvement.

Category 5.0 dealt with quality assurance and was also worth 150 points. Here the criteria asked how the organization got information on customer requirements and customer satisfaction and how it used that information; how it included customer requirements in the planning of new products and services; how it established quality objectives for new or improved products and services; what measurement systems the organization used to ensure that production and service processes were monitored and controlled; how audtis were conducted; and how the organization inspected or validated its finished products and services.

Category 6.0 was worth 100 points and dealt solely with results. The criteria asked for tables and graphs showing trends in such areas as the reliability and performance of products and services; reductions in scrap, rework, and rejected products and services; reductions in claims, litigation, and complaints from customers; and reductions in warranty or guarantee claims and field support work required to fix quality problems.

Finally, Category 7.0 dealt with customer satisfaction. It was worth 300 points, the most of any category. It covered areas such as scores the organization had received on measures of customer satisfaction; how the organization's products and services compared to those of its competitors; how the organization handled customer complaints; and how the organization had improved its product/service guarantees and warranties.

Each category also contained a subcategory asking for a description of unique or innovative approaches the organization had used to address the items covered in that category. Additionally, each subcategory had a set of scoring criteria. For example, the examination item on Customer Views of Quality of Products or Services (7.1) had three scoring criteria:

1. Validity of customer satisfaction measures and correlation with customer quality requirements, i.e., performance, reliability, durability, etc.;

2. Evidence of high level of customer satisfaction; and

3. Trends in customer satisfaction over three years.

Overall, the criteria were very comprehensive. They were also somewhat difficult for Bauer and his team to understand. As a result, much of the team's time was spent discussing and debating the meaning of the questions.

1988 EXAMINATION CATEGORIES/SUBCATEGORIES
Malcolm Baldrige National Quality Award

		MAXIMUM POINTS
1.0 LEADERSHIP		**150**
1.1	Senior Corporate Leadership	50
1.2	Policy	30
1.3	Management System and Quality Improvement Processes	30
1.4	Resource Allocation and Utilization	20
1.5	Public Responsibility	10
1.6	Unique and Innovative Leadership Techniques	10
2.0 INFORMATION AND ANALYSIS		**75**
2.1	Use of Analytical Techniques or Systems	15
2.2	Use of Product or Service Quality Data	10
2.3	Customer Data and Analysis	20
2.4	Supplier Quality and Data Analysis	10
2.5	Distributor and/or Dealer Quality and Data Analysis	10
2.6	Employee Related Data and Analysis	5
2.7	Unique and Innovative Information/Analysis	5
3.0 STRATEGIC QUALITY PLANNING		**75**
3.1	Operational and Strategic Goals	20
3.2	Planning Function	20
3.3	Planning for Quality Improvement	30
3.4	Unique and Innovative Planning	5
4.0 HUMAN RESOURCE UTILIZATION		**150**
4.1	Management and Operations	30
4.2	Employee Quality Awareness and Involvement	50
4.3	Quality Training and Education	30
4.4	Evaluation, Incentive, and Recognition Systems	30
4.5	Unique and Innovative Approaches	10
5.0 QUALITY ASSURANCE OF PRODUCTS AND SERVICES		**150**
5.1	Customer Input to Products and Services	20
5.2	Planning for New or Improved Products or Services	20
5.3	Design of New or Improved Products and Services	30
5.4	Measurements, Standards, and Data System	10
5.5	Technology	10
5.6	Audit	15
5.7	Documentation	10
5.8	Safety, Health, and Environment	10

5.9 Assurance/Validation   15
5.10 Unique and Innovative Approaches   10

6.0	**RESULTS FROM QUALITY ASSURANCE OF PRODUCTS AND SERVICES**	**100**

   6.1 Reliability and Performance of Products or Services   25
   6.2 Reductions in Scrap, Rework, and Rejected Products or
       Services   20
   6.3 Reductions in Claims, Litigation, and Complaints Related to
       Quality   25
   6.4 Reductions in Warranty or Field Support Work   20
   6.5 Unique or Innovative Indicators of Quality Improvement or
       Economic Gains   10

7.0 CUSTOMER SATISFACTION	**300**

   7.1 Customer Views of Quality of Products or Services   100
   7.2 Competitive Comparisons of Products or Services   50
   7.3 Customer Service and Complaint Handling   75
   7.4 Customer Views of Guaranties/Warranties   50
   7.5 Unique or Innovative Approaches to Assessing Customer Satisfaction 25

TOTAL POINTS   **1000**

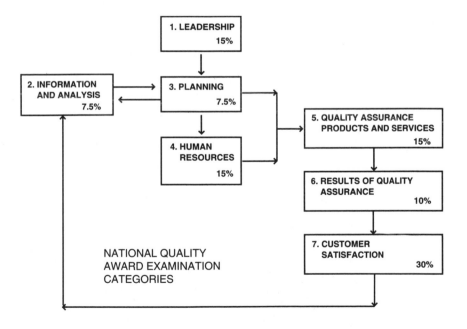

NATIONAL QUALITY
AWARD EXAMINATION
CATEGORIES

Collecting Data to Respond

Reflecting upon Rochester's first exposure to the Baldrige criteria, Bauer later remarked:

> In 1988 the guidelines were messy. They had subsections upon subsections. We were not quality professionals, so all the buzzwords didn't mean much to us. We weren't quality theorists. We were just in there looking at quality from a business standpoint, trying to interpret the guidelines, figuring out what they were asking, and then asking ourselves "Can we answer this question, and what kind of supporting data and information do we need?"

Eventually, the team reached some agreement on what they thought the criteria meant and started collecting whatever data they could find to address the issues raised in the criteria. They gradually assembled enough data to fill six three-inch binders. There was no flow to what the team had assembled, just data arranged in tabs in the binders by subcategory. There was no narrative or story to what they had assembled, and the whole effort had been given only scant attention by Furey, Osterwise and the other senior managers at Rochester. They had just left the matter up to Bauer and his team. "Pull together what you can," they had said. Furey, Osterwise and the others had "more important" things to do.

The Leadership Isn't There

When the corporate review team arrived to conduct their review, they were escorted into Bauer's office and shown the binders. Furey and Osterwise were nowhere to be found. To put it mildly, the corporate quality team was not impressed. Rochester just didn't seem to be taking this whole issue of a quality award very seriously. Certainly, the leadership of Rochester wasn't. "If that is the case," decided the corporate review team members, "we shouldn't even waste our time." They marched to a telephone and called headquarters.

"They aren't ready for us," the team leader said to Tom Burcak, a corporate quality consultant who was coordinating the various corporate site visits. "They've delegated the whole thing down to lower levels and we're leaving. We're not even staying to look at what they've got."

At Burcak's insistence, the review team did stay and examine what Bauer's team had assembled. They had to admit that Rochester did have some good information. They could show some real improvement in quality. And, as a result of the AS/400 development efforts, they had implemented some innovative approaches that were getting results. Of course, there were gaps in what Bauer and his people had assembled that would have to be filled, and it would have to be presented in a way that a group of examiners, perhaps with little technical knowledge, could understand. Still, Rochester was a strong candidate to be IBM's applicant. There was just one problem. It was obvious that the minds and hearts of Rochester's leaders just weren't on winning the Baldrige award in 1988, even though they and the corporate review team thought Rochester probably could win. There was one not-so-simple reason for not trying—the AS/400.

The Decision Not to Compete

Rochester's new product line was scheduled for release in just a few months. No one had the time to reduce six volumes of data to a seventy-five-page application. Plus, what good would it do anyway? If Rochester wrote the application and submitted it in May, as required, it would, by necessity, address Rochester's quality experiences with the System/36 and System/38, the predecessors to the AS/400. Then in June the AS/400 would be announced, and they would start shipping it in August. By the time award site visits could be scheduled, the examiners would no longer be interested in the old products. They would want to know about the AS/400, but the AS/400 would be so new that even Rochester wouldn't know how well it was satisfying customers. "What could we do when they ask about the AS/400," asked Osterwise, "just shrug our shoulders and say, 'Beats the ———— out of me'?" After three weeks of effort, the answer was "No,

Rochester would not compete." The honor of applying in 1988 would go to another IBM site, Endicott, New York. Rochester would focus on bringing out the AS/400. It could always go after a quality award later.

5

The 1989 Baldrige Application

While "Fortress Rochester" was busy launching its AS/400, IBM's Endicott, New York, site, one of the other six sites Talbot and Akers had been considering, was busy writing a Baldrige application and undergoing the site visit required for all Baldrige finalists. But 1988 was not to be IBM's year to win the award. Instead, the Baldrige judges picked Motorola, Westinghouse's Commercial Nuclear Fuel Division, and a little-known Beverly, Ohio, manufacturer of iron-based and silicon metals, Globe Metallurgical.

There was very little doubt that IBM would try for the award again in 1989. After all, Talbot couldn't ignore the Milliken challenge. More importantly, Endicott had received a positive feedback report from the Baldrige examiners, and, even though they didn't win, the Endicott team was enthusiastic about the whole Baldrige experience. Even in losing, they had learned a lot. "Forget the award," the Endicott team raved. "Just do the self-assessment. It will change you forever."

The Decision to Compete in 1989

If IBM was going to try for the award again, and it was, the question of which site should apply remained. Although the Endicott team highly recommended a self-assessment, even without an official application, Akers, Talbot and the rest of IBM's senior management team wanted to win. They could go with Endicott again or they could go with another site. They chose to go with Fortress Rochester. An IBM executive who was involved with the selection process explained the decision to have Rochester apply:

> There were five or six locations that were considered to apply in 1989. [We] made the decision that Endicott would not apply in 1989. Part of the reason that Endicott did not win was that they did not have enough market segmentation, not enough customer involvement, and they did not have a track record of revenue improvement. The Endicott product line was highly successful but not growing. [We] made the decision from reading Endicott's [Baldrige] feedback [report] that we weren't going to do better. The share was what it was. The product line was what it was. The industry was what it was.
>
> Rochester had the whole deal. For Rochester's AS/400, you could find lots of people to talk to because it was a different industry. [We] felt we had a better chance of doing what was expected from a Baldrige perspective—doing everything from suppliers to customers and infrastructure—at Rochester.

The final decision was still pending with IBM's senior management committee when Osterwise received a call from headquarters asking him to apply. "Isn't this a corporate decision?" asked Osterwise, to which the caller responded, "Let me put it this way, there are some people in IBM with very low serial numbers who think you ought to apply. So, while we still have to present it to the management committee, I think you should go ahead and start doing some work." Osterwise knew very well who had "low serial numbers." That could only mean the very top executives of IBM.

Osterwise wasn't arguing or trying to find a way out, like he had the year before. In fact, based on the success of the newly released AS/400, Osterwise was pleased to have an opportunity to document their achievements and, of course, win an award. He and everyone else at Rochester knew that this traditionally good site was better than ever—maybe even a sure winner.

Organizing to Write the Application

If Rochester was going to write a seventy-five-page application and pull together the six binders of documentation Bauer and his team had assembled in 1988, adding new material, Osterwise knew he needed someone in charge, and he needed to assemble a team of people who could be freed up to work on the effort. He couldn't just turn the assignment over to his quality organization, because he didn't have one. In one of a long series of reorganizations, the Rochester quality group had been disbanded by 1988 and integrated into manufacturing, as part of the *quality-is-in-the-fabric-of-the-business* movement. There was, however, a small group that had been retained to focus on product assurance and strategic site-wide issues of quality, led by Joe Rocca, manager of IBM Rochester's product assurance department. Osterwise was still busy with the AS/400, so he turned the application process over to Rocca and his team.

Assessing what had to be done, Rocca and his team made two critical decisions that were to have important ramifications for the 1989 application effort. First, they decided to appoint category owners for each of the seven Baldrige categories. Each category owner would be allotted a specific number of pages, equivalent to the relative point value of the category, in which to write his or her section. Thus, the Category 1 owner would have responsibility for a category worth 120 of the possible 1,000 points, or 12 percent of the total. He or she, therefore, would be allotted nine pages to write the category, or 12 percent of the maximum seventy-five pages. It would be the same for each category. Category responses would be written independently and later merged into a final document. Second, to help the category owners and do some preliminary scoring, Rocca and his team asked Talbot to send down a corporate review team, including someone who had been involved in the Endicott effort.

By December, Rocca had his category owners appointed and had brought in representatives from Endicott to review their experience in writing an application. The Endicott experience, though, would not be a one-to-one translation for Rochester. Not only did the two sites manufacture completely different products, but Endicott's application was based solely on manufacturing. Rochester's application would have to encompass manufacturing, development, customer satisfaction and customer involvement. In addition, the Baldrige award criteria had changed significantly from the prior year. The architects of the Baldrige award considered process improvement as important to enhancing the quality of the award itself as it was to enhancing the quality of applicants' products and services. Therefore, they provided for process review and modification of the award criteria after each year's awards had been presented. Rochester would be applying under the newly modified procedures and criteria.

The 1989 Criteria

Three major structural changes were made to the award criteria between 1988 and 1989. First, the number of examination items was reduced from sixty-two to forty-four, primarily by eliminating redundant or overlapping items. For example, the seven items which had asked about unique or innovative approaches were eliminated as individual items and replaced by the general instruction to discuss innovation in the sections to which it might apply. The second change in the criteria was an increase in emphasis on quantitative approaches and the use of comparative or benchmark data. And last, the scoring criteria under each item were replaced by "items to address." Whereas in 1988, applicants were expected to reply to all scoring criteria, the areas to address allowed applicants to ignore "areas" that were not relevant to their business and simply to explain why the particular "area" did not apply.

Perhaps the most significant change came in the actual scoring of the application. Starting in 1989, the scoring for each subcategory would be based on three evaluation dimensions: Approach, Deployment, Results. In other words, an applicant's score for Category 4.2, Employee Involvement, would be based on a determination of the following:

1. Did the applicant have an approach, method, or process by which employees were involved in the various activities or aspects of the business?

2. To what extent was the approach, method or process deployed within the company? Is it just deployed at the manufacturing level, or has it been deployed to areas like human resources, finance and marketing?

3. Are there demonstrable results, outcomes or effects from the deployment of this approach?

So, all Rochester had to do was figure out what "Approach, Deployment, Results" meant and respond to the criteria.

1989 EXAMINATION CATEGORIES/SUBCATEGORIES
Malcolm Baldrige National Quality Award

	MAXIMUM POINTS
1.0 LEADERSHIP	**120**
1.1 Senior Management	30
1.2 Quality Values	20
1.3 Management System	50
1.4 Public Responsibility	20
2.0 INFORMATION AND ANALYSIS	**60**
2.1 Scope of Data and Information for "Management by Fact"	25
2.2 Data Management	15
2.3 Analysis and Use of Data for Decision Making	20
3.0 STRATEGIC QUALITY PLANNING	**80**
3.1 Planning Process	30
3.2 Plans for Quality Leadership	50
4.0 HUMAN RESOURCE UTILIZATION	**150**
4.1 Management	25
4.2 Employee Involvement	40
4.3 Quality Education and Training	30
4.4 Employee Recognition	20
4.5 Quality of Work Life	35

5.0	QUALITY ASSURANCE OF PRODUCTS AND SERVICES	140

5.1	Design and Introduction of New or Improved Products and Services	25
5.2	Operation of Processes Which Produce the Company's Products and Services	20
5.3	Measurements and Standards for Products, Processes and Services	15
5.4	Audit	20
5.5	Documentation	10
5.6	Quality Assurance of Operations and Business Processes	25
5.7	Quality Assurance of External Providers of Goods and Services	25

6.0	QUALITY RESULTS	150

6.1	Quality of Products and Services	70
6.2	Operational and Business Process Quality Improvement	60
6.3	Quality Improvement Applications	20

7.0	CUSTOMER SATISFACTION	300

7.1	Knowledge of Customer Requirements and Expectations	40
7.2	Customer Relationship Management	125
7.3	Customer Satisfaction Methods of Measurement and Results	135

TOTAL POINTS　　　　　　　　　　　　　　　　　　**1000**

The 1989 Application Team

Rocca had assigned category ownership, at least in name, to Rochester site managers and executives, who quickly decided that this was a task that would be *delegated*. The real task of writing the application would fall primarily to a small group of young, enthusiastic employees:

Category 1: **Leadership**
Joe Rocca, assurance manager
Ken Syring, senior engineer
Pat McCracken, site communications manager

Category 2: **Information and Analysis**
Dave Case, staff planner
Linda Elsbernd, associate planner

Category 3: **Strategic Quality Planning**
Greg Harper, planning manager

Category 4:   **Human Resource Utilization**
Bruce Brandvold, advisory quality engineer
Mel Larson, advisory quality engineer

Category 5:   **Quality Assurance**
Gordy Haubenschild, information development
manager
Ben Persons, retired IBM employee
Art Hamburger, retired IBM employee

Category 6:   **Quality Results**
Lori Kirkland, senior associate quality
engineer

Category 7:   **Customer Satisfaction**
Mike Jacobson, advisory planner

They were good people who could be counted on to work hard at whatever they were asked to do. They might have little knowledge of the site as a whole, but they were available. They were people like Lori Kirkland and Mike Jacobson.

Kirkland, who was in her late twenties at the time, had grown up just thirty or forty miles from Rochester, the daughter of a farming family. After two years of college, she had quit school and gone to work for IBM Rochester in 1979 as a data entry clerk. A few years later she had gone back to school and gotten first her bachelor's degree in accounting and then a master's in business administration. After completing her graduate work, Lori rejoined IBM in systems manufacturing quality and had just taken a new position in Rochester's Production Management Center in late 1988. Her expectation was that she would be doing traditional quality work in the manufacturing area, not writing an award application. But the timing was right and she was the perfect choice. She was also smart, hard-working and, perhaps most important, available for assignment. She got Category 6, Quality Results.

Mike Jacobson joined IBM as an engineer immediately after graduating from college in 1974. By 1987, he had held first- and second-level management positions on a variety of engineering and product assurance projects and completed his M.B.A. At that time, he took a leave of absence to participate in the President's

Commission on Executive Exchange, a White House–sponsored program where private sector employees spend a year working in a government agency, while federal employees spend a year in the private sector. Jacobson had just returned to Rochester after spending a year with NASA. He was on temporary assignment to Rochester's customer satisfaction organization. He seemed a natural choice for Category 7, Customer Satisfaction.

With little training or guidance and almost no planning, Kirkland, Jacobson and the others started gathering information and writing their sections. Kirkland was most familiar with manufacturing and started immediately to pull together any data she could find on defects, yields and other traditional measures of product quality. With a broader category covering everything from how customer needs and expectations were determined, to how complaints were handled, to how customer satisfaction was measured, Jacobson's task was somewhat more difficult. He explained his approach in a later interview:

> It was a new arena for me. Most of my career had been in manufacturing and, prior to that, in a development/product assurance organization. So most of what I was doing was foreign to me. I had a general idea of where the sources might be, but I didn't know many of the individuals except by name or socially. I had never had any reason to research it. As it turned out, I had an M.B.A., which might have given me a little better background than some other people with more technical degrees.

Jacobson started by reading the application and trying to understand the questions. Then he attempted to identify Rochester's strengths and weaknesses in the area of customer satisfaction. Unlike some other category workers, he didn't have much difficulty in understanding what he believed to be the intent of the questions:

> First, I made a list of what I thought were our strengths relative to those questions. And then I made a list of areas where I thought we were vulnerable or not as strong as I thought we might have been. Then I started drawing up a list of names of people that might have data on our strengths and people who were responsible for processes or data where I thought we had weaknesses.

There were some problems getting information, but being a "fairly persistent sort," he was able to get what he needed. "A lot of them didn't understand why I wanted it. Some of them were protective of it," he explained. For example, he found getting complaint information one of the things that was most difficult. "People weren't willing to share that and didn't understand why I needed it. They felt threatened by the fact that I was asking for it. In cases like that I had to be a bit more assertive than in others."

Once he collected or coerced the data from his sources, Jacobson began the writing process, which, he recalled, didn't go smoothly at first. He was basically working alone on Category 7, using information that, on the surface, had little to do with the other categories, and taking his own path. He explained:

> I started out trying not just to blindly answer the questions. I tried to get behind the intent of the questions and answer what I believed the intent of the questions was, making sure that I had the data to support the answers. So I didn't collect a lot of information. I had a relatively small pile of information, because I had really pinpointed what I wanted to go after.

The Low Score

Throughout December and into January, Kirkland, Jacobson and the others collected their data, wrote and revised their sections. By early January they had something to submit to Osterwise for his review. Osterwise later recalled his initial reaction to this early draft, which he took with him on a midwinter trip to Duluth. "It was cold and snowy. I checked into the hotel and stayed up until about two in the morning reading the document. It was painful, boring reading, and I had a hard time staying awake. I had the questions on one side and the document they had written on the other, and I wrote on both."

When Osterwise returned from that trip, he sat down with each group and went over their section with them. The fundamental message he gave to each of them was that they didn't answer the questions. He asked them, "Do you know what this reminds me of? It reminds me of a college exam where the professor gives you examination questions and some blue books. Then, you choose to take the blue book and not the exam." They had just written what came into their minds. Some of it had no relationship to the questions. Osterwise sent them back to "take the exam" again. What he didn't realize at the time was that they *couldn't* take the exam, because they really didn't *know* the answers to the questions.

By late January, the application team had a new draft and they were ready for the first corporate review. The review team arrived, spent three days reviewing the draft application, and pronounced their score. "Mid to high two hundreds," they said, "maybe."

It wasn't at all what the Rochester writing team had hoped for or expected. They were angry and hurt. After two months of work their score was not just low, it was so low it wouldn't even get them consideration for a site visit. Les Papay, a member of the 1989 corporate review team, recalled the Rochester reaction:

> It was after midnight and particularly cold. The wind chill factor was about minus forty degrees. People were bitter and frustrated. They had spent so much time on this and now a bunch of guys were coming in and destroying their work product. Of course they associated it with themselves, so they took everything we said as a very critical statement of their work and their ability.

The Fundamental Problems

There were really two fundamental problems with Rochester's draft application. First, the writers were fairly low-level employees who knew their own areas but had little perspective across the entire site. Second, the application, as they had written it, explained *what* Rochester had done but not *how* Rochester had done it. Both weaknesses were critical.

Jim Grace, another member of the 1989 corporate review team, recalled:

> In 1989 I would characterize Rochester as being very good at what they did. They were very quality conscious and very hard working. They were as committed as any group of IBMers I had ever had any

experience with. But, in terms of Baldrige, they didn't know what was going on in their own shop. They didn't make all the connections and they didn't really have a common purpose. Their crowning achievement during that time was bringing out the AS/400. They really did some great things in terms of reducing cycle time and getting focused on quality and producing a lot of work with a few people in a short time. But when it came time to describe that in terms of processes—"here is how we did it"—they could tell you what they did but they couldn't describe how they managed to accomplish it.

The corporate team was trying to draw out of them the answers to the questions in the context of what they had already done. Grace described the typical review as follows: "We would ask them, 'How did you do that?' and they would tell us what they did. They would always tell you, 'Well, we took four guys and we went and did this . . . ,'" but they didn't think of it in terms of a process or approach, which is critical to the scoring." Grace continued, "So that is what we spent most of our time on—trying to define the processes they used, the data and inputs to those processes, the way they managed within the process, and the deliverable that came out."

The corporate review team found it difficult to get the Rochester team to think in terms of process instead of results. When asked a process question like "How did you do this?" they would respond with an example or anecdote about what happened. "They were the best in the company at doing what they did," said Jim Grace, "but they simply couldn't explain *how* they did it. In some cases, the Rochester team could not answer the questions at all or they didn't know where to get the data they needed to answer them."

Tom Burcak, another member of the corporate review team, had "the honor" of reviewing Category 1, Leadership. After going through the document with a highlighter and making notes in the margins, he sat down with the individual who had compiled the document, Ken Syring. Burcak recalled what happened then. "We got to about the third page and Ken stopped me. He said, 'Tom, I've got to stop you. I understand what you are saying. I understand your questions. But I can't do what you are asking me to do.' When asked why not, Syring replied, 'You're asking me to describe what is in the mind and heart of Larry Osterwise. I can't do that. I *cannot* do that.' "

Burcak understood. "It was the same problem with the other people working on the categories. Category 5, for example, was written by a highly technical person who was a software engineer, a programmer [Gordy Haubenschild]. He wrote Category 5 like it was a programming application." Burcak explained, "They were super technical people, but they could not write about the visions and the strategy for the Rochester site, because they really didn't know what they were."

Papay's "Predictable Process"

As it turned out, the whole Rochester experience with the first few drafts of their 1989 application was typical of what hundreds of companies and most IBM sites were to experience during their first brush with the Baldrige award. Of course, neither IBM nor Rochester knew what the "predictable" or "typical" experience would be like in 1989, because the award was so new. It was only years later, after many tries at writing a Baldrige application, that the pattern began to emerge. Les Papay, director of quality for IBM's World Trade Organization in 1989 and later director of market-driven quality assessment, explained in a 1992 interview what they eventually learned about the "predictable process":

> It begins when management assembles a team of young, enthusiastic people to write the application. Normally, these are people who have relatively few years in the company and who don't have a key role in running the operation, so they can be taken out of the job for a period of time. They interview people and write an application which is essentially no more than the story of their site, location or organization they have always wanted to tell. When the "work product," the application, is evaluated, it rates low on the Baldrige scale.
>
> Their first reaction is "Okay, it needs some work, but once we embellish it, enhance it, and put a good flow into it, our score will be higher." They rewrite their application and get assessed a second time. Their score is better but still not very good.
>
> With this second low score, there is a very predictable reaction.

First, they question the credentials of the examiners. "What do you know about quality?" they ask. So the examiners have to prove that they do have some credentials and know something about quality. At that point, the application team questions whether the examiners really understood the story the team wrote. The examiners say, "Yes, we understood the story" and then begin to explain the ratings they have given. At that point, the application writers get very defensive and say, "Well, we have a quality organization, so the Baldrige criteria are wrong, because we have a good story, and, clearly, the criteria don't fit it." Now, most of the application team members probably only read the criteria once or twice, so the examiners have to explain it to them.

By this point, the examiners have proven that they have credibility, that they understand the story the application writers have been trying to tell, and that the Baldrige criteria aren't wrong. The application team then gets very dejected. They have been working long hours. They are tired and ready to quit. "We are so bad," they start saying. "I don't want to be any part of this." They become very demoralized. At that point, somebody finally realizes the problem.

The problem is that management really hasn't been involved. They've left it up to these young people who have written a lot of things that sound good but clearly don't stand up to the Baldrige criteria.

Papay's "predictable process" is exactly what happened at Rochester. It resulted in the corporate review team calling Bob Talbot to complain, "We've got a problem out here. Larry [Osterwise] ain't playing. He's just not involved in this thing the way he should be, and we've got to get someone to give some direction—some common theme to this thing."

Talbot hopped a plane to Rochester. He recalled later:

It was winter and freezing cold. The car I was driving had just been washed, and it was so cold that ice was all over it. I couldn't get the door open that morning. So I wasn't happy when I got to the plant.

I go in and have a closed-door session with Larry, saying, "Look, the word's out that you ain't playing."

In response, Osterwise complained, "I've got all these other things going on. I'm so busy . . . ," to which Talbot retorted, "Let me understand this. You're too busy fixing problems to stop and figure out how to do things right?!" End of discussion. Osterwise decided to get more involved. He also decided that he needed to bring in some higher level managers who could provide site-wide input to the writing team. He brought Roy Bauer back into the effort.

Bringing the Application Together

After having led the 1988 effort to pull together some information to assess Rochester against the Baldrige criteria, Bauer had gone on to other assignments. In late November 1988, he had been approached by Joe Rocca and asked to write one of the sections for the 1989 application but had begged off, citing his responsibilities in getting a newly reorganized lab up and running. He had little or no involvement with the 1989 application until February. Then he got a call from his boss, Vic Tang. Tang explained that there was a meeting on the Baldrige process and the project was not in very good shape. Several names had come up as those needed to pull the process together. Tang said, "Your name came up to write Category 1 and mine came up to do Category 3." Bauer responded, "Well, Vic, you've got to get me out of this thing." Tang assured him that he didn't think he would be selected.

By the time of the meeting, Bauer had accepted the inevitable. He would agree to take the week or two necessary to shape up Category 1, then return to his lab duties. That, of course, was before the meeting. Bauer remembers:

> There was not a lot of happiness in that room. I could see it in the faces of the people. I didn't know too many of them at the time. The reviewers were sitting in there, and there was all kinds of contention between the reviewers and the team. There was no love lost. Some of the reviewers, over the course of the week, had developed contention among themselves over whether someone was making a point or not making a point. I sat in there and listened to the meeting, and right away, it became fairly clear that there wasn't any constant theme and that no one knew what they should be writing about or what points they should be making. This was Thursday morning.

At the conclusion of the meeting, Bauer agreed to try to put together the common theme of the document. He planned to meet with Jim Coraza, the AS/400 system manager, at 3:00 that afternoon. "We wanted to put together one flip chart that would tie everything together," he said; "then we would get back with everybody on Friday and set the common theme."

Bauer spent the time between the morning meeting and his 3:00 working session with Coraza playing counselor to the application team. "We had all these morale problems with people wanting to get off the team, get out of this thing," he recalled. He also spent time with the reviewers to try to understand what they thought the problems were. There was even contention and frustration among review team members.

Finally, at 3:00 Bauer and Coraza closeted themselves and began trying to make sense out of this chaos. Bauer remembered the effort as follows:

> We asked ourselves, "What is this place all about?" What we came down to was that we had been on a quality journey. We knew Rochester had been very good over time. We needed to show what we had done and why, and we needed to demonstrate it with facts. Also, we felt we needed to show where we were going, because we felt we had a pretty good idea of where we were headed. There were also innovations like customer involvement and other big ticket items we felt we needed to feature.

The result was a presentation which provided an overview of Rochester's quality journey as it related to each of the seven Baldrige categories. They had one flip chart page per category and were ready for the Friday morning meeting.

Rochester's Market-Driven Story

Lori Kirkland attended that Friday morning meeting and remembered it, with lingering agitation, as follows:

> Roy gets together a team. There was Roy, Vic Tang, Jim Flynn, Jim Coraza. They came into the conference room and gave about an hour and a half spiel. Jim Flynn gave this big presentation on what

we did with the AS/400 and how we accelerated things. Joe Frankowski, one of the corporate review team members, just kept yelling "Amen" like it was a Baptist sermon, because Flynn was hitting all these points on the head that we weren't capturing. That's what he [Frankowski] kept saying, "You're not capturing all of this."

Then Roy got up and went through his presentation and . . . [Frankowski] kept saying, "*Ahhhh,* why isn't this all documented? This is exactly what we need."

The presentations that Kirkland and the other team members heard highlighted Rochester's major initiatives within each of the seven Baldrige categories:

- *Leadership.* Schwartz, Osterwise and Furey had created and communicated a vision for producing a standard-setting computer. They had taken Rochester from being product-driven to being market-driven. They had put customer satisfaction first. Furey had reorganized the lab and created a crossfunctional management group to ensure that the vision was realized.

- *Information and Analysis.* Rochester had used research and modeling to segment their market by enterprise and location, industry, subindustry and size. They developed target markets in which they would compete. They had analyzed their competitors and compiled their market and competitive information into an electronic data base, accessible to managers throughout the site.

- *Quality Planning.* They used their market segmentation and information on target markets to allocate resources and set priorities. They included customers and business partners to validate their plans and strategies. They had positioned the AS/400 to differentiate it from the competition.

- *Human Resource Utilization.* Rochester had launched aggressive employee communication efforts to share the vision. They had empowered the work force to make changes and to solve problems. They had encouraged innovation and invested in education and training.

- *Quality Assurance.* Rochester had moved to parallel development and implemented leading-edge technology to simulate the computer system early in the development process, in order to design out defects.

- *Quality Results.* The AS/400 had been enormously successful. Rochester had regained market share and enjoyed double-digit sales growth. They had developed a computer in half the time it normally took. Engineering changes had been reduced by 45 percent. Scrap and rework had been reduced by 55 percent. And delivery time had been cut from three and one-half months to just two weeks.

- *Customer Satisfaction.* Rochester had involved customers and business partners extensively in the development process. They had created councils of customers and business partners to obtain customer input. And Rochester had created customer satisfaction teams, empowered to do just about anything necessary to resolve customer complaints. Finally, Rochester had begun calling customers ninety days after installation of the AS/400 to say "thank you" and to gather information on customer satisfaction, needs and expectations.

When the meeting ended, Jim Grace asked the members of the application team to think about what they had heard and send him their comments. Lori Kirkland, for one, didn't have to wait. As soon as the meeting ended she went up to Roy Bauer, whom she had never met before, and said, "I don't need to wait to send my comments in. I think you're absolutely right. My only comment is where the hell were you two months ago when we should have been planning?" Bauer was taken a little off guard and didn't quite know how to respond. The only thing he knew was that he had talked himself not just into writing Category 1, but into coordinating the entire application.

The very next morning, Bauer started meeting at 7:30 A.M. with the entire team for one hour per day. He also spent an hour per day with each one of the category teams, working through their sections. It was a seven-day-a-week job that started early in the morning and often went late into the night. No one on the team, including Bauer, was excused from their normal job responsibilities, and there was never any discussion about bringing in consultants or outside help. This was their story, and they intended to tell it themselves. They would simply have to balance their regular jobs with "the Baldrige application stuff."

The Importance of Linkage

As Bauer worked with the teams, he quickly began to learn something about the Baldrige criteria that he hadn't realized before. In the past, he and everyone else at Rochester had treated the seven categories as separate and distinct. Consequently, they made little effort to try to tie the sections together. Bauer learned that such an approach just would not work. The Baldrige criteria asked for much more. The criteria were constructed in such a way that there were linkages between sections. "What I found, and I didn't realize," recalled Bauer, "was that the linkage between the strategy section and the human resources section, for example, was such that you couldn't do one until you did the other. They want to know how your human resources plans were derived from your strategic plan, so you had to have the strategic plan piece written first." It was a major revelation about the Baldrige award and quality, although Bauer didn't necessarily recognize it as such at the time. It would take a year before Rochester began to see how important linking discrete activities was to total quality improvement. The corporate reviewers had tried to explain. They had said, "You need to describe the process and you need to have a common theme that runs through this thing that describes how you pull everything together."

The corporate reviewers were trying to make the point that most quality initiatives fail because they aren't part of a systematic, planned process. Instead, most quality efforts U.S. companies tried, such as IBM's Cost of Quality and Quality Focus on the Business Process programs, had been piecemeal programs. Real quality improvement would come about only when these piecemeal, programmatic efforts were brought together under a strategic plan for quality improvement. It was a key lesson of quality improvement Baldrige sought to teach, but Rochester was only beginning to understand.

The Second Corporate Review

The corporate review team returned to Rochester at the end of February to take another look at the document. The score had improved to the 500-point range but still had problems.

Lori Kirkland, for instance, had scored very well in the 200-point pass. This time, after a lot of "help" from Bauer, she got a *lower*, not higher, score. Kirkland was extremely upset with the news. "She was just about in tears," said Bauer, "and so mad at the examiners. If looks could kill, they'd all be dead. I remember her sitting in the conference room eating M&M's like she would often do in meetings. She was across the table from one of the reviewers, clutching those M&M's in her hands. She was so mad she wouldn't even share the candy with him. That wasn't at all like Lori."

It wasn't just the low score that bothered Kirkland. She had worked hard to get her section in shape because she had planned on taking a Florida vacation. She was to leave on Sunday, but this was Friday, and she had just been told that her score was lower. Worse, one of the corporate reviewers told her that she was not to leave for her vacation until she got her section in shape. The question was how she could get the necessary changes made in just one day. Bauer and some others offered to help.

The Need for Better Measures

Kirkland's section was Category 6, Quality Results, which asked for measures of product and service quality and the results Rochester had obtained. It was the old "linkage" thing again. It wasn't enough just to show that Rochester was measuring quality and had some positive results. They had to tell *why* they were measuring what they were measuring, and they had to show *how*, for example, their internal measures of quality, such as defects, related to external measures, like customer satisfaction. "As we started rationalizing why we were measuring what we were measuring," recalled Bauer, "we began to realize that the measurements we were showing in the application should be different. So we had to go back, get more data and do a lot more work on her section."

It took all of Saturday to rewrite Kirkland's section. They found better internal measures that seemed to have a closer linkage in their customer satisfaction measures, and they put them in Lori's section. When the revision was completed, Bauer read it over and thought it was very good, but he decided not to tell Kirkland that. Instead, he told her she could go on her vacation but that she was to phone him every day while she was gone. Bauer explained that what she had written had scored higher but would need more work. Therefore, they would need her to be available to answer questions. Bauer chuckles when he recalls, "It was really a bluff on my part. I actually thought the new draft was pretty good. I just didn't want her to be cut out of the process." Kirkland later admitted that she really appreciated being kept a part of the effort, even in her absence.

The Final Push

While Kirkland was on vacation, Bauer and the others kept massaging the document. It got better but still wasn't where it needed to be. Eventually, Bauer decided that too many people were working on it. He decided the time had come to get the category owners out of the rewriting and just work on the revisions himself, with the help of two or three other people. They would make the final changes and resolve the remaining problems.

Kirkland returned from her vacation just in time for the final push. Bauer and his small group had polished the document as much as they could. They wanted to do more, but they were running out of time. Since most of the team was now exhausted from the last-minute effort, Bauer put Kirkland to work doing some final cleanup. She began the tedious process of going over the application with a fine-tooth comb, finding words that were wrong or out of context and those last-minute things that needed to be changed. At that point, the document had been set for print, so all she could change were single letters or words, not whole phrases or paragraphs. The graphics people had given them a schedule showing that they needed three weeks for final printing. Says Kirkland, "We kept squashing it down until they had just no time to turn this around. The graphics people ended up getting squeezed tremendously in time."

Finally, there was no time left and the document had to go as it was, whether Osterwise and Bauer liked it or not. The application team gathered in Osterwise's office for a signing ceremony. There was cake and picture-taking with the whole team together. Then, with mixed emotions, they packed the application in an envelope and sent it out by Federal Express. It was the night before the deadline.

Rochester's 1989 Application

No one on Rochester's application team could be sure how the Baldrige examiners might respond to Rochester's quality story. Still, most of the application team members believed they had a strong application. They were proud of Rochester's quality journey and felt they had clear strengths in each of Baldrige's seven categories.

In Category 1, Leadership, they had shown an eight-year quality journey. It had begun in the early 1980s with a focus on increasing product and process effectiveness and efficiency. With the development of the AS/400, Rochester had expanded its quality focus to include suppliers, business partners, and customers in what the application team referred to as a "Strategic Circle of Quality." They had shown how site executives were personally involved in formulating quality plans and programs, participating in site-wide kickoff meetings for the programs, reinforcing quality improvement, and conducting ongoing reviews of progress toward meeting quality objectives.

Steve Schwartz, Tom Furey, and other executives had conducted informal employee roundtables, or forums, where employees were invited to ask questions and discuss site goals and objectives. Larry Osterwise had spoken at management colleges, new-employee orientations, and employee symposiums. In 1988 alone, he had personally responded to over five hundred messages site employees had sent him as part of Rochester's "Speak-Up" program, a site-wide on-line system through which employees could express concerns and/or ask questions of management.

Rochester had also created two cross-functional executive management teams (the Rochester Management Committee and the Rochester Management Board) to provide guidance for improving quality processes, providing resources, empowering employees, and fostering team spirit throughout the company.

In Category 2, Information and Analysis, the application team had documented Rochester's world-class, worldwide information and analysis system, which included such major information systems as (1) an on-line Executive Support System providing managers with easy access to competitive market research, customer demographics, customer satisfaction, market segmentation, sales, and other information; (2) an engineering design system and software development system that automatically converted designs to manufacturing process data and transmitted the data to all worldwide development and manufacturing locations; (3) an electronic data interchange that linked Rochester to its suppliers; and (4) an electronic customer support system that linked Rochester to its customers and business partners. Finally, the application team had outlined a seven-step process Rochester used for analyzing and using the data it collected and showed how that analysis had led to a more effective and trouble-free operation of Rochester's internal processes, a shorter cycle time, and improved customer satisfaction. For example, Rochester had developed an Artificial Intelligence (AI)-based Order Configurator that had been effective in eliminating order inconsistencies that could cause customer problems when equipment was installed.

In Category 3, Strategic Quality Planning, the application team had shown how Rochester developed detailed five-year strategic plans that were supported by two-year operating plans and how these plans focused on Rochester's achieving leadership in quality and customer satisfaction. The application described how employees actively participated in the planning process and how principal quality priorities and plans were set up with an emphasis on the early detection and removal of defects, the integration of customers, suppliers, and business partners in design validation, and increased availability of on-line data to each area. Finally, the application showed how Rochester benchmarked its competition and how it used leading-edge techniques for analyzing data it obtained. For example, Rochester used a market research tool to weight customer and business partner buying preferences and to assess whether Rochester's products matched the customers' buying preference.

In respect to Category 4, Human Resources, the application team had shown that all Rochester employees had a career development plan prepared in cooperation with their managers. They showed how 35 percent of employees were directly involved in cross-functional teams performing process evaluations, developing proposals, conducting pilot tests, and implementing improvements. Rochester's lost time and turnover rates were shown to be extremely low compared to industry averages, and, according to employee opinion survey results, the Rochester employee job satisfaction and morale were more favorable than any other IBM manufacturing and development site. Finally, the application team reported that the average cost of education and training to employees at Rochester over the past three years had represented 4 percent of the IBM Rochester payroll—four times higher than the national average.

In respect to Category 5, Quality Assurance of Products and Services, the Rochester application team had been able to document early and continuous involvement of customers, internal organizations, business partners, and suppliers in the design and development of product lines, particularly the AS/400. Cross-functional teams developed hardware, software, manufacturing processes, and customer service systems concurrently with an emphasis on defect prevention rather than the removal of defects at the end of the line. The application team had noted:

> [W]e put major emphasis on preventing defects and driving defect detection to the earliest possible point in the process. When we find a defect, our first priority is to find out how it happened and to prevent further defects from occurring. If the defect is a workmanship error, we contact the individual to determine if the process needs to be enhanced. If the problem is with a purchased part, we contact the supplier. The supplier reviews the defect and responds with the process changes necessary to prevent a recurrence. We require all suppliers to use statistical process control or other structured analysis to control key processes.

In respect to Category 6, Quality Results, the application team had been able to point to consistent improvement on a wide range of indicators of product and service quality since 1984, at the same time as product complexity and capability increased. Operational and business process quality trends and competitive comparisons had shown dramatic improvements. In particular, Rochester had significantly shortened the time it took to manufacture a new system (start-of-build to placing in finished goods inventory ready for shipment) and could point with pride to the development cycle time of its AS/400, which was equal to or even slightly better than its smaller "niche" competitors.

In respect to Category 7, Customer Satisfaction, the application team had shown how, with the development and introduction of the AS/400 system, IBM Rochester had changed its management philosophy from being technology-driven to being customer-driven. Customers had been involved early in the design and development phases of the AS/400; they assisted in field tests of the AS/400; and they served on an advisory board. Business partners had been involved early on to assure that application software they developed would meet customer requirements. Finally, Rochester regularly used a number of IBM surveys, independent surveys and analyses to determine customer satisfaction and its competitive position. Results of these surveys and analysis showed that Rochester products had been among the best in customer satisfaction from 1984 through 1988.

Overall, Rochester had an excellent record. The application team had developed what they felt was a good application documenting the site's accomplishments. The question remained whether it was good enough. No one knew. What happened next would be out of their hands.

6

The 1989 Site Visit and Verdict

After Rochester submitted its 1989 Baldrige application, members of the writing team returned to their normal day-to-day jobs. Each had different views of their probability of passing the examiners' screening and getting a site visit. Lori Kirkland was perhaps the most confident. "I thought we had a pretty good document," she said later. "I felt sure we had a good chance. Of course, I didn't know much about scoring at that point because I was just a category owner, and I was a little myopic. But on the whole, I thought we were in good shape."

Mike Jacobson was a little less certain about Rochester's chances. He recalled that he had felt good about the application and thought it was competitive. "I didn't necessarily think we had a winning application," he remembered, "but I felt we had nothing to be ashamed of."

Osterwise and Bauer were hesitant to count on anything. "We knew where we should score based upon our own scoring," said Bauer, "but we weren't at all sure whether we would get a site visit. We didn't have any clues. So we made a conscious decision not to do a lot of preparation for the site visit before we were officially informed that we were going to get one."

Waiting to Hear

May dragged on into June. Finally in late June, Rochester got its first notification. It had passed the first-stage review. Still, there was no word about a site visit.

June passed, then July. Rochester waited and did little to prepare for a site visit, should it come. Mike Jacobson recalled the period as follows:

> We would convene every couple of weeks because there were a number of things that were identified during the preparation of the application that clearly needed some follow-up work. In anticipation of a possible site visit, a number of activities were underway to make sure we consolidated all the backup data we needed to make our tables and references in the application current. In my area, for example, I had a terrible time getting complaint information, so that was one of the areas that I continued to work on. But there was really no news during that period, and it was not until we heard that we had been selected for a site visit that interest picked up again.

Preparing for the Site Visit

Finally in August, Osterwise got a letter informing him that Rochester was a finalist and requesting possible dates for a site visit. Bauer and Osterwise met and decided to push the site visit out as far as possible to give themselves time to prepare. They requested a mid-September visit, then got the application team together again. Jacobson remembered the meeting and what happened next:

> We had to make sure that all the data and information in the document were updated. Others on the application team spent a lot of time just organizing their files. I didn't have the voluminous data that some of them had. The other thing that we did during that time was to make sure that our own executive management team was prepared and briefed on the information. We believed that the evaluation team would focus on the executive team, so the executives felt they needed to be able to present all of the data in a great deal of detail.

Because of the way the 1989 application had been written, updating data turned out to be an ordeal. Lori Kirkland later recalled:

> I was putting together all the supporting documentation behind everything that I could. It wasn't easy to do. In 1989, as we put all this stuff together, we wrote first, then collected all the data. Therefore, when we started preparing for the site visit we had to recreate everything. I spent a lot of time trying to figure out where I got something, how I calculated it, and who I got the data from. Then I put together a book for the site visit on about any question that I thought they could possibly ask me about my category.

When the application writers had all their data updated, they spent two weeks educating site executives—the same executives who should have been the category owners but who decided to delegate the responsibility—on the entire application. The team had to explain, "Here is what we said and why we said it, and here's the supporting data." There was a *lot* of data. Much too much for anyone to understand, and few of Rochester's executives did understand it. Neither did Rochester employees.

The Employee Reaction

Rochester's three-day site visit was scheduled for September 18–20, 1989. No one at Rochester knew quite what to expect, but Osterwise and his team had updated their data, prepared formal presentations (in case that was what the examiners wanted), briefed site managers and executives on the contents of the application, and, just in case the examiners might want to talk to employees, posted notices and ran PA announcements informing employees that examiners might tour the site and approach them informally with questions. Employee response was the first sign that the visit might not go as well as it could. Karl Shurson, Rochester's production facility manager, recalled the employee reaction to the 1989 site visit as follows:

> We told our people that the Baldrige examiners were going to be here at a certain time and that they might stop and talk to them in

the hallway. "They may go to the cafeteria and ask to eat lunch with you. They may come into your department and talk to you about what you are doing." That week the hallways were empty, the cafeteria was bare, and people didn't seem to be available.

The Site Visit from Hell

From the beginning, the 1989 Rochester site visit was traumatic. Kirkland recalled:

> The examiner team got to Rochester, and they were extremely disorganized. The makeup of the team had changed from what we had been told just before they got to Rochester, and a new member had been added. The team members apparently had never spoken to each other prior to the visit, so they all got there with their own agendas, and they were all different. They had personality clashes and they had viewpoint clashes. We just sat there watching the dynamics of all of that and trying to keep our sanity. It was hard.

Roy Bauer added, "Confusion reigned supreme the first hour or so." The examination team wanted a half-hour tour of the facility. The Rochester team finally convinced them that the plant was simply too large to cover in that amount of time, and they agreed to an hour tour. Bauer described the whirlwind tour:

> We ran them through the Software Partner Lab, where we bring customers into the laboratory. Then we ran through Marketing Support Center. We took them through the hardfile storage device manufacturing area and the AS/400 manufacturing area. Also, we set up presentations and demonstrations of key things we wanted to feature, for example the Executive Support System.

Everyone had been prepped for the tour. Second-line managers and above had been given packages on who the examiners were and the key points of each of the categories. They, in turn, had briefed their people. Joe Rocca prepared a thick book with key data for each of the category owners, but most of them never had a chance to use it.

Once the tour was completed, the nature of the site visit changed. The examiners were ready to start question-and-answer sessions. Here is a typical category session, in the words of Roy Bauer:

> When we got into the session, they had the questions they wanted to ask and we tried to give them stand-up presentations for answers. It ended up taking too long, and some of the presentations didn't go very well.

One of the examiners pressed on every point and actually irritated both the Rochester people *and* the other examiners.

Bauer later admitted that the category owners weren't answering the examiners' questions "crisply." "We were most concerned about our ability to answer the questions in a way that non-computer people could understand. We didn't know how knowledgeable they would be about our business." Bauer continued:

> We were always trying to read their faces between the answered questions. They were excellent at providing stoic facial expressions. You went from highs to lows, because there were a couple of examiners who, from offhand comments, made you feel you were doing real well. Then, of course, we had one examiner who kept raising issues in every session he attended, so none of those sessions went well. We were really at a loss to determine how the site visit was going.

These sessions continued for two long, grueling days. In hindsight, Bauer commented:

> I would like to be able to say that when they asked a question we responded, "This is what we do—boom, boom, boom, and, by the way, here's the supporting evidence," and that they looked at it and said, "Fine," and then went on to the next question. But that wasn't what happened at all. Instead, they asked, "How do you do this?" and somebody would get up and give a presentation. There were too many people in the room, because we brought in everybody and anybody who might have something to say about the item that was being reviewed. What happened was the presenter would finish and then somebody else would chime in with a remark, and that would open up another question from the examiners. Then all of a sudden we were in a mess.

It wasn't just a question of presentation. The Baldrige examiners were asking questions about things that Rochester managers had never considered.

The Need to Close the Loop

Bob Griffin, an IBM marketing director and a member of the Rochester application team in 1989, recalled trying to explain Rochester's approach to handling customer complaints:

> It was late the last night, and I was presenting the complaint process that we had. That complaint process put the responsibility on the branch office and the local marketing rep[resentative]. Whenever you got a customer complaint in the branch office, whether it came directly to the branch office or to John Akers's office, it was treated with a high degree of sensitivity. There was a special yellow form called a Customer Complaint Form. The secretary would pull it out, log it, and assign it to a manager. The manager had to respond to the complaint, send an acknowledgment back to the customer, and close the complaint in so many hours. Then it was filed in the branch. Our view was that you should drive responsibility down to the branch office level.
>
> What they [the examiners] kept asking and asking was how we captured and used *all* of that information. I was waxing eloquently on our process for handling complaints, but I was seeing the trees and not the forest. I really believed we were doing the right thing. I thought, "Obviously I didn't explain it very well, because I didn't convince them." I could tell there were questions in their minds.
>
> I kept focusing on the fact that we had an excellent track record, because it was audited and we had a system to follow up on customer complaints. I just wasn't hearing the question. They wanted to know how, at Rochester, we were sure we were capturing and using all of the complaint data, not just some of it. There could have been issues that the branches learned about that never got any further. I was missing their point.

Griffin *was* missing the point. The examiners wanted to know not only how the branch office and Rochester handled complaints, but how they compiled, analyzed and used the data they could gather from customer complaints. Correcting a customer's problem rapidly was good, but it was also important to "close the loop" and insure that there was constant feedback to those who could make a difference and *prevent* problems from occurring.

The Need for Senior Executive Leadership

Another issue the examiners focused on was "leadership." Phil Thompson, Rochester's low-end storage products plant manager at the time, recalled some of the examiner questions on leadership as follows:

> They were trying to understand, in greater detail, how thc leadership got involved in the day-to-day operational management, as well as in the strategic management of the site. What quality data did they see? What action did they take based on what they saw? How did that filter its way down into the organization? Then they peeled us down to the very lowest level, to what the people were empowered and authorized to do within their own realm of responsibility.

Rochester didn't exactly pass the "leadership" test with flying colors, and Osterwise later admitted that they didn't deserve to:

> To begin with, we utilized individuals in 1989 who were good people—in fact I refer to them as *available,* good people—to write our applications. But the executives really weren't involved to that great an extent. I was perhaps most involved, but even I didn't own it. I had "other things to do."
>
> When we got the word that we were going to receive a site visit, it actually took about two weeks of cramming by many of the executive team to feel even reasonably confident about being interviewed by the examiners.

It was perfectly obvious to the examiners. Rochester senior executives not only weren't fully involved in the Baldrige application, but weren't fully involved in quality improvement efforts. It was a major negative.

Waiting for the Verdict

The six weeks after the site visit were almost worse than the visit itself. Rochester waited to hear the results. Would they win or lose? There was a wide range of opinion from supreme confidence to extreme doubt. For Lori Kirkland it was a "sure thing" or as nearly sure as it could be. "I didn't feel we left too many points on the table," she said later, "but then I'm either all over the floor about things or all over the ceiling. After we submitted and had gone through the site visit, I assumed we would win since we *always* won."

For Roy Bauer, it was altogether a different story:

When the examiners left, Larry and I didn't know whether we had won or lost. We didn't know whether we did well or poorly. We just didn't have a feel for it. On the one hand, you would think of something that went really well in the site visit. Then you would think of this disaster with something else. I felt we had a shot, but I had prepared myself to be surprised if we won.

I didn't know all of the companies who were in the running, but I knew that Xerox and Milliken were, so I knew the competition was going to be tough. Then I saw an article in *Electronic Business* with David Kearns from Xerox on the cover. The scuttlebutt was that *Electronic Business* would try to find out who was in the running for the Baldrige and who had the best chance, then put them on the cover. When I saw that article, I said to myself, "We just got outpositioned." After that, I sort of expected not to win. Then something else happened that made me even more pessimistic about our chances.

What happens in the process is that the examination teams validate examination issues and then make a decision as to whether or not a company should be considered for the award. Then they pass their recommendation on to the judges. One judge looks at everything, then makes a presentation before the panel of judges.

During the time frame of the judges' discussions, the senior examiner from the Rochester site visit called Larry a couple of times to ask him questions. One question he asked was whether or not we were a bona fide business unit, whether we had profit responsibility. I heard about that question, and that was the second thing that led me to believe that we weren't going to win. You have to turn in an eligibility form, and they told us we were eligible. "Why are we now having this discussion?" I asked myself.

I decided the reason was they were trying to differentiate between the winners and the losers. That whole thing led me to prepare myself and say we're not going to win this deal. I never said that to anybody, but that's what I thought.

The Call from Curt Reimann

The folklore of the Baldrige award is that if you receive a site visit and get a call from the secretary of commerce, then you know, just on the basis of who is calling, that you have won. If you get a call from Curt Reimann, the director of the Baldrige award, then you have lost. In early October 1989, Larry Osterwise got a call. It was Reimann:

There was a meeting going on in my office, so I took Reimann's call in the open area outside my office at my secretary's desk. Reimann told me that we had not won and said he was sorry because he knew we were great and so on. He told me how tough it was for him to make the call. I felt like telling him, "You have no idea. You should be on this end." I was trying to look poker-faced because people were sitting there across the room watching me take the call.

I finished the call and went back to the meeting. Reimann had told me that the winners weren't going to be announced for a week and that I should tell as few people as possible. I sat there thinking, "Oh, wonderful!" I called Joe Rocca, because he was the owner of this process, and Roy. And I called Akers, Schwartz, and Kuehler and told them. I told Schwartz he could tell whoever else he thought should know but that it should be kept to a very narrow group. No one else knew. I don't even remember telling my secretary, Dar.

Learning from Losing

Losing the Baldrige award was disappointing to Osterwise, perhaps the biggest disappointment of his career. What did it all mean, and how was he going to tell his people? He recalled tough nights pondering those questions:

I spent the next four nights trying to figure out what it all meant and how we were going to handle this. My typical routine then was that I would work until about 7:00 and then go home and spend a couple of hours having dinner and being with the kids. Then everything would begin to quiet down, and I would go through my mail and watch TV, or whatever.

For the first four nights after I had learned that we had lost and I still couldn't tell anyone, I went out and sat in the hot tub on our deck with all the lights out in the place. This was October in Minnesota! I sat there and stared at the stars and said to myself, "There's got to be more to this." Sure, it was only a trophy, but when you think of the commitment of the people and the effort they put forth to try to win and what winning meant to them, it was really something. It was like losing the Nobel Prize or the World Series. So I sat out there, night after night, trying to figure out what it all meant and what I was going to tell our team.

By the time I got to the third or fourth night, I started to feel a little better. I began to think, "Okay, maybe it is better we didn't win." If we had won, IBM would just sorta say, "Well, that's nice. We won. I told you we were great." But I knew we could be better. By the fourth night, I decided that we were just going to redouble our efforts. We were just going to be that much better. Whether we won or lost didn't matter. We learned a lot and we're going to continue to get better. I had this mental image of what I was going to tell people about our loss and about our future. We were just going to keep plugging and driving.

Telling the Troops

Osterwise developed a plan for telling his people about the loss. He decided he would make a formal announcement over the PA, orchestrate it and do it in the right way. But a story in USA Today changed all of his plans.

The week after Osterwise had received his call from Reimann, Rochester was holding one of its biannual management colleges. Osterwise had started the management college just that year, as a way of bringing in outside speakers to talk to Rochester's management team about quality. It was the morning session and Osterwise had just introduced a speaker. He was sitting in the front row. Osterwise tells what happened then:

Pat McCracken, our communications director, came in and sat down beside me. She whispered, "I've got to talk to you." I whispered back, "No, this person has just started speaking. It wouldn't be polite to leave, and there are four hundred people back there who'll see me get up and leave and say, 'Well, if Osterwise doesn't care anything about what this guy has to say, why should I?' So I can't leave."

But Pat insisted, "Larry, I've *got* to talk to you *now*." I said, "Is the place burning down?" as I got up and followed her to a little anteroom.

Then she told me, "We haven't got it yet, but I've heard that *USA Today* is saying that Xerox and Milliken are going to be announced as the winners of the Baldrige award for manufacturing. It won't take a genius to figure out that if they won, we didn't. So you've got to do something, or people are going to find out by reading the paper, and we don't want them to learn that way."

We scribbled a few words on a piece of paper, and we arranged for the site to tape a message from me to the troops that they could play over the PA system at a given time. I decided that I wouldn't just make an announcement from the podium to the people attending the management college but that I would tell them right after this speaker. They were about to go to small breakout groups, and I decided what I would do is go from session to session and tell them in their breakout groups.

I went into each breakout session and said, "If you haven't heard already, you will see that *USA Today* reports that we didn't win the Baldrige award. I can't verify it, but *USA Today* says it is going to be Xerox and Milliken. I can verify that it is not us, since I've already gotten the call from the Department of Commerce telling me that we did not win. So we didn't win. But, on the other hand, we learned a tremendous amount about ourselves through this process. It is going to enable us to get better. I'm sure our not winning is a large disappointment to a lot of folks, but life goes on. Let's just pick up the pieces and keep going."

Lori Kirkland, who was now a manager, was in one session that I went to. It was obvious that she was devastated by the loss, so at lunchtime I sought her out. I sat down next to her and said, "Lori, I know what you put into this, but it is not the end of the world. We learned a lot about ourselves. We're better. Think about it from the glass-is-half-full perspective."

Osterwise didn't know it at that time, but Kirkland had already heard about the loss. In fact, she had known for several days. Kirkland explained:

I found out on a Thursday morning, the week before Larry told everyone else. I was in Palisades, New York, in a class and Roy [Bauer] called and told me. I hadn't wanted to go to the class that week because I knew we might hear soon. I was afraid I would be away and miss hearing, so I made Roy promise to call and tell me if he heard anything.

When he told me, I didn't believe him at first. I thought he was teasing. He said, "Lori, we didn't win Baldrige," and I said, "Yeah, right." Then he said, "I'm serious, we didn't win. Curt Reimann called Larry and told him we lost—told him we didn't win."

I was in this class with my manager. Roy had told me, "Lori, you can't tell *anybody*. This isn't released, so you can't tell anybody." When I saw my manager, he asked me, "What is the matter?" He could tell by the look on my face that I was upset. I just said, "Nothing. It's personal."

When the class was over on Friday, I came home, and the next night my husband and I were getting ready to go out for dinner. I had showered and was sitting on the bed, and I just started crying. My husband came out of the bathroom and said, "What is the matter?" I said, "What is absolutely the worst news I could get? What is the worst thing that could happen in my life?" He said, "Your Dad! Something happened to your Dad." I said, "No, it's not my Dad. We lost the Baldrige." All he would say was, "Well, why are you crying?" He didn't understand, but for me it was really emotional. It's like a child. You've seen it from its inception all the way through, and you don't want to let go of it. To have lost it was just unbelievably horrible. Then I found out that Roy and Mike had been smart enough to prepare themselves for a loss. Dumb me. I never even toyed with the idea that we might not win.

Larry announced it in management college during the breakout session. He just walked into the room and said, "I want to read this announcement. Today it will be announced that these were the winners." He was incredibly somber. Very, very somber when he read this.

At noon, Larry caught me and said, "Listen to Vidmar's message. I know you'll understand. Just listen to him. I can't say that it will make it easier, but just listen."

We had a gymnast by the name of Peter Vidmar at the management college that day. He talked about one year's world championships in which he had felt confident, and he hadn't prepared as much, so he lost. He said that losing that year had been the absolute best thing that had ever happened to him, because after that, he resigned himself to being the last one in the gym every night.

Of course, at that point in time, it was hard for Lori to accept that anything good could come out of Rochester's losing. As it turned out, she was very wrong about that. Losing was one of the best things that could have happened to Rochester—and perhaps to IBM.

The 1989 Baldrige Feedback Report

The application feedback report from the Department of Commerce praised Rochester for their many accomplishments, but it also confirmed what the application team already knew or, at least, were forced to admit. They did not fail to win the Baldrige award because they had not written a good, concise application. They did not fail to win because they were not a good, a very good, company. Rochester did not win the Baldrige award because they were not yet a world-class company. The feedback report simply exposed many of the "warts" that the team had found for themselves and hoped that the examiners would not see:

- Rochester's leaders had not provided a clearly defined quality policy, goals or guidelines. Rochester had a lot of good, strong leaders who were all doing a lot of great things. The problem was that they were all acting independently and without a unified vision.

- Only 30 percent of employees had participated in the suggestion program or on a quality team.

- Because the AS/400 had been on the market for only one year, Rochester could not demonstrate sustained (two to five years) world-class quality levels for its primary product.

- They did not have a comprehensive system for gathering and analyzing all customer complaints.

- Their benchmarking efforts for nonmanufacturing areas were limited to other IBM locations.

The Baldrige application process and feedback report had clearly spelled out what stood between Rochester and world-class quality. In Baldrige terms, it wasn't enough just to have a good product like the AS/400. That was important, true, but what was equally important was knowing exactly *why* you had a good product. If you didn't know what you had done to make it happen in the past, then how could you make it happen again in the future? Rochester was beginning to learn an important lesson. The pursuit of world-class quality required more than just discrete actions or flowery language. It required a strategy for bringing all of the discrete initiatives one might take to improve quality and customer satisfaction into focus. It also required senior management's commitment to implement that strategy. Rochester had pursued a limited vision, the AS/400, and had taken action to fundamentally change in order to realize that vision. Consequently, it had become good. It was not yet great. Something was missing. If Rochester was to become great, it needed a broader vision and a strategy to realize that vision. So did IBM.

7

Market-Driven Quality

It was difficult for many at IBM to accept Rochester's losing the Baldrige award. For the second time in as many years, an IBM site had gone for the award, gotten close, but lost. For Akers it was just another frustration in a long series of frustrations. For four years he had been trying to find out what was wrong with IBM and what he could do to fix it. He knew that Rochester and a few other sites like Endicott were doing something right. But what, exactly, were they doing, and was it transferable to the rest of IBM? Akers didn't know, but he did know that IBM as a corporation was running out of time.

A Vision Without a Strategy

In 1987 and 1988, Akers had sent his top team, including IBM's president, Jack Kuehler, out to talk to customers in a series of forums, hoping that they would learn more about what was wrong and how to start making things right. The message the IBM executives heard from their customers was the same everywhere they went. "IBM has a long way to go to improve itself and be much more customer-driven." "You have to be quicker to the marketplace with new products." "You have to be more responsive to what we want and need." The feedback from the customers was strong, direct, and much worse than Akers and his team had expected. More importantly, they had invited IBM's *best* customers, not its worst ones, to these forums. The message was coming from customers who still liked IBM and wanted to help. Their message to IBM was, to say the least, candid: "You had better listen to us and make some changes or we're going to give you some very sad news."

Responding to this message and the results of many quality audits that revealed that dramatic change was needed, Akers decided that IBM had to be more customer-focused. He announced that IBM would become a market-driven company in an Executive Instruction issued in May 1989. He followed the announcement with a requirement that all IBM executives attend a two and one-half day "retreat" that would be hosted by senior executives and include intense training on what it meant to be market-driven and why a vigorous effort to deploy quality processes was important. During the "retreat," the executives were asked to identify concrete things they would do in their own organizations to improve customer satisfaction, market share and quality. To accommodate the large number of executives who were required to attend, IBM conducted thirteen such "retreats" during 1989. These "retreats" turned out to be the most extensive and exhaustive such training in IBM's history up to that time. Still, little changed.

In retrospect, most IBMers came to realize that the market-driven principles—"make the customer the final arbiter, understand our markets, commit to leadership in the markets we choose to serve, and execute with excellence across the enterprise"—were nothing more than a slightly modified restatement of IBM's basic beliefs. The principles sounded good, but offered no specific strategy. "What exactly are we supposed to do to be market-driven?" And, "What does it mean to be market-driven in an area like manufacturing?" IBMers wanted to know. It would take an extremely unpleasant "trip to the woodshed" and a trip to a former Baldrige winner for IBM to begin finding the answers to these and many other questions.

Taken to the Woodshed

Throughout 1989, Akers had become more and more frustrated with IBM's quality problems and the fact that his market-driven initiative appeared to be going nowhere. Finally, in the fall of 1989, Akers decided to do something he had never tried before. He would hold quality reviews. All IBM executives would be brought in to confront the company's quality problems. These quality reviews became a series of meetings no one at IBM would ever forget. Later, IBM executives referred to their experiences in these meetings as "being taken to the woodshed."

The "woodshed" meetings were held in various locations during the fall of 1989. Top IBM executives, many of whom had not wanted to come, were forced to attend the meetings and report on product quality as seen through the eyes of their customers. Each meeting lasted three days, and each was painful because most of the discussion focused on what had gone wrong. An executive who attended these meetings recalled what happened at one of them and his own reaction:

> They started off the meeting going through all the things that were going wrong. We were told that some of our hardware wasn't as good as our competitors'. Our software had problems. Maintenance people were getting parts that were defective. They talked about what the leading companies were doing, and they told us IBM was in trouble.
>
> The immediate reaction was denial. "That's not so! Who said that!" But John [Akers] wasn't having any of that. He forced us to start talking about the problems, going through sector by sector.
>
> The room we were in was really too small. After about the first hour, it got so hot you could hardly breathe. Schwartz and Osterwise ended the presentation part of this meeting covering shortcomings, but they also described a customer- and quality-focused system they were using at Rochester that was showing signs of working. They provided the only glimpse of hope in the meeting. But, on the whole, everybody was embarrassed. We weren't used to talking about our problems.

When the "woodshed" meetings were over, Akers insisted on two follow-up meetings to continue the discussions. He made it clear to his team that he wasn't happy with the results he was seeing with his market-driven effort and that, if the executives couldn't fix the quality problems, *they would be replaced.*

One executive later reflected on the whole "woodshed" experience as follows:

> Going through all of that was painful, but it was something that had to happen. It was a lot like the experience of alcoholics. People could talk to us until they were blue in the face, but nothing was going to change until we were willing to admit that *we* were the problem. Then we could start the long journey back.

Like Rochester, IBM executives had finally come face-to-face with a crisis, and it was a very personal one. After the trip to the woodshed, IBM was ready to begin the journey back. But first it needed a plan, a road map for change. Not just any plan would do. "We started thinking about what kind of comprehensive, corporate-wide program we could kick off that would be an eternal journey," said Terry Lautenbach, IBM senior vice president, "not just a short try-to-fix-it-in-thirty-days program." An IBM vice president then stepped forward with an idea. It involved a trip to Motorola, one of the 1988 Baldrige award winners, and it would lead to IBM's finally developing a strategy for fundamental change.

Learning from Rochester and a Baldrige Winner

Throughout 1989, Heinz Fridrich, IBM vice president for manufacturing, had been struggling with the problem of how to make IBM's manufacturing business more "market-driven" but, like many others, he had found it difficult to translate market-driven concepts into actions his people could take. Rochester, of course, was farther along the road to being market-driven than any IBM site, and IBMers had visited Rochester to learn. Still, there were questions. "Was the AS/400 just a fluke?" "Was it just something about the Rochester site or the midwestern work ethic of the people that enabled them to accomplish what they had?"

"Would Rochester's approach work elsewhere within IBM?" The rest of IBM wasn't sure. Maybe Rochester was on the right track. But then, maybe it wasn't. The rest of IBM needed some confirmation that what worked at Rochester would work elsewhere. Plus, the whole concept of being market-driven just seemed to fit better with what marketing or service people did than with what manufacturing people did.

Gus Vassiliades, who worked for Fridrich, was aware of the progress Motorola had made in improving quality and knew that they had won the Baldrige award in 1988. He also knew that Rochester and some other IBM sites had visited Motorola and had come away with some good ideas. So he suggested to Fridrich that the two of them make a trip to Motorola and visit a couple of people he knew there: Tommy George, vice president and assistant general manager, Motorola Semiconductor Products; and Scott Shumway, vice president and director of quality, Motorola Semiconductor Products. Fridrich agreed.

In August 1989, Fridrich and Vassiliades made their first trip to Motorola. They came away impressed. "We were sitting there having this very informal conversation with George and Shumway," Vassiliades recalled, "and halfway through the meeting they started grabbing people and bringing them in to tell us about quality and what they were doing. It didn't take long before we began to realize that there was something really different at Motorola. Everybody had the same theme and objective. They all understood it and were anxious to tell us what they had learned."

As Fridrich and Vassiliades listened to the Motorola story, they were struck by two things. First, many of the quality tools and techniques Motorola was describing, such as quality measurement, cycle-time reduction, striving for aggressive goals, linking design and manufacturing, employee involvement, and so on, weren't new. Rochester, for example, had used many of these same tools and techniques in designing, developing and manufacturing the AS/400. But the second thing they noticed was that there was something different about Motorola. They had a strategy, an overall plan for change and for tying these various tools and techniques together. It was something that was missing at IBM and even at Rochester. In Baldrige terms, what Motorola had was a strategic quality plan, an approach that addressed in detail how the company would pursue market leadership through

providing quality products and services and through improving
the effectiveness of all operations of the company on a continuous basis.

Fridrich and Vassiliades came away determined that other executives at IBM needed to learn more about Motorola and that
IBM needed its own strategic quality plan. They immediately arranged for two representatives from Motorola to speak before a
conference of IBM plant managers. While the Motorola presentation was well received, Fridrich and Vassiliades knew something
more was necessary. After all, these plant managers had heard
presentations about quality improvement techniques before.
They had heard about what Milliken was doing and what Xerox
was doing. They had heard about Rochester. And they had heard
about the ideas of Deming, Juran, Crosby, Feigenbaum and all
the other quality "gurus." Still, nothing much had happened.
What Fridrich and Vassiliades wanted to do was to take a group
of IBM executives to Motorola and let them spend a day or two
listening to Motorola's entire story, not just a short presentation.
"Then," Fridrich and Vassiliades thought, "what if we could spend
another day or so with these executives and get them to take
what they had heard from Motorola and discuss how they could
apply it in IBM?"

It was a good idea, but how could Fridrich and Vassiliades get
such a task force assembled? How could they get the thirty or so
IBM executives they felt should be on the task force to agree to
spend two or three days at Motorola? While Fridrich and
Vassiliades were pondering these questions, IBM executives were
suffering through their "trip to the woodshed," being presented
with their own personal crises, and being motivated to find answers. Fridrich and Vassiliades saw an opportunity to sell their
idea for a trip to Motorola, and they took it.

They approached Terry Lautenbach with their idea.
Lautenbach listened and agreed, and Fridrich arranged a two-day
meeting at Motorola for thirty-one IBM executives, including
Bob Talbot. Fridrich also took along Larry Osterwise to provide
the Rochester perspective. "I was asked to go and be supportive,"
said Osterwise in a later interview. "When anybody brought up
something negative about what they were hearing from Motorola,
I was supposed to tell them, 'Not only does Motorola have it
right, but that's how we do it at Rochester and, indeed, it does

work.' Then I did the closing presentation, after Motorola, on what we had done at Rochester and what we had learned from our Baldrige experience."

The plan was simple. The first day and a half, the IBM executives would be briefed on Motorola's quality story. Then they would go into breakout sessions and review what they had heard. They would try to come up with a plan for taking what they had learned and adapting it to IBM.

When they arrived at Motorola University at Schaumburg, Illinois, the IBM executives settled in for their meeting, not knowing quite what to expect. They certainly didn't expect that what they heard from the Baldrige winner would change the course of IBM. Nor did they expect that what Motorola would tell them would be things they already knew, or at least should have known, but just weren't applying. Based upon the recollections of people who were at this meeting, this is a synopsis of what they heard:

> In order for a business to survive today, it must provide its customers with a quality product, at the right price, and on time. There are two keys to making that happen: six sigma quality and total cycle-time reduction.
>
> What we mean by six sigma quality is near perfection—just 3.4 defects per million opportunities—and that is what customers are expecting today, near perfection. Not only do customers expect quality approaching zero defects, but defects are expensive. They drive up warranty costs, cause more scrap, force you to maintain excessive inventory, and make your overhead costs higher than they should be. In short, eliminating defects is not only important for satisfying your customer, but it's important if you want to reduce your costs.
>
> The term, "six sigma," that we use refers to a measurement or characteristic of a process capability. It helps us all use the same language and measure, with the same yardstick, when we talk about defects. And it helps us to define how far we have come and how far we have to go to eliminate defects.
>
> To help you understand six sigma, we'll give you some examples. Today, we estimate that the average American company is operating at about four sigma. That translates into about 6,200 defects per million units or operations. It is about the defect or error rate you see in restaurant bills, doctors' prescriptions, payroll processing, reject rates for purchased materials in manufacturing, and a host of

other things. Now contrast that with domestic airline flight fatalities, a major defect if there ever was one. People are killed in airline disasters only about 0.43 times out of every million flight segments. That's still not perfect, but fortunately it is a lot better.

Another way of thinking about this is to consider what we normally think is good quality. In the past, a lot of us have said that 99 percent good quality is pretty good. We know being 99 percent defect-free isn't very good at all, certainly not compared to something like six sigma, which means being 99.99966 percent defect free. Think about it this way. If, in the United States, we accepted 99 percent defect-free as good enough, it would mean:

- 20,000 lost articles of mail per hour;
- unsafe drinking water almost fifteen minutes each day;
- 5,000 incorrect surgical operations per week;
- two short or long landings at most airports each day;
- 200,000 wrong drug prescriptions each year; and
- no electricity for almost seven hours each month.

Would that be good enough? We don't think so, and that is the reason we are pursuing six sigma quality in everything we do.

To achieve six sigma, we have designed a course for all of our employees called "Understanding Six Sigma." It is a basic course we are requiring every employee to take, and it covers six steps that we want our people to follow to improve the way they do their jobs. First, we teach them to identify the product they create or service they provide. Second, they identify the customer for their product or service, either external to Motorola or within their own organization, and determine what their customer considers important. Next, they are taught to identify what they need to provide a product or service that satisfies the customer, and they sit down with their suppliers and tell them what they need to do to improve. Fourth, they define the processes they use for doing their work. They break down their entire operation into steps and tasks and identify in detail the inputs and outputs of each step or task. Next, they are taught how to redesign the process they use to make it mistake-proof and to eliminate wasted effort. That might involve simplifying tasks, increasing training, changing methodologies or just stopping doing tasks that don't add value. Finally, they measure, analyze and continue to improve their processes.

A second key element of providing customers with a quality product, at the right price, and on time is what we call total cycle-time reduction. What we are trying to do with total cycle-time reduction is cut the total time for development, production and delivery of the product or service. The way we look at it, every activity has a cycle time that can be reduced by following the same steps we follow to achieve six sigma. In fact, six sigma defect elimination and cycle-time reduction are closely linked. When we decrease defects, we reduce cycle times, since we have few defects to correct. But it is also true that, as we reduce cycle time, defects are also reduced, because the processes we use are simplified, and that leaves us with fewer opportunities to introduce defects in the first place.

The Motorola people then went on to discuss other parts of their approach to improving quality.

When the Motorola presentations were concluded, the IBM executives heard from Osterwise about Rochester's experiences, and then went into their breakout groups. For the rest of that day and half of the next, they debated and discussed what they had heard. Many were convinced that six sigma was *the solution* for IBM—that they could simply implement six sigma and that would do the job. Others weren't so sure.

Bob Talbot later recalled a breakout session in which he participated and the reception he got when he commented, "You've got to understand, fellows, six sigma alone won't get you there. Sure, you'll make really good stuff, but, if you aren't listening to your customers, you're not going to have that sparkle in the marketplace." These were development and manufacturing executives who had been struggling futilely with the nebulous concept of being market-driven, and they were in no mood to hear what Talbot had to say. Talbot remembered one particularly irritated plant manager telling him:

> Bob, I went to your class on being market-driven, and I came back to my plant saying, "I want to be market-driven. I want to be market-driven!" But I didn't know what to do next. My job is putting tops on bottoms, so I went back to what I knew—putting tops on bottoms. Now, when you talk about six sigma, that level of specificity, I *know* what I'm supposed to do.

The Motorola trip concluded with agreement that Motorola's six sigma approach would be valuable but disagreement over whether six sigma by itself was enough. Further discussions culminated in a closed-door meeting between Bob Talbot and Heinz

Fridrich. Talbot and Fridrich concluded at this meeting that in order for a new IBM quality initiative to work it needed both a market-driven element, with attention to customers' wants and needs, as well as the discipline of defect-free processes offered by the six sigma approach. Working with Bill Rich, who was at the time secretary of the IBM Corporation, Talbot and Fridrich began to flesh out the architecture of what was to become a program known as Market-Driven Quality.

Fridrich and Talbot decided to test the water by presenting their recommendations to Terry Lautenbach's general managers. Lautenbach's monthly general managers meeting was well known as a highly interactive forum in which ideas could be presented for comment. It was the perfect place to start.

Steve Schwartz recalled the initial meeting in which Fridrich and Talbot presented their findings:

> They were very excited about what they saw at Motorola. We had some real problems in the corporation that year, both in the area of defects and in cycle time, and they were excited because this looked like a very good approach to getting everyone's eyes in focus on those two things. The gist of the conversation that day was "that's terrific. We agree, but we need to broaden the scope."

Schwartz raised the issue of self-assessment. His experience with Rochester had convinced him that self-assessment against the Baldrige criteria was crucial to IBM's continuous improvement. Jim Coraza, who had been part of the Application Business Systems (ABS) team at Rochester and who now worked for Talbot, suggested that process management and improvement needed to be incorporated into any comprehensive program. Others interjected that Motorola and Rochester had also done a lot of training, and they had both involved their employees. Rochester had also done a lot of work on segmenting their market.

After a couple of working sessions with Lautenbach's managers, the proposal for Market-Driven Quality began to emerge as a comprehensive, strategic-quality plan. It was a plan based not just on what IBM had learned at Motorola, but on what it had learned from Milliken, Xerox, other Baldrige winners, and, of course, Rochester. It encompassed all of the good intentions of being market-driven, but it contained the two new and essential elements—specific actions and measurement. This new Market-Driven Quality was received with enthusiasm by IBM's corporate management board.

Market-Driven Quality

Market-Driven Quality (MDQ) was officially announced at IBM's January 1990 senior managers meeting. The key to MDQ, the senior managers were told, was "Excellence in Execution" achieved through two critical paths: (1) six sigma quality, and (2) total cycle-time reduction.

Achieving six sigma would be challenging, they were told. Some initial calculations showed that at the beginning of 1990, IBM had a defect rate around three sigma, or 66,810 defects per million opportunities, slightly worse than the average American company. IBM had to play catch-up and it had to do it fast. IBM needed to be at six sigma by 1994. Using 1989 year-end defects as a baseline, that meant they had to reduce the number of defects by ten times by year-end 1991 and by 100 times by year-end 1993. It wasn't going to be easy, and they needed more than six sigma and cycle-time reduction to get them there.

How were they going to reach that ten times and one hundred times improvement and six sigma quality by 1994? IBM would get there through MDQ, which had three major components: (1) a set of five initiatives that encompassed the market-driven principles laid out in 1989; (2) a system for analyzing key business processes and making changes that were necessary; and (3) a method for measuring progress.

The Five Initiatives

The five MDQ initiatives would be the basis for transforming the organization and achieving total customer satisfaction. To insure that the initiatives were carried out, each would be assigned to an executive who would be the corporate owner of the initiative and provide leadership across the organization. The executive

MDQ Framework

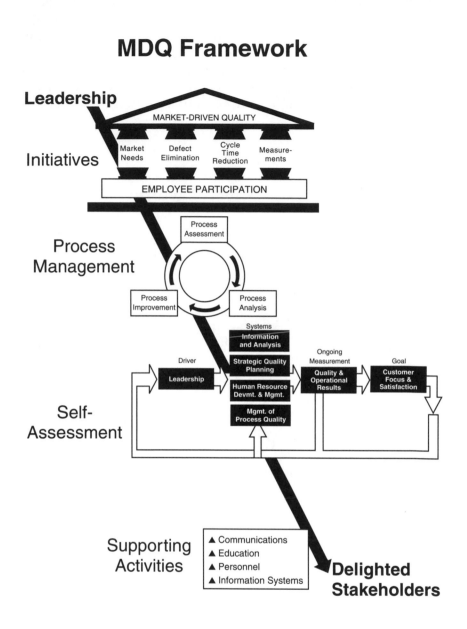

Leadership

MARKET-DRIVEN QUALITY

Initiatives

| Market Needs | Defect Elimination | Cycle Time Reduction | Measure- ments |

EMPLOYEE PARTICIPATION

Process Management

Process Assessment

Process Improvement

Process Analysis

Self- Assessment

Systems
Information and Analysis

Driver
Leadership

Strategic Quality Planning

Human Resource Devmt. & Mgmt.

Mgmt. of Process Quality

Ongoing Measurement
Quality & Operational Results

Goal
Customer Focus & Satisfaction

Supporting Activities

▲ Communications
▲ Education
▲ Personnel
▲ Information Systems

Delighted Stakeholders

would be responsible for establishing a management system for overseeing the implementation, supporting deployment of the initiative, reviewing results, and reporting on progress. The five initiatives were:

1. *Define Market Needs.* IBM would research, understand and segment total market needs; commit to leadership in selected markets; and deliver the right solutions at the right time. IBM, as a company, would now seek to develop a strategy to address its approach to the market, similar to Vic Tang's strategy for Rochester's AS/400.

2. *Eliminate Defects.* IBM would work to eliminate defects in everything it did, based upon analysis and measurement. MDQ approaches and measurements, such as six sigma, would be used to analyze and measure each process or work activity to identify the cause of defects and to establish a plan to eliminate and ultimately prevent virtually all of them. IBM would need to reach Rochester's "constant state of discontentment," which led Rochester to continuous improvement.

3. *Cycle-Time Reduction.* IBM would seek to cut the total time between determining customer wants and needs and fulfilling them to the customer's total satisfaction. The cycle time of every work activity would be shortened through process simplification, the elimination of steps in the process that didn't add value, and the elimination and prevention of defects. They would have to emulate Rochester's efforts in continuous flow manufacturing, design for manufacturing, and engineering and software process reengineering.

4. *Measure Progress.* The company would establish MDQ measurements, based on what customers thought was important, and compare itself to its competitors on these measures. In addition to end-result measures of total customer satisfaction, each unit would have a set of 5-Ups, approximately five measures of key customer satisfiers or irritants/dissatisfiers it could track and display on wall charts. The original concept of 5-Ups was adopted from

Motorola, but was expanded to be more customer-focused. Motorola's 5-Ups concentrated on cycle-time and defect reduction, but, based on Rochester's enhancement of the concept, IBM would link the 5-Ups to what was important to the customer.

Five-Ups would show IBM how well its processes were conforming to customer requirements. They would be "customer-defined," not "internally defined," measures of performance. Ideally, a 5-Up would define a defect as the customer saw it. For example, 5-Ups might measure missed delivery dates or promises to the customer that were not kept. Organizations were asked to express their 5-Up measures as fractions, showing the total defects (such as missed delivery dates) divided by total opportunities for defects (for example, total delivery dates) so that resulting performance could be converted to a sigma value. Most importantly, 5-Ups were to be selected for their ability to predict customer satisfaction. Thus, if the trend on the internal 5-Ups measures was improving, then total customer satisfaction would also improve, albeit perhaps at some later date. Each organization would have different 5-Ups measures but all 5-Ups were required to meet these criteria. For example, a marketing and services organization might have 5-Ups covering such areas as warranty costs, on-time delivery, billing accuracy, and speed in fixing customers' problems. Such measures would be acceptable as 5-Ups because they were important to the customer.

5. *Employee Involvement.* Employees would be urged to participate in decisions that affected them or their customers; would be empowered to take ownership of their jobs, understand and improve their work processes, and make and implement decisions either individually or as part of a work team. The goal was to achieve a level of employee involvement and morale like that at Rochester.

Enterprise Processes

In addition to the work employees would be doing within their own organizations to improve work processes, and thereby improve quality and reduce cycle time, IBM identified twelve (later expanded to fifteen) corporate-wide processes that would be subject to the same process reengineering that would be undertaken within units. Each enterprise process would have an executive as the process owner who would have responsibility for, among other things, defining the process goals and objectives, ensuring that the process was effective and efficient, and continually improving the process. Process owners would report regularly to Terry Lautenbach on their progress in quarterly reviews.

ENTERPRISE PROCESSES

- **Strategic Opportunities:** Develops and communicates the strategic intent of the enterprise, creates strategies to achieve that intent, and defines a management system to insure the strategics will be implemented. Assesses major new business and market opportunities and changes the enterprise portfolio mix through entering and exiting business and/or markets. The output of this process establishes the strategic framework and goals for the remaining enterprise processes.

- **Market Information Capture:** Collects relevant and accurate market data and makes it accessible on a timely basis to people in IBM who need it to make market-based decisions. Included is information on competition, market segmentation, market share, customer wants and needs, and opportunity sizing.

- **Market Management:** Identifies, prioritizes and selects market opportunities. Develops and ensures implementation of plans for selected markets that provide customers with solutions to meet their needs and wants. Requirements are generated to support the various elements of these solutions. Identification, definition, and prioritization of markets and solutions are performed within geographies and lines of business.

- **Commitment Management:** Prioritizes solution and technology candidates across IBM units to guide IBM in making investment decisions that will allow the company to compete successfully in selected markets. Optimizes investments including those associated with marketing, services, development, and manufacturing functions. Supports operational planning and implementation of decisions by providing a plan management framework for synchronizing commitments, developing measurements, and monitoring performance.

- **Offering Information:** Satisfies the needs of customers and customer contact people worldwide for information about IBM's offerings. Determines what information is needed and how customers want to receive it. Responds to requests for specific offering information. Serves market owners by helping them plan the most effective mix of information deliverables. Creates and delivers offering information to target audiences that is accurate, relevant, and easily usable.

- **Customer Relationship:** Establishes a long-term relationship with each customer by providing expert assistance and premier offerings that integrate the full range of IBM and business partner skills, products and services. The goal is the customer's total satisfaction. This process provides the enabling processes and management system that support the IBM team responsible for addressing the customers' needs.

- **Service:** Delivers hardware and software maintenance services that maximize IBM product availability and minimize customer operational costs. This includes service planning, service delivery, call management, parts logistics, reclamation, service feedback and software service education. The goals are total customer satisfaction, increased market share, and profitability.

- **Hardware Development:** Establishes processes for hardware product and technology development that can be applied across the company and that meet or exceed customer requirements and IBM goals for defect elimination and cycle-time reduction. It starts with requirements definition for products along with a financial commitment, and results in the development of manufacturing processes and delivery of engineering data to production. It also includes processes that support the product life cycle until withdrawal of the product from the marketplace.

- **Software Development:** Establishes processes for software development that achieve IBM defect elimination and cycle-time reduction goals while contributing to the cross-company development of solutions that meet or exceed customer needs. Includes the architecture, design, and development of software programs and documentation based on established requirements, and results in the release of products and publications to the production process.

- **Services Development:** Develops services products that meet or exceed market and customer requirements and provides the services to customers. Begins with a validated requirement for a services solution and results in a services product developed and available for sale to customers, and in delivery of that service.

- **Production:** Manufactures and distributes hardware, software, and publication products that meet or exceed customer demands and requirements. The process includes early involvement with product development and continues with planning, management, and fabrication of products. The execution of these processes will allow production to achieve the overall goal of delivering defect-free products in world-class cycle times.

- **Customer Fulfillment:** Assures that customer expectations are fulfilled or exceeded in requests for IBM products, services, and solutions. Includes announcement support activities, order entry, contract management, timely scheduling and shipment of products, invoicing and accounts receivable. The process continues with final payment to IBM and validating the fulfillment of customer expectations.

- **Solution Integration:** Tracks the progress and manages the assembly of all the elements of a solution until it is available for delivery. Includes managing the business process, verifying that products and services meet the requirements, and assuring that all elements—hardware, software, and service—work seamlessly as a total solution to customer needs.

- **Financial Analysis:** Provides financial analysis as the foundation of a management system for selecting strategic investments and providing products and offerings that maximize customer value and IBM's worldwide financial returns. Includes establishing product, service, and solution prices, and providing financial analyses and recommendations. Results in the release of approved prices and terms and conditions or recommendations for executive decisions to proceed on proposed investments.

- **Customer Satisfaction Management:** Consolidates and analyzes information obtained from various sources, including customer-initiated feedback, IBM-initiated survey data, and internal measurements. The resulting customer issues will be used to determine ownership of identified problem areas. The process will ensure ownership is assigned and accepted, and that the owners develop and execute action plans which will resolve the issues. Finally, there is continuous measurement in order to determine the success of the action plans in improving Customer Satisfaction. Because the "voice of the customer" is essential to Market-Driven Quality, the Customer Satisfaction Management process cuts across all other enterprise processes in the IBM management system.

Self-Examination

Finally, each organizational unit within IBM would assess its progress on implementing a management system based on the MDQ strategy. Since both Endicott and Rochester had reported the significant benefits of their Baldrige experiences, IBM chose the Malcolm Baldrige National Quality Award criteria as the basis for the assessment and diagnostic tool IBM units would use to measure their progress toward MDQ. Within IBM, they would be rewarded for their efforts in achieving higher levels of performance on the Baldrige criteria through an MDQ Assessment

Achievement Level Recognition program, patterned after the Baldrige award.

In summary, that was Market-Driven Quality. First and foremost, its primary focus would be customer satisfaction. It would be driven by leadership. And it would be strategically supported by the five initiatives, continuous process improvement, and self-assessment.

It was to be the road map for IBM's long journey back, and IBM would have a new navigator to plot its course.

A New Chief Quality Officer

Shortly after the conclusion of the Strategic Planning Conference in 1990, Akers decided that IBM needed a senior line executive as the chief quality officer. That person turned out to be Steve Schwartz.

Schwartz recalled the day he got the call from John Akers offering him the job:

> I was sitting in my office one day at the end of March, and I get this call from John. I said, "Well, I could juggle a few things around. I'll come up right away." You know, when the chairman calls, you juggle a few things on your calendar.
>
> We [Schwartz and Akers] have known each other many, many years, and I knew if he called me directly, it was something important. So, as I'm driving from Somers to Armonk, I'm asking myself, "I wonder what he wants to talk to me about?" ABS was doing very well. We had just come off of two banner years in a row with volume shipments of the AS/400 in 1988 and 1989. We were gaining market share. We were profitable. I was having a lot of fun.
>
> When I went in to see John, he said, "We've launched this Market-Driven Quality initiative. It's terribly important to the success of the business. I really want to drive this very hard, but I think I need help. I think I need an executive reporting to me who has been there. Someone people respect, who has been all around the business." I said, "Now wait a minute, John, I feel a setup coming." So, he said, "Will you come do this?" He just felt very comfortable because of our long relationship. He felt we looked at things the same way. Our priorities were very similar. We were very open and honest

with each other, and he thought my background and experiences would give me the credibility that the job required. So, obviously, I said, "Yes."

Within one week, Steve Schwartz assumed responsibility as IBM senior vice president for Market-Driven Quality. Schwartz's first activity on assuming his new position was to find out what had been done to get this program off the ground since the January announcement. He found that most of the efforts had been directed toward development of education and trying to answer the question "How are we going to roll out MDQ education to every IBMer in every country and try and do it within twelve to sixteen months?" The MDQ staff had begun developing a two-day "awareness" course which had the sole purpose of familiarizing everyone with the market-driven concepts and defining the terminology. This education, however, was a prerequisite to everything else they wanted to accomplish. Managers could not be asked to develop plans for defect elimination if they didn't understand the fundamentals of six sigma, and virtually no one had ever heard of 5-Ups measurements.

By the time Schwartz began his new job, they were getting ready to do a pilot of the class. He recommended that they do the pilot with his old ABS team because, as he told them, "One of the great things about that crowd is they'll tell you exactly what they think of it, and they'll do it in a constructive way." So the first class was held in Rochester for the top forty executives and managers of the ABS team. Schwartz recalled, "It went pretty well, and we got a lot of good suggestions about how to make it better, just as I thought." But providing training for forty executives in one location was one thing. How were they going to provide this training to more than 300,000 people in locations all over the world?

The answer they decided upon was to train the most senior executives of each business unit and to have them train those employees who reported directly to them. The newly trained employees would repeat the process with their direct reports, and so on until everyone had received the training. It was a very ambitious project and one which probably would have failed without a direct mandate from John Akers. As Schwartz put it, Akers made attending the training "a condition of employment." As a result, the top eleven hundred executives in IBM received their initial two-day training by July 1990, and, although they missed their target of training all employees by the end of 1990, they only missed that target by four months.

To compound the difficulties they were already facing, Schwartz and his staff determined that they needed to provide leadership development training as well. Suddenly, they were asking employees to become more involved in the decision-making process and to take more responsibility for their work. They were also asking managers who had grown up in the old school of top-down management to *encourage* such behavior. This was *not* going to happen without some intervention, so they "borrowed" and expanded a course in transformational leadership from IBM Canada.

In his "spare time," Schwartz also worked with people like Heinz Fridrich, Terry Lautenbach, Pat Toole, and Larry Osterwise to put together a framework for the six sigma, the 5-Ups and cycle-time reduction activities, so they could be rolled out in an organized fashion to the whole business. Schwartz summarizes the activity of the first six months of 1990 as really being spent "in all the foundation work, the detailed education, the detailed process for putting all the meat on the bones of what we had decided on. It's one thing to decide on it. It's another thing to get it rolled out in a company of our size."

But it was beginning to roll out. The question was which unit would take the lead in implementing MDQ? Where would Schwartz and Akers find an IBM site that could serve as the model for the rest of IBM? How could they prove to the skeptics that MDQ would, indeed, work in IBM? And there was a related issue. IBM did want to go for the Baldrige award again and had already selected a site to compete in 1990. They didn't know it yet, but the Baldrige site and MDQ model would turn out to be one and the same: IBM Rochester.

8

The 1990 Baldrige Application

After failing to win the Baldrige award in 1989, Rochester began almost immediately to try to get over its shock and grief. They were determined to make something positive out of the experience and began to struggle with the question of what to do next. Should the site volunteer to make another run for the award in 1990, or should it just try to put the loss behind it and get on with the task of fixing what the Baldrige experience had told them was wrong? A lot, probably most, of the people at Rochester didn't want to apply for the award again. The application process in 1989 had been a lot of work, and most just didn't want to have to start immediately to go through the whole process again. Plus, as Pat McCracken was to recall, "There was the feeling that if you lose once you can say to yourself that you learned a lot and the loss built character. But what do you say to yourself if you lose a second time? There was this whole morale issue."

Additionally, many on the Rochester application team felt Rochester would be better off spending its time fixing some seventy-one "warts" identified as a result of the 1989 site visit and application development. Mike Jacobson was one of those opposed to trying for the award again so soon:

When I took a look at all of the data, I thought it was premature for us to apply again in 1990. I felt it was going to take a tremendous investment of resources to prepare the application. I approached the leadership team and told them I felt we would be better off spending our resources working on the things that we knew were problems, rather than working on writing an application. I never expressed my feelings about that directly to Larry Osterwise, but I did to others.

If Jacobson had gone to Osterwise with his concerns, it probably would not have done much good. The informal vote in Rochester was ten to one against applying for the award again. Just about the only person at the site who wanted to apply again was Osterwise. He had his concerns, but he was really just waiting to be asked. It didn't take long, as Osterwise recalled:

I had gone out to the airport to pick up IBM Senior Vice President Terry Lautenbach in December of 1989. He was coming to present Rochester with its IBM U.S. Quality Award. I would usually pick him up when he came, because I would use the time during the drive in from the airport to brief him on what was going on and issues he was likely to encounter during his visit. We got in the car and started to leave the terminal. Terry asked me, "Well, Larry, how are things?" I said, "Well, Terry, you know, we are struggling mightily here. It looks like 1989 is going to be a good year for revenue and profits. It looks pretty good right now, but people have been working so hard and the fulfillment just isn't there. We lost the Baldrige award. The financial pressures in IBM are such that we've got the hatches battened down tight. So, it's been tough.

Terry asked me what influence I thought the Baldrige award had and I told him, "You know it was a downer not to win, finding out that we had lost all of a sudden and not being properly conditioned to the fact that we might not win. That was a shock. But I think people are now getting around to the fact that we learned a lot. After all, wasn't that what we were in it for? I mean, it would have been nice if we had won, but we weren't in it just to win a trophy. We learned a lot. We're getting better and people are starting to feel good about that. I think, if the corporation asked, we'd do it again because we like to win, but more importantly, we like to learn. About the only negative we can see in running again would be another shot to morale if we were to lose a second time. Other than that it's all positives."

Terry turned to me and said, "That's what we wanted to hear. You've got enough guts to be ready to fight and not just roll over in spite of the bad odds." So I told him, "Well, consider that we are ready to go."

When Lautenbach left, Osterwise gathered his team together to tell them the "good" news. They were going to try for the award again. Emotions were mixed. Mike Jacobson had just gotten married and was headed off to a new job with IBM in Gaithersburg, Maryland. While he had been opposed to trying for the award again, his only regret, now that the decision had been made, was that he might not be asked or be able to be part of the new effort. Characteristically, he decided that if Rochester tried again without his involvement or Lori Kirkland's or that of the others from the 1989 application team and lost, it would be because the leadership didn't take advantage of their expertise. If Rochester won without their involvement, then it only meant that the 1989 team had provided such a good foundation. That was Jacobson's way of looking at the situation.

Senior Executives Own the Categories

Having been through the 1989 experience, Osterwise had learned a few things about writing Baldrige applications and about the award itself. One of the things he had learned, and that the Baldrige examiners had stressed, was that leadership was more important than even Osterwise had thought it was. If Rochester was to go for the award again in 1990, Osterwise wanted to start the effort a little differently than he had started it the previous year. In January of 1990, he called a meeting to lay out just what he had planned:

In 1989, we found seventy-one "warts" and the Baldrige people told us about five other things. But the people who owned the categories in 1989 didn't have the power to change what they found wrong with what we did. At a staff meeting I put up a chart and said, "Here are the owners of the categories." Listed there were senior executives and the categories they owned. I said to them, "Look folks, we are in this thing again because we agreed that we learned from the 1989 experience and that we were going to improve. You are the owners because we got feedback in each of the categories, and you are going to have to take that feedback and change our business in these categories.

"A second point I want to make is that we are in this again because some of us around here don't like to be losers, and the second time around, if we lose, it's going to be a lot more painful in terms of morale. This time around, we are going to score a thousand points. How are we going to score a thousand points? We are going to do it by reading those questions and knowing what they mean. If we don't do things the way we think we should, not the way *they* think we should but the way we think we should, then, damn it, fix it! You've got the power and you've got my mandate. So, let's do it. I'll do it in leadership. You do it in data and information. You do it in strategic planning. Whatever has to be changed, change it."

Then I went on to say, "Now, I'll make you another deal. If you tell me that something needs to change, but you are here in January and it is not going to really change 'til June or July, you and I can meet on the plains of Lexington, so to speak, and reach this little agreement. I'll let you write it like we do it the way you plan for us to do it, provided I have your commitment that you will make sure that we will do it just the way you write by May, June, or July. As it is being read and reviewed, it *will* be the truth.

In other words, it had to be deployed before a Baldrige site visit.

Many of the category owners assigned by Osterwise had also "owned" categories in 1989. The difference was that they all understood that there would be no delegation of responsibility in 1990. They were each personally responsible, both for the content of the application category, and for assuring that the "warts" and weaknesses in their area were corrected. This executive team would not have to be briefed on what was in the 1990 application the way they were in 1989. This time they would *own* what was in it.

1990 CATEGORY OWNERS

Category 1: Leadership
            Larry Osterwise, site general manager
Category 2: Information and Analysis
            Greg Lea, site controller

Category 3:   **Strategic Quality Planning**
                Roy Bauer, manager, engineering, planning
                and operations
Category 4:   **Human Resource Utilization**
                Rick Martino, site personnel manager
Category 5:   **Quality Assurance**
                Kevin Anderson, senior engineer
Category 6:   **Quality Results**
                George Moore, manager, systems
                production management center
Category 7:   **Customer Satisfaction**
                Erv Bernhardt, manager, ABS system
                assurance and customer satisfaction

More Than Just a Simple Update

Although most of them were new to the Baldrige application process, since they had only minimally participated in 1989, the Rochester executives didn't see writing the 1990 application as such a difficult assignment. After all, they already had a high scoring application from 1989. And they had feedback from the Baldrige examiners and their own internal analysis of weaknesses from 1989. It should be a relatively easy process of updating, clarifying and polishing the 1989 application, they thought. No one got too excited about what had to be done. No one thought writing the 1990 application would be difficult or that they would run out of time. They were all wrong.

The Rochester team experienced at least three totally unexpected challenges in writing their application in 1990. First, they soon realized that they had indeed learned a lot from the 1989 losing effort, so they had much more data and a much bigger story to tell in 1990. Yet they were still locked into a maximum length of just seventy-five pages to tell their story. Finding enough space to tell their story would be a constant problem. Second, Osterwise had given them the task not just of writing the story, but of making any and all necessary changes to fix what was wrong. That meant that they simultaneously had to change the way they ran the business and to document what they were doing or would be doing as soon as the changes were accomplished. Finally, they didn't expect the collaboration and the linking of sections to be as difficult as it had been in 1989. After all, they had the 1989 application to serve as a guide, and it contained all the work Bauer and his team had done to provide the common themes. It didn't turn out that way, because of something they should have anticipated. The Baldrige criteria had changed again.

The 1990 Baldrige Criteria

The changes in the 1990 application criteria were not as extensive as they had been in 1989. The number of examination items had been reduced further from forty-four to thirty-three, reflecting, as the application explained, "the aggregation of related themes to minimize overlap and to afford applicants more page space per item." The new application had also been made more generic, eliminating special requirements for certain types of business and quality systems.

1990 EXAMINATION CATEGORIES/SUBCATEGORIES
Malcolm Baldrige National Quality Award

	MAXIMUM POINTS
1.0 LEADERSHIP	**100**
1.1 Senior Executive Leadership	30
1.2 Quality Values	20
1.3 Management for Quality	30
1.4 Public Responsibility	20
2.0 INFORMATION AND ANALYSIS	**60**
2.1 Scope and Management of Quality Data and Information	35
2.2 Analysis of Quality Data and Information	25
3.0 STRATEGIC QUALITY PLANNING	**90**
3.1 Strategic Quality Planning Process	40
3.2 Quality Leadership Indicators in Planning	25
3.3 Quality Priorities	25

4.0 HUMAN RESOURCE UTILIZATION	150

4.1	Human Resource Management	30
4.2	Employee Involvement	40
4.3	Quality Education and Training	40
4.4	Employee Recognition and Performance Measurement	20
4.5	Employee Well-Being and Morale	20

5.0 QUALITY ASSURANCE OF PRODUCTS AND SERVICES	150

5.1	Design and Introduction of Quality Products and Services	30
5.2	Process and Quality Control	25
5.3	Continuous Improvement of Processes, Products and Services	25
5.4	Quality Assessment	15
5.5	Documentation	10
5.6	Quality Assurance, Quality Assessment and Quality Improvement of Support Services and Business Processes	25
5.7	Quality Assurance, Quality Assessment and Quality Improvement of Suppliers	20

6.0 QUALITY RESULTS	150

6.1	Quality of Products and Services	50
6.2	Comparison of Quality Results	35
6.3	Business Process, Operational and Support Service Quality Improvement	35
6.4	Supplier Quality Improvement	30

7.0 CUSTOMER SATISFACTION	300

7.1	Knowledge of Customer Requirements and Expectations	50
7.2	Customer Relationship Management	30
7.3	Customer Service Standards	20
7.4	Commitment to Customers	20
7.5	Complaint Resolution for Quality Improvement	30
7.6	Customer Satisfaction Determination	50
7.7	Customer Satisfaction Results	50
7.8	Customer Satisfaction Comparison	50

TOTAL POINTS　　　　　　　　　　　　　　　　　　**1000**

As much as they liked the idea of having more space per item, the veteran application writers knew that this meant a major effort. Information would have to be reshuffled, eliminated, enhanced and written from scratch. More important, the linkages that had been so laboriously built in the 1989 application would be broken, and they would have to go through the process of rebuilding them.

Lack of Progress

By late January, the application team had still made little progress. Applications were due at NIST by April 25. There were only a couple of months left before the application had to go to the printers, but so far there wasn't an application or even the beginning drafts of one. Bauer recalled going to Osterwise to express his concern that time was running out:

> Larry still believed that, based on last year's stuff, we ought to be able to write this thing in no time. He told me he could write Category 1 [Leadership] over the weekend—this was a Friday—so I said, "Okay, you go write Category 1 and bring it in Monday morning." We basically threw out what he wrote Monday morning and told him, "You're not answering the questions." He invested a tremendous amount of time. I give Larry credit for that. But he finally realized, when he got through, that there was a lot more to doing an assessment than writing fancy words.

It soon became obvious to Osterwise that, as he had in 1989, he was going to need an overall architect, and he knew exactly who he wanted, Roy Bauer. So once again Bauer was called in to run the process.

The Drop-Dead Dates

Bauer's first step was to set drop-dead dates for all the tasks. "You've got February and March to write your sections," he told the category owners. The first corporate review team scoring would be at the end of February. Then, by the first of April, the category owners had to be finished. With some final polishing by a small team of people who had worked on the 1989 application, the publications people would get the final document by April 15 and have just ten days to get the application printed and ready to mail. It was a workable time frame, Bauer thought. It actually turned out to be a much tighter time line than he had anticipated.

With clear drop-dead dates and pushing from Osterwise and

Bauer, the category owners finally began making progress, but it was not without some effort and a much larger commitment of their personal time than they had anticipated. The first two weeks after receiving their drop-dead dates, the executives began blocking out an hour here and an hour there each day to work on the application. Pretty soon they were blocking out a half a day and then a whole day at a time. Still, they weren't getting it right.

Rethinking How the Business Is Run

Writing the application forced a lot of them to rethink how things were run. *How* thinking was hard for these IBMers. Just like the 1989 application team, they could describe *what* was done but not *how* it was done. Frequently, it was just a matter of getting beyond IBM's technical jargon so an examiner could understand the answers to the questions. Tom Burcak, a member of the corporate review team for both 1989 and 1990, recalled a particularly frustrating experience he had working with the talented, but much too technical, owner of one category in 1990, Kevin Anderson:

> Category 5 [Quality Assurance] came out and it was brilliant. It was well written. It was powerful. The problem was, I don't think any Baldrige examiner in the country could comprehend it. In fact, it made your head hurt. We critiqued the section and suggested some changes. Then we got it back a couple of days later and looked at it, and it still made your head hurt. He had taken scissors and tape and repackaged it, but it was the same stuff. It took a number of tries, but eventually he got it down to the right level, and it was okay. But, at the end, . . . [Kevin] looked across the table at me and said, "You know. This was one heck of an experience. I learned a lot. But let me tell you guys, I would rather suffer the pain of a double root canal than go through the pain that I faced writing this section again. There's got to be a better way."

Changing the Measures

George Moore, ABS systems production manager at the time, had ownership of Category 6, Quality Results, the same category Lori Kirkland had struggled with in 1989. Moore described his experience with the 1990 application in a later interview:

> The first go-around for the quality-results section, we asked ourselves, "What do we have quality measurements on?" It soon became clear to us that we had to get out of the mind-set of "what kind of data do we have that looks good" to "what is really important from a customer's point of view?" When we started looking at it that way, we discovered that a lot of the things that we measured routinely and looked at every day were not important to the customer. Other data would be there. You could go get it, but it wasn't what you had been looking at every day. That forced us to change not only what we were measuring but also what we were looking at.
>
> For example, in measuring software quality, we measured defects per million lines of code. The problem is that the defects per million lines of code may come down, but the customer may still be unhappy. So what we looked at is requests for assistance [the average number of times a user requested IBM's assistance per month and the type of assistance requested]. When we started doing that, we found that code defects were a very small piece of what people were having trouble with. Instead, they were calling us and saying, "I don't understand the manual," or "You sent me an update where you found a problem that I haven't encountered yet, but I still have to go to the trouble of updating my system so I won't encounter the problem in the future." We began to realize that we needed a measurement process to focus on the customer view of software quality, not just our view. As a result, the process of writing the application ended up forcing us to change the way we ran the business.

Kirkland had encountered similar difficulties the prior year and had readjusted the available information the best way she could. That was all she had the power to do. This year, when George Moore found this "wart," he had been empowered to do something about it, and he did. Eventually, Rochester was able to tie its internal measures to the key elements of customer satisfaction, which they identified through customer surveys, interviews with customers and business partners, analysis of customer com-

Figure 8.1
Elements Important to the Customer

Customer View
Responsiveness
Ease of doing business
Technical ability and coverage
Knowledge of customer's business

Administration	Marketing and sales offerings	Technical solutions	Delivery	Maintenance and service support

• Terms and conditions (no hidden costs)
• Order accuracy
• Billing accuracy
• Late billings
• Complaint management
• Telephone support
	• Expectations defined and set
	• Wants and needs understood
	• Solutions and applications provided
	• Solutions affordable
	• Products announced on time
	• Trial period permitted
	• Channel management
	• Sales and volumes increased
	• Customer education
	• Gain and loss management
		• Low price and high performance
		• Quality and reliability
		• Low cost of ownership
		• Solutions available
		• Incorporate wants and needs (accurate specifications)
		• Easy to use
		• Reduced cycle time (rapid product introductions)
		• Rich functions
		• Easily migratable
		• Connectivity with vendors
		• Easy to use documentation
			• Complete shipments
			• Shipped on time
			• Order-to-invoice time shortened
			• Upgrade
			• Reduced complexity
			• Reduced time
			• Flexible policy
			• Installability
			  Short time
			  Not complex
			  Free of defects
				• Single person to contact
				• Problem source identified quickly
				• Knowledgeable customer engineer
				• Excellent hardware and software service
				• Parts available
				  Free of defects
				  Sufficient quantity
				  Near customer's location

plaints, consultant reports, and other means. As shown in Figure 8.1, IBM Rochester would now measure and focus on improving what the customer thought was important—not on what IBM thought was important.

Preparing the Final Application

By the end of March, Rochester's category owners had been through several drafts of their sections. Still, the application was far from being something that could be submitted. Some sections were still too long. Some were still too technical. Some still didn't address the Baldrige questions directly. As in the previous year, Bauer finally decided he needed to take the category owners out of the process and bring in people who could begin to pull the final application together. Two of the people he turned to were Mike Jacobson and Lori Kirkland.

Bauer and Osterwise had reached an agreement with Jacobson's new bosses in Gaithersburg that they could call him back to work on the Rochester Baldrige application if they found they needed him. By March it was clear that Jacobson would be needed, so Osterwise placed the call and Mike found himself back in Rochester. Jacobson was surprised at what he found when he returned. He had expected the application to be much farther along. But it was late March and the document didn't appear to Jacobson to be coming together very well at all. There was a lot of work remaining, and Jacobson found himself in the middle of an intense effort for the next two weeks.

Kirkland might not have become involved at all if Roy Bauer had not asked her to do him a favor. Bauer had been writing a book about the AS/400 development project, which would later be published under the title *The Silverlake Project*. He had a draft manuscript and asked Kirkland to read it from a layperson's perspective and tell him what she thought. Kirkland read it and, in the process, made a number of editorial comments. When she returned the marked-up manuscript to Bauer, he took one look, said, "Hey, that's pretty good," and handed her a draft of Category 3, Strategic Quality Planning, of the new Baldrige application. Not having been called in to help to begin with, Kirkland was a little hurt and not too sure she wanted to be pulled into the process at the last minute. She took a look at what Bauer had handed her and said, "Okay Roy, I'll take a look at this for you. But I'm giving it back to you when I'm through and no one is to know that I've worked on it. I'll do it on my own time and just for you—*but just this once.*" It didn't turn out that way. When Kirkland handed back her marked-up copy of Category 3, Bauer gave her Category 5, Quality Assurance. She edited it, and, before she knew it, she was back in the thick of things.

The Final Push

Even with Jacobson, Kirkland and others to help him, Bauer still found it difficult to pull the final application together. He recalled the final push several years later:

> The team that I pulled together at the end of March took what the category owners had given us and went through it with a fine-tooth comb. We would go back to them with comments like, "You didn't answer this question, because you didn't give trends. Let's go get trend data." So the category owners became runners for the "enhancement team," trying to get the data we needed.
>
> We tore up one section two nights before we had to be ready to go to press. It was so bad we had to rewrite a large part of it right at the last minute. We worked all night and finally got it ready.

George Moore recalled the difficulties the team had reconstructing the linkages:

> Coordinating the different sections was also very difficult. We would have a meeting every week where we would try to relate to each other what was going on in the sections. We would talk about tie-ins between categories. There is a thread between Categories 3, Strategic Planning; 5, Quality Assurance; 6, Quality Results; and 7, Customer Satisfaction, that has to tie together. I had to be very aware of what was going on in 3, 5 and 7.

They finally constructed a massive chart of all activities, tools, techniques and programs which were crosshatched with each category, subcategory and area to address. That allowed them to identify the linkages that they wanted to document. For instance, the chart showed "Awards" in Categories 1, Leadership; 4, Human Resources; 6, Quality Results; and 7, Customer Satisfaction, while the QFBP (Quality Focus on the Business Process) program was discussed only in Category 1, Leadership, and had no linkages.

Moore also recalled some of the more petty things that came up during the final push on the application:

> Of course, there were things that you were wild about and wanted to keep in, but they got taken out. Roy Bauer and I got into some real arguments. For example, there was one chart I wanted to leave in that took up half a page, and they wanted to take it out because they needed the space for some other category. Somebody had to make that decision, and that was Roy's job. We had to go back and look for ways we could take three charts and combine them into one.

But Roy had more to worry about than whether they could combine three charts into one:

> All along, I was worried whether we could make it in time. There were a couple of days when I went home very depressed, wondering if we were going to make it or not. I just didn't feel that we were going to get there. The whole thing was eating at me. I didn't want to go into this twice and lose. If we hadn't gotten a site visit, I would have felt that I had let down not only the whole IBM Corporation but also the people at Rochester. They were counting on me.

Osterwise felt the same. He recalled later that during the last two weeks before the application was due, he was away from Rochester, but he was still involved and he also felt that everything was on the line:

> I turned my category over a couple of days before I was to go to Florida on a two-week vacation with my family and some of my children's friends. We desperately needed the vacation, so I went even though everything was coming down to the wire.
>
> When I went on that vacation I not only took a personal computer, but also had a FAX machine installed at my parents' house, where we were staying. They only had a single phone line into their

house, so every evening at about ten o'clock we would turn the phone line over to the FAX machine. Roy would FAX me the entire Baldrige document. I would read and edit until the wee hours of the morning, turn the FAX machine back on and send it back. When I got up in the morning, I would rehook the line to my parents' normal phone. For a period of two weeks, I probably reviewed and altered the document ten out of the fourteen nights like this.

There was no letting go at that point. We were striving for excellence. We were striving for perfection. We were writing an application for an award, but we weren't just writing an application. We were changing. Everything that I had stood for and taught throughout Rochester—"you must be better," "the bar of excellence always gets raised," "there is no excuse for anything short of total success"—all of that was on the line. We were changing, but I didn't know if we were changing fast enough. And we weren't sure we were going to make it.

But the enhancement team did make the deadline and submitted the application. Still, they wished they could have had just a few more days.

9

A Different Rochester

Rochester's 1990 experience with the Baldrige award was quite different from its 1989 experience. In 1989 Rochester executives had turned loose an energetic corps of young people to document Rochester's quality achievements in the hope of winning an award. The executives themselves had little involvement in application development, since they were "too busy running the site." In 1990 that all changed. That year, the executives were directly involved, not only in writing the application but, more importantly, in using the award criteria as a diagnostic tool. Based upon what they were learning, they were changing the way the business was run. Tom Burcak noticed the change soon after arriving for the first review in late February 1990:

> The second year I was out there, I remember one evening being in a room with this guy, and I made a comment. I said to him, "This is driving me crazy. Last year I was out here and you were the biggest obstacle to figuring this thing out. You were argumentative. You were obnoxious. This year you are like a different person. You are cooperative. You understand this stuff. You are the biggest Baldrige proponent I have run into in two years. What happened?" He responded, "When I saw what going for that award did for this facility, I became a convert. It is as simple as that." We saw that in the whole team. The people had changed. They saw the value in going through it.

The second year was a dream for the corporate review team. They would go to a meeting at seven o'clock in the morning, and Osterwise would be there with his entire management team. The corporate reviewers had no trouble getting support or getting someone to listen to their advice. It was a different world. Finally, the leadership of Rochester was getting involved, not just to write an application, but to change the site in fundamental ways. Osterwise had given his executives marching orders to exercise authority to change the site consistent with Baldrige or, if not consistent with Baldrige, consistent with what they thought was needed. And they had a lot to go on, as Osterwise explained in a later interview:

> One of the things about striving for the Baldrige award is that the examiners give you feedback. They come in and give you a rigorous examination. They poke around everywhere. Then they tell you how what you are doing stacks up. So, in 1990 when we were deciding what we needed to do, we had a lot to go on. Basically, the Baldrige people had told us that we were weak in four areas. Now, these were pretty basic areas. I mean, these weren't just minor, nitpicky problems. They were major weaknesses. It's just that we couldn't see them. We might never have seen them if we hadn't gone for the award in 1989, and we might never have fixed them if we hadn't been pushing so hard to go for the award in 1990.

Weakness #1: Leadership

The first thing the Baldrige examiners told Rochester's senior executives was that they weren't providing consistent leadership. Osterwise recalled that his first response to this criticism was, "What do you mean not providing leadership? That's a pretty rough thing to say. We're leaders. We're doing things. Look at how much we've got going on." Plus, Osterwise kept thinking, "I'm the one who has been here as site general manager for the last five years. So, it's not like you're talking about some manager I just replaced. You're talking about *my* leadership!"

It was a hard thing for Osterwise to accept. But, finally, he had to admit that it was true. He got some help in coming to that conclusion from two Rochester employees, Lyle Dockendorf and

Dan Rand, who decided to write Osterwise a letter, telling him exactly what they thought of his quality improvement efforts. Osterwise remembered the letter well:

> In a reasonably polite way, they told me that I had been talking a good game, but that I had really not been paying the appropriate attention to quality improvement. It was sort of like saying, "The emperor has no clothes." Among other things, they said that the fear of reporting bad news continued to result in upper management receiving a distorted view of the business; that we emphasized improving our appearance rather than addressing the real issues; that the major portion of quality activity had been directed at perception rather than action; that emphasis had been placed on trying to "look good" for the Malcolm Baldrige Quality application; and so on. Then, they went on to say, "In our implementation of quality, we need to go beyond slogans and posters. Quality must begin with understanding. . . . Without a clear, directed and committed strategy, we face confusion, inefficiency, and perhaps failure."
>
> It wasn't exactly an "open letter" telling me what a great job I had been doing!

It wasn't that Osterwise didn't have a vision for the site. Back in 1988, Steve Schwartz had asked him what it was he thought was most important for the site. After giving the question some thought, Osterwise had developed a three-part vision. First, he told Schwartz, he wanted to enable, empower and excite his people. To do that, he wanted to provide them with the best tools and support facilities, enhance their skills, facilitate teamwork and insure open, two-way communication. Next, Osterwise and he wanted to provide the leadership, strategies, goals and results across the business in quality, responsiveness, cost and volume to "meet and make the market." Finally, Osterwise told Schwartz, he wanted Rochester to be a leader in the community, and, to that end, he was going to do whatever he could to enhance the site's community image.

It was a good vision. Osterwise understood it well, and he ran the site in accordance with it. Therefore, he was surprised when the Baldrige examiners criticized him for inconsistent leadership. In 1990, as he tried to deal with this leadership issue in writing the leadership category, he had several discussions with Roy Bauer and others. "How could the Baldrige examiners say I'm not providing consistent leadership when I have so much going on and know exactly what I'm trying to do?" he asked. Their response came as a shock. "You know, Larry," they said, "you are absolutely right. You do have a lot going on and you know where you are going. There is just one problem. You haven't codified these ideas anywhere and shared them with anybody. It is not truly visionary until you get people to buy into it."

On reflection, Osterwise had to admit that they were right. He later recalled:

> I finally had to accept that we didn't have a strategy and we didn't have a focus. Sure, we were doing a lot of things, but all we really were doing is continually firing off some gigantic shotguns. We had little pellets of activity flying all over the place. Sure, some of them were hitting the target, but they weren't doing much good.
>
> We needed to bring things into focus. We needed a rifle, not a shotgun. If we were going to get serious about total customer satisfaction and total quality, then we had to concentrate our firepower where it could do some good. We had to hit the target solid with all the power we had, not just pepper it with buckshot. To us that meant that we had to communicate a clear and consistent vision to our people. So one of the changes we made in 1990 is that we developed our vision.

Osterwise took the entire senior management team and spent the equivalent of four or five days in half-day and full-day segments over the course of three months learning what a vision was. One by one the team then started describing their own personal visions. There wasn't much agreement, Osterwise recalled:

> The lab guys got up first and said their vision was to have the AS/400 be the be-all and end-all, the lifeblood of the computing world. When the lab guys got through presenting their vision for the AS/400, I remember Dick Lueck, the manager of site operations, got up and said he disagreed. The AS/400 wasn't his vision for the site. The lab guys sort of looked at him like "You're the outcast from Poker Flats, man. What do you mean you don't buy the AS/400 vision? Shoot him! This guy's not on the team!" Lueck took some real abuse for a couple of hours. After Dick opened up, then the DASD guys [from the disk file storage area], who had been just sitting back in the corner, said, "It's not our vision either." The laboratory people

were astonished at that. They couldn't understand how the whole world was not on their AS/400 vision. "What do you mean? The AS/400 is larger than life. There isn't anything more important than the AS/400," they said. Well, the DASD products people said, "No, that isn't our vision. I mean we like good storage devices to go in the AS/400. But give us a break. It's just not our vision."

There were other people in the room who said, "We don't care what the vision is, but we are going to be the best manufacturers known to man in cycle time, defects, cost, etc." Then, there were others in the room, like myself, who said, "All of that is interesting, but I just want to have a very successful business. I don't care what it is. I just want people to revel in what they do, just be excited about it and have fun."

It was obvious that we didn't agree. By the afternoon everyone was saying, "We don't have a vision here. It's no wonder we are screwed up." It was a really eye-opening day. Everybody left frustrated but much more knowledgeable about each other.

It took four or five meetings and hours of debate about the fine points of words and phrases. It also took countless discussions and debates with employees in meetings, in roundtables and even in the cafeteria over lunch, but Rochester ultimately developed its vision.

A VISION FOR IBM ROCHESTER

Customer—The Final Arbiter:

Customers are our partners, they will be the focus of all our work. They will be an integral part of every step of our process. We will serve our customers with a passion for quality and excellence. We will provide products and services that enable solutions which will make our customers more successful and more competitive.

Quality—Excellence in Execution:

Every customer will be totally satisfied with our products and services. Through continuous improvement, we will have defect-free processes and products, including those we obtain from others. Every employee will be committed to quality and excellence and take pride in their contribution to our quality reputation.

Products and Services—First with the Best:

Through our products and services, IBM Rochester will be recognized as the world leader in providing information solutions. Our innovation will set the standard for all criteria of importance to the customer, our business will be healthy and growing, and our long-term projections will be bright.

People—Enabled, Empowered, Excited, Rewarded:

Each of us will continue to be part of a highly motivated, knowledgeable team, a team committed to excellence. Our environment will be one of mutual trust, confidence, support, and delegated authority and responsibility. Each individual will have the required tools, training, and understanding. Each individual will be appreciated and rewarded.

When the exercise was over and Osterwise looked at what his team had agreed to, he couldn't understand at first why it had taken so long. He said to himself, "We spent all this time doing this? Come on. There is nothing intellectually deep here." The vision Osterwise and his team had developed for the site wasn't really new or different, at least not to IBM. It was, in reality, just a reaffirmation of IBM's Basic Beliefs, which had been formally expressed back in the 1960s: respect for the individual; best customer service in the world; and, the pursuit of excellence. As Osterwise explained:

After all, what did we mean by "Customer—The Final Arbiter"? It was "Provide the best possible service." What was "Quality—Excellence in Execution" if not the "Pursuit of excellence in all our endeavors"? And "Products and Services—First with the Best"? That was "Provide the best possible customer service" *and* the "Pursuit of excellence in all our endeavors." Finally, "People—Enabled, Empowered, Excited, Rewarded" was just our way of expressing "Respect for the individual."

It was true. The site vision Osterwise and his team had developed was nothing more than an expression of IBM's Basic Beliefs and MDQ principles. Couldn't they have just copied down the

Basic Beliefs and let it go at that? With hindsight, Osterwise would say he didn't think so:

> I think it was important for us to express our vision in our own terms. It had to be our guiding principle—what *we* wanted to be. And we had to be completely committed to it, because, if we weren't completely committed, there was no way our people would be. They had to see us working together as a team and setting an example, or they wouldn't feel inspired to take the vision and what we were trying to do seriously.

Weakness #2: Supporting Teamwork

The Baldrige feedback report had also pointed out that only one-third of Rochester's employees had been involved in their suggestion program or on a quality team. While that's a respectable percentage for many U.S. companies, it was not competitive with other Baldrige applicants, and especially not with the winners. Companies like Xerox and Milliken reported and demonstrated employee participation at much higher levels. Rochester had convinced the 1989 examiners that, even though they didn't have a formalized team participation plan, they did, in fact, have teams. It was described as "just the way we do business here." However, there was no indication in 1989 that participation in teams exceeded that 33 percent mark.

Rochester immediately set out to change that, and it was easier than anyone expected. They began rewarding team efforts. Osterwise and his managers began seeking out teams that were doing good things and began rewarding and recognizing them. In 1989, Rochester executives participated in the presentation of over two hundred awards, ranging from simple thank-yous and time off, to monetary awards totaling over $1.5 million. For example, Keith Slack, Rochester's engineering lab director, awarded $38,500 to an eleven-member team for their improvement of a key development process. "It was the old thing," said Osterwise, "actions speak louder than words. We had to show we supported teams, not just say that we did."

Rick Martino later recalled:

Larry [Osterwise] used this example with me about forming teams. When you're a kid forming a baseball team, you pick people, and there are always those people who are picked last. As you are starting to form teams and make changes, you can either be part of the change or you can sit around and complain about it. Most people, as they saw others form teams and make changes, wanted to participate. The peer pressure and seeing the success of teams got them there.

The whole concept of teams and team recognition not only caught on but caught fire at Rochester. Teams quickly began creating their own internal recognition and awards systems. One three-shift operation in the hardfile manufacturing area was concerned that employees on different shifts had no personal contact with each other. In fact, they may never have even met. Their solution was to put everyone's picture and name on a bulletin board. They reasoned that even if the employees didn't have one-on-one contact, they would at least be able to put a face with a name. The same group later expanded the idea to include posting the pictures of all new employees as well as employees who had received an award or recognition.

Another group in the hardfile area created its own peer award for customer service. Members nominated each other to the group manager, and, when a member received five peer nominations for outstanding customer service, he or she received a special "trophy." The "trophy" was actually a disk platter, which looks like an audio compact disk, with the recipient's picture and name in the center. The words "IBM CUSTOMER SERVICE AWARD: For continually providing the utmost service to my customers at all times" encircle the picture. These trophies are proudly displayed throughout the team's work area.

During 1990, Rochester created and recognized hundreds of such teams, with members trained in MDQ process improvement techniques. It would make a real difference in the Baldrige site visit.

Weakness #3: Benchmarking

Another thing that Rochester changed, based upon what it learned from the 1989 experience and examiner feedback report, was its approach to benchmarking and learning about the competition. Like the rest of IBM, Rochester had done competitive analysis for a long time. For example, Rochester knew about Hewlett-Packard, Digital Equipment, Olivetti, Nixdorf, Fujitsu, Hitachi and the other companies that directly competed with them. But Rochester hadn't been looking beyond its direct competition to find out what the best companies were doing. The Baldrige examiners had criticized it for that. "You have to look at whoever is the best at any functional thing, try to learn what they are doing, and see how you can adapt what they are doing to help you get better," said the examiners. So that's what Rochester did. And it even went to what some thought was an unlikely source for help, as Osterwise recalled:

> The Baldrige examiners had told us that we weren't finding the best company at each functional thing and learning from them. For example, we knew how Digital Equipment distributed its product, but we weren't searching out companies like, say, L. L. Bean, that might be better at distribution than either Digital or us, and learning from them. So, we decided that was something we needed to do, and we started asking ourselves who did that kind of functional benchmarking very well. One name we came up with was Xerox, so we decided to invite David Kearns, the CEO and chairman of Xerox, in for our 1990 kickoff meeting to talk about what they did.
>
> The fact that we would consider inviting Kearns in to talk to us is, I think, interesting. You have to remember that this was 1990 and Xerox had just beaten us in the Baldrige competition the year before. In fact, when I checked with Corporate to see if it would be all right for us to invite Kearns to speak, the response came back that we could go ahead and invite him but "didn't we have some hard feelings concerning Xerox since they had just beaten us in the Baldrige?" My response was, "Who better to learn from than someone who just beat you?" Anyway, we invited Kearns to speak.
>
> The day Kearns arrived, I went out to meet him to escort him into the site. I don't know exactly what I had expected Kearns to be like. After all, he was chairman and CEO of a company and a busy guy. In fact, when I had invited him, I hadn't really expected him to

come all the way to a place like Rochester, Minnesota. But here he was, and he came across as this very amicable, slightly graying, sixty-year-old guy who put you at ease just shaking his hand.

I walked up to Kearns and he said, "Larry, thanks for inviting me. Let me tell you why I'm here."

I was a little confused at that. I said, "Well, David, I think I know why you're here. We invited you to talk to my team."

Kearns said, "Yeah, yeah, but let me tell you why I'm really here. I asked around among my friends in Xerox if I should visit Rochester. Their view was 'Oh heck, yeah. Rochester is a very good place and a leader in many aspects of manufacturing. You can learn from them.' So," Kearns continued, "I'm counting this as one of my 1990 benchmarking visits."

He was benchmarking us! We had invited Kearns to learn from him, but he came with the attitude that he was going to learn something from us. It was a clear example of just what benchmarking was all about.

Rochester also expanded their benchmark efforts to include nonmanufacturing areas that had been ignored in the past. Areas like personnel, public relations and site services were trained in benchmark techniques and then compared themselves against best-of-breed companies. A Site Services team visited Hewlett-Packard. Administrative Services compared notes with Honeywell and came back with an improved way of writing job descriptions for secretaries.

A Facilities Management team was faced with the problem of decontaminating the bath that was used in a nickle-coating process in the hard-disk file manufacturing area. The volume of disks they were selling was going up and they were reaching capacity on their ability to treat waste from the process to make it environmentally sound. They did some benchmarking and learned that Northwest Airlines did nickle plating in its engine overhaul area but used a different method for treating the waste. As a result of that visit, the Rochester team uncovered a process for treating chemical wastes that resulted not only in an improved process, but in a $200,000 savings.

Weakness #4: The Closed-Loop Connection

Still another thing Rochester did in 1990 because of the feedback report was to start getting a closer, closed-loop connection to customers. The Baldrige examiners had said, "You send your stuff off the loading dock, somebody installs it, maintains it, but in some respects you don't care who. What you measure and manage is what you do in Rochester. You don't know when you have a marketing rep or systems engineer talking to a customer and that customer says, 'I don't like this system because . . .' You never know that conversation happens, so you don't have a 100 percent closed-loop understanding of the customer."

Again, the criticism came as a surprise, since Rochester had customer advisory councils and focus groups to provide input on products and had a lot of data from IBM sales and service personnel in the field. The site was also making customer follow-up calls ninety days after installation to find out what customers liked and didn't like. Everyone at Rochester thought they were doing a pretty good job of staying in touch with their customers. Yet the Baldrige examiners criticized Rochester for not doing enough.

In 1990, Rochester started to get a much more closed-loop, connective system to tap into what IBM marketing and service people were hearing by holding quarterly meetings with marketing and service people from other parts of IBM. Rochester manufacturing and development people would attend these meetings and talk to their sales and service counterparts face-to-face about customer interactions and what customers were saying. As a result of these meetings, Rochester began not only to close the loop, as the Baldrige examiners had suggested, but to develop a better relationship with IBM's marketing and service personnel. "Before we started having these meetings," Osterwise recalled, "marketing and service might hear something customers were saying about one of our products, but they didn't really see it as their job to make sure the conversation got reported back to us. After we started these meetings, marketing and service became much more attuned to what customers were saying and realized that what they were saying needed to get back to us so that if there was a problem we could get it fixed. After we started reaching out to them to ask for their help, it was a totally new relationship."

That relationship was not the only thing new at Rochester. The category owners took their assignment to find and fix "warts" very seriously, and this commitment went well beyond the criticisms in the Baldrige feedback report.

If You See a Wart, Fix It

One of the issues that arose during application preparation concerned education and training. That concern, like most of the feedback criticisms, came as a surprise to many at Rochester. After all, they did a lot of training. But the application team was concerned that training wasn't focused or consistent. Rochester employees just picked what they wanted to take. "It was," admitted Osterwise, "like picking from a college catalog." Very little was mandatory or targeted. As a result, there was no consistency in what people learned about quality. To change that, Rochester launched a program of mandatory and targeted quality training in 1990 and, in conjunction with the rest of ABS, piloted corporate MDQ training. In one year they put all eight thousand Rochester employees through one to two days of intensive quality training. And they did it in a way that sent a clear message to employees, as Osterwise explained:

> We did the training in a roll-down fashion. I educated my people about quality; they educated their people; and so on down through the entire organization. By doing the training that way, we accomplished two things simultaneously. First, we demonstrated the buy-in and support of managers, since they did the training. Second, everybody got the training twice. They learned it once and taught it once.

In addition to this focused quality training, Rochester continued and expanded other education and communication efforts in 1990. For at least a year, Rochester had been holding management colleges at which outside consultants and college professors would lecture about the concepts and ideas behind the quality transformation Rochester was attempting. In 1990, these were expanded into all-employee colleges where the concepts and ideas behind the transformation were shared with everyone.

Osterwise was later to remark that he felt one of the keys to Rochester's success was the effort expended on education and communication. He said:

> As our people were making transformations from being product- and technology-driven to being market- and customer-driven and from autocratic management to participatory management, the education and communication we conducted helped them understand why the transformations needed to occur. They began to understand the concepts and what they needed to do differently. Then we began to have an actual behavioral shift that culminated in results.
>
> In these forums, I stressed to everyone that the spirit of the individual—the resilience, the capability, the power of teams—would accomplish more than we could even imagine. These all-employee meetings were my opportunity to explain to individuals, to encourage them and to implore them to reach new heights. They also served to stimulate some bottom-up pressure for change.
>
> We pulled no punches in these sessions. Often we talked about our position with our customers in the marketplace. In fact, we typically had presentations from customers and from economists about the problems we were facing. But we also had the inspirational presentations. For example, we used a Joel Barker video to explain paradigm changes and how you had to anticipate the future and be innovative and strive for excellence. We had Peter Vidmar, the Olympic gymnast, come in to talk about taking risks, the importance of originality and virtuosity, and what it took to be a champion. So we exposed our people to all of these ideas.

One concept to which Rochester managers and employees were exposed was that of "empowerment"—giving employees the authority and responsibility to take action on their own to solve problems when they saw them. Empowerment was a concept foreign to "traditional" IBM, and not everyone in IBM was comfortable with the idea of empowering employees to take action without getting prior approval. But empowerment was something Osterwise believed in, and it was to become especially important at Rochester. Osterwise recalled an example of the difference "empowered" employees made:

> This particular incident occurred on a weekend. A woman in the plastics area was putting together some parts for a storage file. To do this, she had to attach a vendor-supplied part to an IBM-

manufactured part. In the process, she noticed that the color of the vendor-supplied parts didn't exactly match the color of the IBM-manufactured parts. It wasn't too much of a mismatch, since the parts were basically just two shades of gray. But it didn't seem right to her, so she took it upon herself to stop the production line. She called over one of her peers to look at the parts, and, together, they agreed that the parts didn't seem right. They decided to call an engineer at home and ask him to come in and check the parts. He came in and looked at them. Although he couldn't see anything wrong with the parts, he agreed to run some tests. As it turned out, the women had been right. The parts were bad. Something in the vendor's process had changed, ever so slightly. The net result of that change was that the parts would have passed all of our tests and worked fine in the device for a while. But then, one of the chemicals in the parts would have outgassed and created a film on the hard disk. That film would have caused the hard disk to crash. The customer would have lost data, and the disk would have to have been replaced. It would have been a very costly problem for us and the customer. As a result, we probably never would have regained the customer's confidence. People ask me how important empowerment is. Well, I tell them it is hard to put a dollar figure on it, but when you consider what it could have cost us, those women catching that single problem saved us enough to cover our entire training bill for 1990.

With empowered employees and all of the other changes, Rochester, a site that was already good, was getting much better. But even with these changes would Rochester be good enough to win the Baldrige this time? No one knew.

10

The 1990 Site Visit

Osterwise and Bauer were more nervous in 1990 than they had been in 1989. It wasn't that they thought their application was that bad. They had been worried about it. There had been a last-minute rush to get it out. And they knew that they had run out of time and that there were other refinements they could have made. But overall, it was a good application, at least as good as the 1989 application. Perhaps that was the problem. They knew that being as good as they were in 1989 wouldn't be good enough. They had been good in 1989 and had gotten a site visit, but they hadn't won. They knew the bar was being raised. The award was getting tougher. There was more competition. They also knew that more was at stake in 1990. Helping people deal with the 1989 loss was hard enough. How could they handle a second loss? Osterwise kept thinking, "If we lose again, how do I tell the people? How do I tell Lori Kirkland we didn't make it again?"

There was nothing to do but wait. They knew that from the year before. April dragged into May and then May into June. Then in July, they heard. They had made the first cut—again. Rochester would get a site visit for the second time in two years.

Preparing for the Site Visit

In 1989, much of the preparation for the site visit had involved reconstructing the evidence for what they had put in the application. Not this time. In 1990, they had been smarter. Early on, Bauer had told the category owners that they had to put their evidence file on the table when they submitted drafts of their sections. He made it clear that there would be no repeat of the 1989 experience where everyone had to go back and collect evidence to support what they had written. "If you can't substantiate it with evidence," said Bauer, "you don't put it in the application." So Rochester had its evidence together this time. Of course, they had to update some of the information, but it was nothing like what they had to do the year before. This time Rochester could concentrate on more important things.

They planned how the site visit would go, who would be in the room with the examiners, and who would answer the questions. They decided to limit the number of people who would be in the room. Answers, they decided, would be given by the category owners, and, to support each category owner, they would prepare a box of files with all the evidence. Each category owner would carry his own box of evidence files into the room. If a question came up, he could reach in the box, extract what he needed, and give it to the examiner. There would be no long-winded presentations, just short, direct answers to specific questions.

Then they got into the details of the visit itself. Lori Kirkland led a team to make sure everything was "just so." She rode around the site with the maintenance people, spotting trash she wanted picked up, holes she wanted filled in, and things she wanted generally spruced up for the visit. They checked out the hotel where the examiners would be staying, to make sure that the accommodations were just right and that the hotel staff knew who the Baldrige examiners were. Just as they did for customers and other important visitors to the site, Rochester got limos to bring the examiners in from the airport and to take them back and forth between the site and their hotel. Someone even noted that the computer keyboard in the IBM display at the local airport was dirty. So they sent someone out to clean it.

They even went over what everyone would wear. In a little back room, they gathered extra scarves for the women and extra ties for the men, in case anyone spilled something on their clothes during the visit and needed to change. They stocked the room with shoe-shine kits, combs, brushes, and any little thing someone might need for a quick touch-up. They decided no detail was too small to be left to chance. So they left nothing to chance. Then they did something that they had never thought about in 1989. It turned out to be, perhaps, the most important thing that they did and just the extra touch that they needed to win.

Simply the Best

It started out as an effort to find out about their competition. In 1989, Bauer and Osterwise had the feeling that the winners had done a much better job not only of preparing for the site visit, but also of learning about who else might be getting a site visit and how they could position themselves to show off their strengths. This time Bauer and Osterwise wanted to make sure they knew something about their competition, so Rochester could be better prepared.

Shortly after they learned that Rochester would get a site visit, Osterwise put out some feelers to IBM's marketing and service people. He said, "We've been putting notices on our bulletin boards to let people know where we stand on this Baldrige thing. If we are doing that, others probably are too. So let us know if you see or hear anything that makes you think somebody is in the running and is going to get a site visit."

Soon, the word started coming in. There were rumors that a division of AMOCO, a division of Westinghouse, and several others were supposed to get site visits. Then they found out that Cadillac was in the running and was holding pep rallies to psyche their people up. "We talked about it," said Osterwise, "and we decided, 'Why should our people be acting normal if everybody else is going to be acting like they are at a Super Bowl or something.' " Rochester decided to create its own excitement.

Over Labor Day weekend, Rochester's communication team

got together to decide what they could do to turn Rochester people on to this award and this site visit. They worked over Sunday and Monday. Tuesday, they came in with a plan. They had two ideas.

First, they wanted to make a videotape. It would be about five minutes long and have Osterwise out in the plant. He would talk about the award and winning. They envisioned a presentation based on "positive visioning," like in sports, where players get themselves prepared mentally to compete by picturing themselves going through the motions, executing the play and getting everything right. The video would end with a wide shot of a whole group of people and the closing line would be "Picture yourself in the winner's circle."

Their other idea was a little different. They wanted to run morning announcements over the site PA each day for eight days prior to the site visit. The announcements wouldn't begin with the standard "May I have your attention, please; may I have your attention, please." Instead, they would start with just a few clicks of the microphone and a short burst of music. That would be followed by a short discussion of what was important about each of the seven Baldrige categories, one category each day. The last day they would bring in Peter Vidmar, who had spoken at one of the all-employee colleges. Vidmar would end the series of announcements with one devoted to his ideas about how to relax, be yourself and compete as if you were just practicing. Both ideas were adopted, and communications was sent off to make the video, arrange for the announcements and pick the music.

A few days later, Osterwise was meeting in his office with the site personnel manager, Rick Martino. Doug Miller and Tim Dallman, from the communications department, came in with a couple of music selections they wanted Osterwise to hear. "Which one should we use for the PA announcements?" they wanted to know. One was, in Osterwise's words, "dentist's office music." The other was a song by Tina Turner. Martino and Osterwise listened to short segments of both and agreed immediately. The Tina Turner song was the obvious choice. They approved it and went back to their meeting, without listening to the entire song. They didn't have any idea what they had done.

Eight days before the site visit, Osterwise got ready for the first PA announcement. He clicked the microphone a couple of times to get everyone's attention. Then across the site, out of every speaker in every conference room, office, lab and manufacturing area came the sound of Tina Turner, louder than anyone had ever heard her before. Somehow, the volume had gotten turned all the way up. The song started with a heavy drumbeat, then the lyric, "You're simply the best . . ." The song faded out in a few seconds and the short presentation on the category began. *No one* missed it. It was so loud, how could they? Some liked it. They thought it was about time stale old IBM began announcements with rock and roll. Others thought it was all wrong. "Tina Turner isn't appropriate for the workplace," they complained. "That music's too loud," others said. Some just thought it was funny. "Hey, Larry," they asked, "do you really know what she's singing about that's 'the best'?" Of course not. He'd never listened to the whole song. When he did—Oops! Oh, well, the important thing is they paid attention.

Later, when the examiners came, everyone was up for the visit. That year they didn't hide in their offices or avoid the cafeteria, afraid that an examiner might walk up to them and ask them about quality. This year they walked up to the examiners and *told* them about quality. They told them a lot about quality. Some within IBM, Bauer and Osterwise in particular, came to feel later that the Rochester people won the award that year. In their opinions, examiners' visits on the floor talking to the people were the best parts of the site visit. At a minimum, those examiner/employee discussions were an important part of what went right. But, then, a lot went right.

The Site Visit from Heaven

The Baldrige examiners arrived for the three-day site visit on September 18, 1990. Rochester and all of ABS were ready and pleasantly surprised. The examiners came in with a well-thought-out plan. "They were very professional," said Kirkland, "very organized, and very gracious—all of them."

The first day went better than anyone could have hoped. The examiners wanted a short tour of the facility. Then they said they wanted to sit down and start going through the categories asking questions. They wanted to spend a day on Category 7, Customer Satisfaction, and a half day each on the remaining categories. Two examiners would ask questions on each category, so they needed three examination rooms. They had it all planned. They knew exactly what they wanted to accomplish and how they wanted to accomplish it. Rochester was impressed. So were the examiners.

Rochester's planning paid off. After the morning tour, the examiners settled down in their two-person teams with the Rochester category owners and began their questioning. Each category owner carried his or her box of evidence files into the examination room. The examiners had a list of prepared questions. "In item 3.3," they would ask, "you make this statement. Can you show us some data on this?" The category owner would turn to his file, pull out the evidence, and hand it to the examiners. They would look at it, check off their question and hand it back. "Thank you," they would say. "Now, in respect to 3.2 . . ." It went like that all day.

Rochester sent three people to each examination—the category owner, a "scribe," and a "gatekeeper." They had worked it out in advance. In 1989 there had been confusion about who would participate in the examination and who would answer questions. There would be no confusion this time. The category owner would answer all of the questions. The "scribe" would write down every question asked and every answer given. Then, he or she would assign a grade to the answer—"A +" if the question seemed to have been fully answered, "A" if points appeared, from the examiners' response, to have been left unanswered, and so on. The "gatekeeper" controlled the timing and who was allowed in the room. He or she watched the examiners' expressions. Was a break needed? Was it getting contentious? Did they need to stop and get control? Was a certain person needed in the room to help the category owner answer a question? The "gatekeepers" made those decisions. It was all very organized, and the question-and-answer phase went much faster than it had the year before. At the end of the first day, the Rochester team met to assess where they stood. They couldn't have been more ecstatic. It was going better than anyone had ever expected. They had even asked for and gotten support from corporate headquarters.

Corporate Leadership

In 1989, after some debate, Rochester had decided not to invite Schwartz, Talbot and others from IBM Corporate to the site visit. "After all," they had decided, "what could corporate executives add?" Things were different in 1990. Not only did Rochester invite corporate executives, but they came and they helped. Terry Lautenbach came. Steve Schwartz, by then the senior vice president of Market-Driven Quality, came. So did Bob LaBant, the new general manager of Application Business Systems, who had replaced Schwartz. Lautenbach, Schwartz, and LaBant gave presentations to the examiners about what IBM had been doing to improve quality and they *had* a story to tell.

They told the examiners about Market-Driven Quality, six sigma, cycle-time reduction, defining market needs, eliminating defects, measuring progress, employee involvement, enterprise processes and the MDQ self-assessment, which was patterned after Baldrige. Then they told them that "Rochester was the 'rabbit' of IBM, really leading the whole company to the 'Holy Grail' of quality." It was impressive corporate support and commitment.

Excited and Involved Employees

By the second day, examiners were beginning to move to their next step in the examinations process. They wanted to talk to employees. Again, 1990 was completely different. Employees were calling Osterwise's office. "Are the examiners coming to our department?" they wanted to know. "Send them to our department. We want to show them what we've been doing." After the site visit was over, Osterwise was to remember one employee who came up to him and told this story:

> You know, Larry, it must be that I eat alone in the cafeteria a lot, because last year I was sitting in the cafeteria by myself when the examiners were here and the same thing happened this year. Last year when the examiner came up to me, I sorta looked up and then back down, and I hoped that he would go away and not ask me any questions. But he sat down and started talking to me about our quality

and what we were doing. I said some things, but I didn't feel very well prepared. I didn't really know what we were doing so it was embarrassing. This year I saw one of them come into the cafeteria and when they got a few steps away from the table, I stood up, put out my hand to shake his and said, "Sit down, I'd like to talk to you about quality." He sat down and we talked for about forty-five minutes. I felt very much at ease. I knew what I was doing to improve quality, and I knew what the site and IBM were doing. What's more, I knew I had the company's full support. It was just totally different this year.

Indeed it was "totally different." Rick Martino, Rochester's personnel manager, tells a story about the site visit that made a strong impression on him:

The Baldrige examiners . . . walked through my area, and they stopped in the offices of one of our administrative employees [Marlys Perkins in recruiting] and asked, "What are you doing in terms of quality?" She looked at the Baldrige examiner and she said, "I'll show you what I'm doing. This is going to blow you away." She took out a chart and showed it to him. It was an example of some process improvement she had been working on with others in her department. The recruiting organization had mapped their entire process and, with the help of the administrative folks and the recruiters, had changed the process. They had developed this new process that cut cycle time for recruiting supplemental employees by two-thirds. Their customers were happier. They improved their jobs because they had designed them. We had the cycle-time measurements hanging up in the recruiting area, so when people walked by, they could see that it went from six weeks down to two weeks. That's what she was showing the examiner.

It was the same throughout the site. Everywhere the examiners went, they met employees who were involved and anxious to talk about what they had been doing to improve quality. It was very much like what Heinz Fridrich and Gus Vassiliades had experienced on their first visit to Motorola. Even when the examiners eavesdropped on training classes, they found good things happening at Rochester.

Effective Training

Rick Martino was accompanying two of the examiners when they decided to drop in on a training session. Rochester had started sending all of its managers to a training session on transformational leadership, covering the need for change and how to manage the change process. They had a senior manager kick off each session. Martino recalled the impact this had on managers who attended:

> They [the senior managers] talked about survival and really challenged folks to participate and discuss and bring forward issues. So, what you found right up front was executive commitment to what we were trying to do. The comments we got back were "this must really be important for [senior managers] to come to every session."

Additionally, Rochester modified the initial training to have each manager bring a couple of key employees from their department with them to the training. At the end of the class, each manager was asked to sign a contract saying, "Based upon what I have learned in this session, here are the things I am committed to change about the way I manage." A copy of that contract went to the course instructor, who would then send a reminder to each manager thirty days after the training ended asking, "Did you really change the things you said you were going to change?"

In a 1992 interview, one Rochester manager who had attended the transformational leadership training remembered making a commitment in his "contract" to stop "micromanaging" his people. About a week after attending the leadership training, he recalled getting a report from a group of his people outlining what they thought should be done to accomplish a change the department was planning. The manager responded to his people's recommendations in his typical fashion. He took the report, marked it with his own recommendations on how the change should be accomplished differently, and sent the report back to his team. Shortly afterward, he got a note from one of the employees who had attended the leadership training class with him. It said, "We just went to this class and you told me you were going to try to do something a little different. This marked-up report you sent back looks like you really aren't going to try to change like you said you would." The manager had to admit that the employee was right. He hadn't lived up to his commitment to stop "micromanaging." He sent back a note saying, "You're absolutely right. Forget what I wrote on the report. If that's the way you guys think it should be done, then do it." Later, the manager recalled that his team made the changes their way and that the change was a tremendous success. The transformational leadership training had a similar impact on other managers who attended the training.

The Baldrige examiners happened to drop in on a transformational leadership session for a group of programmers. Martino described what happened:

> The class was full. That was the other interesting thing about this class. Doing it with managers and employees together, we were overbooked. Getting managers to management development classes wasn't always easy. I give lots of credit to the management development team in Rochester—Jim Buchanan and his team—they turned that around. The demand for this course was so high we couldn't fulfill the demand. The Baldrige examiners sat in on a class of these programmers with their managers. It was very open. People were laughing. People were joking, but they were talking about serious stuff, and it was even impressive for me to see that team of people sitting there with their managers, all talking about the issues and what they were going to do to solve them.

The examiners were impressed. Yet by the end of the second day everyone was getting tired, and the examiners were raising some issues that obviously concerned them. By the time of the daily recap meeting that evening, Osterwise and his team were becoming concerned.

But Do You Have Teams?

One of the issues the examiners raised on the second day concerned employee teams, the same issue the examiners had raised in 1989. Lori Kirkland remembered the examiners' concerns as follows:

They kept asking about teams. We just answered, "Teams are very much part of our culture. If you need a team, you just go out and form a team." Well, they weren't understanding that, and they kept asking the questions, "Who forms teams? What's the process? What kind of escalation do you go through?" We just kept glossing over it, and it finally became clear to us that they did not understand that this was just part of our culture. If a quality inspector or line person saw a problem and needed a team, they'd call a development engineer. They'd call a line engineer. They'd call a procurement engineer or whomever they needed. They'd fix the problem. They might tell the manager. They might not. Or they might tell him later. And that was just the way it worked. They were looking for some type of formal team system. But we didn't have that.

The examiners actually had two concerns about teams. First, they wanted to know how many teams Rochester had. Second, they wanted more information about how teams went about deciding the root cause of problems, so they could begin to address them. Fortunately, Rochester had struggled with how to respond to the issue of the number of teams before the site visit, so they had data to address it. While Rochester didn't have a formal team system, everyone knew that there were more quality teams at Rochester than ever before. But how many? Rick Martino had surveyed the Rochester managers just prior to the site visit. He had asked them to report how many teams they had. Martino had defined "teams" to mean two or more people within a function or across functions working on a particular project or objective together. He had gotten back fourteen hundred responses, and he had put the responses in a binder. When the Rochester team was asked how many teams they had, Martino simply handed them the binder. That was all it took. That issue about teams was settled.

How Do You Determine the Root Cause of Problems?

Answering the examiners' questions about how teams identified root causes of problems was a little more difficult. Rochester did have a formal process, but they didn't have a presentation to show it. Andy Papamarcos, a member of the 1990 application team, was sent off to prepare one. Essentially what he did was document the five-step Root Cause Analysis Process that Rochester used. As shown in Table 10.1, that involved (1) confirming the details of the problem; (2) probing for any related information; (3) analyzing the data to review frequency and initial trends; (4) correlating the information with recent actions or changes in the processes or materials; and (5) isolating the causes through statistical techniques and controlled experiments.

Andy gave his presentation the next day. The examiners listened politely, and then said, "Thank you very much." They were satisfied. Case closed.

Table 10.1
Root Cause Analysis Process

Confirm
> Recreate problem
> Repeat failure
> Restate process deficiency
> Complete process review
> Visit supplier or customer location

Probe
> Examine with electron microscope
> Examine checkpoints, dumps, and traces
> Examine vital product data
> Find last point before failure

Analyze
> Determine frequency of occurrence (Pareto diagram)
> Review trend data (trend diagram)
> Review statistical process control charts
> Decide how exhibited and how found
> Evaluate single supplier versus multiple supplier
> Analyze execution path, system state, and environment

Correlate
> Correlate supplier, in-house, and customer data
> Find indications of problems in other measures
> Identify recent process changes
> Determine batch, job lot, time stamp, and release level

Isolate
> Isolate possible causes (fishbone diagram)
> Rank by probability
> Perform additional testing
> Perform experiment at suspected point of origin
> Test for stress (heat, voltage, strength, life, etc.)
> Test boundary conditions

An Unexpected Development

It was harder to close the case on another matter, though. Throughout the site visit, Rochester had felt that they were in control, since they had planned so well for the visit. There was, however, one thing that neither Osterwise, Bauer nor any of the others had expected or planned for. They didn't expect the examiners to want to leave Rochester and talk to other parts of IBM.

The issue had come up soon after they had arrived. "In addition to talking to Rochester employees," the examiners had said, "we'd like to talk to some marketing representatives and some systems engineers. We know they aren't part of Rochester, but you talk about your working relationship in your application. What if we went to Chicago and talked to IBM's people there?"

Osterwise wasn't sure how practical that was. Chicago was an hour away by plane, and it was a little late to arrange for a corporate jet. "How about Minneapolis?" he suggested. "We could drive you up there." The examiners wanted to think about it. They still had questions to ask and they wanted to talk to employees. They weren't sure they would even have enough time to visit a branch office. Then, on the second day of the visit, they came back with their decision. Everything was proceeding so smoothly, they would have plenty of time to go to Minneapolis after all.

It wasn't so much that Osterwise was worried about the Rochester/Minneapolis relationship. Rochester's relationship with the marketing and service groups had always been positive and responsive and had improved further with their new customer satisfaction meetings. He felt sure about that. The only thing was that they hadn't prepared for this. They had prepared Rochester managers and employees for the site visit. Everyone had time to reflect upon the messages they wanted to convey. That wouldn't be true at the Minneapolis branch. The examiners would just show up and start asking questions. No one wanted to do anything inappropriate, but it had been clear to the Rochester team, at least since the experience in 1989, that they had to treat the site visit like a marketing event. By that they didn't mean trying to sell the examiners on something, but understanding and preparing for it as an event in which they had to know their customer, had to know what information their customer would be seeking, and had to be prepared to provide that information in the way the customer wanted it and could understand it. They had done that kind of preparation with the Rochester team, but not with the Minneapolis team. They decided they should send an advance man to Minneapolis to get the marketing reps and systems engineers prepared for the Baldrige examiners' visit. Bob Griffin, a member of Rochester's senior management team and later a marketing director for IBM, got tapped for the Minneapolis "warm-up" job. He later described the events of that day:

The examiners were scheduled to be in Minneapolis for an early morning meeting, so I ended up leaving at four or four-thirty in the morning from Rochester. I was concerned about traffic and getting up there before they arrived. They were going to get there at about eight. It's a two-hour trip, so, under this circumstance, I allowed myself two and a half or three hours. I was *not* going to be late to this meeting. As it turned out, I got up there and literally opened the place. I've been in marketing with IBM for twenty-two years. Maybe in some professions people are bright-eyed in the morning, but a lot of marketing people aren't really churning like they should until they have their first cup of coffee. They need to collect themselves before they get hit with a lot of questions, and they need that cup of coffee. So when I got to Minneapolis that morning, the first thing I did was I made sure that everyone had a cup of coffee.

Then, I tried to prepare them a little for the examiners' visit. It was just a matter of taking the time to say, "This is like a marketing event. Treat it like we are presenting a proposal. Just think through the questions before you answer."

As they [the examiners] were coming up the elevator, I left the conference room and went to a private office. The minute they got in there, I left and went back to Rochester.

For the rest of the day, the Rochester team waited to hear how the Minneapolis visit had gone. Osterwise was the first to get some clue. He had been away from the site that day and returned just as the examiners were returning from Minneapolis. As they walked into the building together, Osterwise casually asked one of the examiners, "Well, how did it go?" "Oh, great," he said. Then he took Osterwise by the arm and led him to the side. "You know, Larry," he whispered, "I went up to Minneapolis with high expectations. I'll tell you my expectations were far exceeded. You should call Conrades [George Conrades was IBM's general manager for marketing and services] and your other headquarters marketing folks and tell them just how far this Market-Driven Quality stuff has gone. These people all know it. They are striving to satisfy their customers, and they are connected to you. They understand it. They really do." Osterwise said, "Okay! Good deal!"

It was a very good deal.

Another Unexpected Development

There was just one thing remaining for the Rochester team. They had, it appeared, orchestrated the site visit and brought it off extremely well. Of course, there had been a few moments of concern such as those on the night of the second day. They had discovered, to their horror, that the female examiners were finding it very difficult to climb in and out of the long, low-slung, stretch limos Rochester had so "thoughtfully" provided. The limos were immediately replaced with vans, and things continued to go very well, on the whole. Now they wanted to end the visit in style. They wanted to have an event—something the examiners would remember. The question was what?

They came up with all kinds of stupid, silly ideas. "We could play kazoos," someone suggested, "and sing 'We Love You, Malcolm' as the examiners leave." "Or," someone else suggested, "there's this forty-foot plastic bull they used for that local dairy promotion. We could rent it and stick it in the parking lot with a sign saying something like 'Rochester Excellence, Customer Satisfaction . . . It Ain't No Bull.' " There were other ideas like those. Of course most of them had been suggested toward the end of late-night meetings when people were a little punchy anyway.

Eventually, in the light of day, they rejected all of them. They finally decided upon just having cake and ice cream, a kind of Rochester tradition. Fate, however, had something a little more exciting in mind—a code-44 alarm. It meant trouble. A power outage, burst pipe, or, God forbid, a fire. Osterwise hadn't heard the code-44 over the PA, but the rest of the Rochester team had. All they knew was that they were within an hour of waving the examiners off to the airport, and this was the last thing they needed.

Osterwise recalled the next several minutes:

We were walking between buildings, escorting the examiners to the departure ceremony where we were going to have cake for them. Raul Cosio, our systems plant manager, walked right past me and didn't say a word. I said to the examiner I was walking with, "Wait a minute. Looks like I need to talk to Raul." I caught up with Raul and asked him what was going on. Raul told me, "There is a fire in the Integrated Technology Laboratory. I think we have got it under control, and there doesn't appear to be any lasting damage." Now, in an environment like that, if the fire was serious, you could be down for months. But, Raul said, "I think it is okay now. I'll let you know."

I rejoined the examiner I had been walking with when Raul passed me, and he wanted to know, "What's the deal?" I explained, as casually as possible, "There's a little fire in one of the buildings, but it seems to be under control now."

The examiner asked, "How did you know that? Why did you stop just because Raul walked by?" "Well, Raul is always an upbeat person," I said. "You can't walk by Raul without his smiling and saying, 'Hello.' He is always charged up. If you noticed the look on his face when he passed us just then, it was obvious that something was wrong."

The examiner was amazed. "I've heard about managing by sight, but this is ridiculous. You walk by your employees, and, just by their body language, you can gauge the severity of the activity of the day. This is a team that works together well."

A little later Raul joined us for the final ceremony. Now he was his upbeat self again. The fire had been taken care of, and everything was fine. The examiner who had noticed my "managing by sight," as he put it, came over to me and said, "This is remarkable. Everything is okay now, right? You sure were right about Raul. You can read him like a book."

Well, it was true. Osterwise could read Raul like a book. But he couldn't say that about the examiners. There was no way to tell from their expressions whether Rochester had a chance of winning.

The Examiners' View

What Osterwise didn't know for sure, but was to find out later, was that Rochester's site visit had gone much better than it had in 1989. The Baldrige examiners had found a lot to their liking. In a later feedback report, they said that IBM Rochester had demonstrated "evidence of effective quality efforts in all categories and excellent efforts in Category 1.0—Leadership, Category 2.0—Information and Analysis, Category 3.0—Strategic Quality Planning, Category 5.0—Quality Assurance of Products and Services, and Category 6.0—Quality Results." In particular, the examiners had been impressed with "Senior management's strong leadership . . . demonstrated through a clearly formulated vision based on customer satisfaction and deployed through critical success factors. . . ." Communication of the Market-Driven Quality system, said the examiners, "was outstanding."

The examiners were also impressed with the "high level of sophistication in information systems, data collection and analysis, as well as deployment of databased and analytical tools . . ." that they found at Rochester.

"The quality planning process," said the examiners, "has a strong focus on customer and business partner satisfaction, a structure which ties plans to quality and business priorities and goals and . . . encompasses all internal functions, suppliers, and customers."

Equally if not more impressive to the examiners was Rochester's "strong and long-established focus on IBM 'basic beliefs,' supported by education, open communications, and recognition." That, said the examiners, "has created an atmosphere where customer satisfaction and continuous quality improvement have become a way of life."

The examiners also praised Rochester's extensive involvement of customers and suppliers, worldwide new product introduction, continuous process improvement, audit processes and supplier quality improvement efforts.

Rochester's quality and customer satisfaction results were also impressive. Between 1988 and 1990, Rochester had

- increased revenues from computer and operating system sales by 35 percent per employee;
- increased market share by 16 percent;
- increased customer satisfaction by 8 percent;
- increased its total installations by 25 percent;
- cut inventory by 28 percent;
- improved total inventory turns by 10 percent;
- improved turns on new inventory by 52 percent;
- reduced engineering change scrap by 38 percent;
- reduced obsolete inventory scrap by 24 percent; and,
- cut warranty scrap by 21 percent.

It was an outstanding evaluation, although no one at Rochester knew it at the time. Even if they had known, there was still no guarantee that an outstanding evaluation would lead to an award. Six applicants in the manufacturing category were receiving site visits that year. Most, if not all, of them could be expected to receive positive evaluations, but only two could win. There was no guarantee Rochester would be one of those two.

11

The 1990 Verdict

For the next several weeks, Osterwise went into his office every day not knowing if Rochester had won or lost. He didn't know what to think. The site visit, he thought, had generally gone well, and there was the discussion he had had with Dr. Ruth Haines, the NIST representative on the site visit. She had pulled Roy Bauer and him aside to discuss the responsibilities of being a winner. That was an encouraging sign, right? But the competition, if anything, was much tougher than it had been the year before, and what Larry didn't know was that NIST had decided to discuss the responsibilities of being a winner with all site-visit companies. NIST didn't want anyone to be surprised when those responsibilities came along with the trophy. Osterwise felt that Rochester had a good chance to win, but he wouldn't want to bet on it. So he just went in each day and waited for the call.

The Call from Mosbacher

It was October 9, 1990, about two in the afternoon. Osterwise was sitting at his desk, finishing some last-minute paperwork before going to a meeting. Several people were waiting in the reception area outside his office to attend a meeting with him. Deb Pesch, an administrative assistant, was substituting for Osterwise's regular secretary, Dar Moen. Pesch's phone rang and she picked it up. The caller said, "Secretary of Commerce Bob Mosbacher calling for Larry Osterwise." Pesch put the caller on hold, got up from her desk and went to Osterwise's door. She stuck her head in, caught Osterwise's eye, and mouthed two words, "Bob Mosbacher." Silently, she shut the door.

Osterwise picked up the phone. His hands were shaking and so was his voice. He answered, "Hello, this is Larry Osterwise," to which the caller replied, "Hello, Larry, this is Bob Mosbacher here." "I'm *delighted* to hear from you, Bob," said Osterwise. "Well, I'm delighted to speak to you, Larry," said Mosbacher, "because I get to tell you that you are a winner of the 1990 Malcolm Baldrige National Quality Award."

The only thing Osterwise could think to say was, "*Boy*, am I glad to hear from you!"

The rest of the conversation lasted only a few minutes. Mosbacher congratulated Rochester on its win and told Osterwise that since he knew Rochester had received a site visit the previous year he had wanted to call them as the first winner he would contact that day. Osterwise asked about the other winners, but Mosbacher said he couldn't tell Osterwise their names until all the winners had been called. Anyway, said Mosbacher, the official announcement wouldn't be made until the next day, so, for now, Osterwise should only tell those he felt really needed to know.

At least Osterwise wouldn't have to keep his secret for the long, torturous week he had to keep it in 1989. As a result of the prior year's news leak reported by *USA Today*, the Department of Commerce had decided to shorten the time between notifying winners and losers and the president's announcement. They hoped that would minimize the possibility of additional news leaks. Osterwise was thankful. It would have been much tougher to hide his good news than it was to hide last year's bad news.

Telling the Boss

Osterwise already knew who was on his need-to-know list. It was almost the same list he had called the year before about the loss—John Akers, Jack Kuehler, Bob Talbot, Terry Lautenbach, Bob LaBant and Steve Schwartz. He started with Akers, of course.

Larry reached Akers's secretary, De Anne Spencer, immediately. She told him that Akers was at a strategic planning meeting at the Palisades, IBM's New York training center, and would not be in his office that day. Then it dawned on Osterwise. "Oh! Everybody's there, right?" he asked. Spencer, who had known Osterwise for some time, heard the excitement in his voice and queried, "Larry, do you have good news for us?" Osterwise hesitated. He wanted the group at the Palisades to be the first to hear the news, so he asked De Anne, "Are you ready to sign a nondisclosure agreement [a prerequisite to any confidential discussion with IBM]?" Spencer just laughed and replied, "That's okay, Larry. I don't need to know, and I think I understand exactly what you just *didn't* tell me."

Osterwise then called the Palisades and asked to speak to John Akers. "I'm sorry," came the singsong response on the other end of the line, "we are not allowed to call Mr. Akers or anyone out of the room." "You don't understand," said Osterwise, "I've *got* to talk to someone *now*. Is there any way to get a message in to Mr. Akers that I have to talk to him?"

"Well, we would rather not interrupt Mr. Akers," came the reply. "Is there anyone else in there that we could give the message to?"

Osterwise thought a minute. "Yeah," he said, "my line-of-business general manager is in there. Can you get a message to him?" "Sure, we can do that," the receptionist answered, to Osterwise's relief.

Steve Schwartz tells the story from this point:

When Larry made his call to the Palisades, it just so happened that I was in the middle of making a presentation about Market-Driven Quality, how far we had come and how far we still had to go.

As I was giving the presentation, I saw someone come in and hand a note to Bob LaBant, Rochester's line-of-business general manager. Bob read the note, and it was obvious that something was up, by the look on his face. Bob sat there for a moment and then got up and left the room.

Now this is the type of meeting you don't want to leave. Nobody gets up and leaves a planning meeting ever, because everyone knows that we're talking about the next three or four years of your life. If you leave, something might happen that you're not too happy about. You could come back and find out that it was too late and there is nothing you can do about it. So I was surprised to see Bob get up and leave. It had to be something very important.

I kept going with my presentation. A little later, Bob came back into the room, and everybody was watching him. They were so curious about what was going on, they completely lost interest in what I was saying.

Then Bob went over to Terry Lautenbach and leaned down and whispered something in Terry's ear. You could see Terry's face light up, and he whispered something back to Bob.

By this point, no one in the room was paying any attention to what I was saying, because they were all watching Terry and Bob. I was getting a little disgusted, because I was trying to emphasize how important Market-Driven Quality was to our future. Then I saw Terry take out a little piece of paper and write a note. He folded it up and passed it down the table to John [Akers]. Of course, the note passing in itself caused even more disruption.

John was sitting right next to where I was standing. He took the note and read it. You could see his face light up, and the whole place, with everybody in the room following the passing of the note and looking at John's reaction, was really disrupted.

I still didn't know what was going on. I was just trying to continue with my presentation and get their attention back on what I was saying. At that point, John took the note, folded it, and handed it to me.

I was anxious to see what the note said, but I was almost through with my presentation and didn't want to cause any more disruption. So I decided I would read it after I was finished with my talk. I started to put the note in my pocket, but John stopped me. He said, "No, Steve, read it." So I took the note out of my pocket and started to read it to myself. John said, "No, Steve, read it out loud."

In one of the proudest moments of my professional life, I read the note to the rest of the room. It said, "We've just received word that IBM Rochester has won the Malcolm Baldrige National Quality Award."

With that, every single person, every general manager within IBM around the world, stood up and started applauding.

Shortly after giving IBM Rochester a standing ovation, the whole top management team of IBM assembled in a small room and placed a conference call to Larry Osterwise to congratulate him.

Telling Roy Bauer

Osterwise's first call, after hanging up from the Akers conference call, was to Roy Bauer. He knew he had to reach Bauer soon, because Bauer was getting ready to leave for a few days' work on an IBM task force. Osterwise wanted to catch him before he left. He reached Bauer on the first try. "Roy, are you sitting down?" began Osterwise. "No," said Bauer somewhat sarcastically. "I'm standing up." "Well," said Osterwise, "you had better sit down 'cause I've got something to tell you. I just got a call from Mosbacher." Osterwise knew that Bauer understood what that meant, but the only comment he got back was "Oh, we won." It was just like that. Bauer showed almost no emotion. "I didn't jump up and down," Bauer said later, remembering the call from Osterwise. "I couldn't. The only thing I felt was this big burden being lifted from me. I had been so worried that we might not win. That was the scariest part of doing it twice—worrying about losing twice. When I got the call, all I could feel was relief."

Telling the World

Osterwise wanted to tell the whole site, the world for that matter, that Rochester had won, but he couldn't. He had promised Mosbacher that he would postpone his announcement until the next day when the official announcement would be made by the White House. There was nothing Osterwise could do but just go home that night and wait. Tomorrow he would tell everyone— just as soon as he got word from the Commerce Department that he could go ahead.

Osterwise already knew what he wanted to say. Since the site visit, he had been thinking about the "we won" speech. He had it all worked out in his mind. He would get on the PA system and start slowly and somberly like the year before. He would go over all they had accomplished. He would build the suspense. Then he would make the announcement: "Rochester is one of the winners of the Malcolm Baldrige National Quality Award." He had the "win" version of the announcement all worked out. Thank God they hadn't lost. He had no idea what he would have said if they had. He had never gotten around to preparing that speech. Well, it didn't matter. They had won. He wouldn't have to deliver a "we lost" speech—not this year.

The real question was the timing of the announcement by the White House, and all Osterwise could do was wait. He kept calling the Commerce Department. "No, not yet," they kept saying. Lunch came and went. Then it was early afternoon. Osterwise got word that Cadillac had called a meeting of all of its employees to announce that they had won. He called the Commerce Department again. "Have you heard about Cadillac?" he asked. "Yes," they said, "we have." What's more, they knew the list of winners was going out over the wire services. The White House still had not made the announcement, but "go ahead," the Commerce Department representatives said, "you've got the right to tell your people first before they hear it from the media." "Okay!" said Osterwise.

Osterwise quickly began making calls. He wanted the application team and all the category owners together in his conference room when he made the announcement. He knew one person in particular that he wanted to be there, so he picked up the phone and dialed her extension. "This is Larry Osterwise. May I speak to Lori Kirkland?" he said.

On the other end of the line, Kirkland's secretary asked Osterwise to wait, jumped up from her desk and raced down the hall to Kirkland's office. "Larry Osterwise is holding for you," she said excitedly. After all, the site general manager didn't call every day. Kirkland picked up the phone and heard, "Lori, you took it so badly last year when we lost the Baldrige award, I wanted to be the one to tell you first. It's being announced today that Rochester has won the 1990 Malcolm Baldrige National Quality Award. In about fifteen minutes, I'm going to announce it to the rest of the site over the PA, and I'd like you to be in my conference room when I do. Can you come over?" said Osterwise. "*Could I?*" Kirkland thought. "You couldn't keep me away."

Kirkland would remember later just how wonderful she felt as she raced down the long hallways to Osterwise's conference room. In a few minutes she arrived at Osterwise's office. There, sitting around the conference table, were all of the members of the application team.

At four o'clock, Osterwise began his announcement. He tried to follow his plan to start somberly and build the tension as he went. It didn't work. The excitement in his voice gave him away. Unbeknownst to him, the application team had been handed streamers before they entered the conference room. Larry's secretary, Dar Moen, had made just-in-case plans for a celebration. The cheering had already begun by the time he got to his punch line, "It is going to be announced by President Bush shortly that we have won the Malcolm Baldrige National Quality Award." With that, the celebration began.

The Celebrations

The next day, Rochester held an ice cream social to celebrate. First the local and then the national media began calling the site. Over the next few days Osterwise and Bauer did almost nothing but interviews and site tours for newspaper, magazine and TV reporters. After being almost ignored in 1988, "winning the Baldrige" had become major business news by 1990.

In mid-December, Osterwise took his category owners and application team members with their spouses to Washington to the national ceremony. Roy Bauer was there. So were Mike Jacobson and Lori Kirkland. They were wined and dined and given special tours. Then on Thursday, December the fourteenth, they went to the ceremony. There was electricity in the air and a tremendous sense of pride and accomplishment.

Each member of the Rochester team has his or her own story about that day. They range from tears and lumps in the throat to encounters with the Secret Service. Dar Moen, Osterwise's secretary, had suffered through two years of Baldrige preparation. She had supplied the coffee and junk food that kept the team going on those long days and nights of preparation. Perhaps more importantly, she had conjured up little games and songs to keep their spirits up. And, she would not be denied the experience of seeing IBM accept this award.

When Larry asked Dar to accompany the team to Washington, she did what most other people would do. She went out and bought herself a snazzy new outfit for the occasion. Dar remembered arriving at the ceremony in her new dress:

> I had tears in my eyes. I could hardly talk. I remember that I had brass buttons on my dress, and when I went through security, the detector kept going off. They wouldn't let me in because my buttons were setting off the metal detector! So I told them, "I'll take my dress off and go in my slip, but I'm not going to miss this."

Fortunately for Dar, the Secret Service let her and her brass buttons in.

Dar took her seat and the ceremony began. President Bush took the podium and announced the 1990 winners—Cadillac Division of General Motors; Federal Express; Wallace Company of Houston, Texas; and IBM Rochester. IBM Rochester employees watched the ceremony over closed-circuit TV, as John Akers accepted the award for them and took custody of the award certificate. It was the first live broadcast ever made over the IBM Communications Network. Afterward, Bauer took custody of the actual trophy. Moen remembered walking the three or four blocks from the ceremony to their hotel. "The award was heavy, but he [Bauer] was carrying it through the streets like a baby."

Now it was time to take the trophy home to Rochester. No one wanted to check the award as luggage, and they were not sure if it would fit "in the overhead bins or under the seat in front" of them. "Should we buy it a seat?" they considered for a while; then Bauer came up with the solution. He rode home with it in his lap.

The celebrations continued after they returned to Rochester. John Akers flew in to present the award to Rochester employees. They rented the Mayo Civic Center for two nights of concerts by Beverly Sills and Melissa Manchester, and they invited all of IBM Rochester's eight thousand employees and their spouses.

Following all the celebrations, everyone assumed that the trophy would occupy a permanent place somewhere in the Rochester complex. But that spire of Steuben crystal was in great demand throughout IBM. Everyone wanted to display it for this function or that. Ultimately, the trophy made only a few trips to a stockholders meeting and to a product announcement in New York. They quickly learned that it was simply too fragile to travel.

At first, they put the award in a trophy case in the main lobby but decided that the location wasn't "worthy of the award." So they turned to one of their AS/400 customers, a company which made display cases for the Smithsonian. The new display case was beautiful, though expensive. They reasoned, though, "We aren't going to get this kind of award very often." With glass on all four sides, the case had a centerpiece that would rotate, making the award visible from every angle.

When the case arrived, they placed the award in the reception area of Rochester's main building, just behind two glass doors that serve as the main entrance to the site. It was strategically placed so that visitors could see it through the glass doors, but, more importantly, it was placed where those who had earned this award, Rochester's employees, could see it whenever they passed by. There the award sits today as a symbol of Rochester's quality journey. Behind the glass doors, Rochester's quality journey continues.

And, far away in Armonk, New York, IBM's headquarters, John Akers and Steve Schwartz had what they were seeking. Rochester's success was proof that Market-Driven Quality worked. Now, if they could just get the rest of IBM to follow Rochester's lead, maybe they could finally create a new IBM.

12

A New IBM

Nineteen ninety had been a very good year for IBM. After years of searching, Akers and his team had settled on a plan for implementing fundamental change and had launched Market-Driven Quality. At least the top tier of IBM executives and managers had been trained in MDQ principles; most organizational units had their MDQ plans in place; executives were participating in Terry Lautenbach's quarterly reviews of their progress in implementing MDQ; and quarterly reviews had already been scheduled throughout 1991, emphasizing how serious Akers was about this MDQ stuff.

Teams that had been trained first in MDQ were five or six months into their quality improvement efforts and were already showing results. Steve Schwartz recalled:

> We were starting to see places that had begun working on finding out what their customers felt were the priority things that needed to be fixed as early as June or July of 1990. By the fall, we could visit manufacturing plants and have a very good discussion about their 5-Ups, how they were progressing in their 10X defect elimination plan, what their plans were for reducing cycle time, and so on. Marketing and service units like IBM Taiwan were doing a great job of quickly jumping into looking at everything they did from the viewpoint of the customer, and they started reengineering a lot of their

key business processes in those areas most important to their customers.

Schwartz was pleased with this kind of early progress:

> By the end of 1990 and early 1991, we were starting to get positive feedback from customers about the changes they were seeing. So we had pockets of problem resolutions like that scattered all around that told us MDQ was beginning to have an impact. In most cases they weren't big things. They were small successes.

In addition to these small successes, IBM, of course, had its *big* success at IBM Rochester. Rochester had won the Baldrige award and become the symbol for Market-Driven Quality and, in the words of Schwartz, a clear demonstration of "what an IBM team could accomplish when it focused on quality, process improvement, and customer satisfaction." With Rochester, Schwartz had his MDQ showcase and was busily developing briefing programs to share what Rochester had learned and done with people inside and outside of IBM. "We were using Rochester as our 'existence theorem,' " said Schwartz in a 1992 interview, "to show the rest of IBM that Market-Driven Quality really did work."

Having Rochester as a role model turned out to be good not only for IBM but for Rochester as well. After Rochester won the Baldrige award, Schwartz, Osterwise and others had been concerned about a letdown. Would Rochester keep striving to improve, or would it experience that lull that so often follows victory? As it turned out, Rochester didn't get a chance to sit back and take it easy. As one IBM executive recalled:

> Rochester got roped in as a role model for the whole corporation almost immediately. Since they had become the role model, they couldn't let anyone pass them. So they recognized that they had to work very hard to maintain the image they had built for themselves.

With Rochester's success and small victories elsewhere, there was every reason to be optimistic that IBM was finally beginning to turn the corner. And the optimism didn't stem just from the Rochester experience and the small MDQ successes beginning to surface through IBM. There were other numbers one could look at for comfort. The business results appeared to be turning around.

After four disappointing years, IBM reaped a solid $6 billion in earnings on $69 billion in revenues in 1990. Plus, its stock price started rising in September 1990 and had jumped 31 percent in just two months, based upon a particularly strong fourth quarter performance. *Datamation* reported that, "With a new line of mainframes on the market, and very competitive mid-range and workstation offerings, IBM has strong products in key market sectors." The midrange, particularly Rochester's AS/400, had performed extremely well. Largely as a result of the AS/400, IBM garnered 41.4 percent of the midrange market for the *Datamation* 100 companies (twice the market share of its nearest competitor, Digital) and had increased midrange revenues by over 40 percent since 1989. Not bad compared to Digital's 6 percent growth and losses at Data General and Wang of 30 percent and 17 percent, respectively, between 1989 and 1990. IBM's upsurge continued into the first couple of months of 1991. Then in March 1991 disaster struck. It was all too reminiscent of 1985 when revenues had dropped sharply after a banner year.

The Balloon Bursts

Steve Schwartz recalled the 1991 disaster as follows:

Nineteen ninety had been a good year. We got very close to getting back to our 1984 performance. Our business results were good, and we had won the Baldrige Award. It looked like all the things we had been doing were starting to work. The first couple of months of '91 continued to look good. Then, in a matter of days, it just went to hell in a handbasket. After the Gulf War, the economy took an unexpected nosedive, capital spending plummeted, and our business just cratered. We were all surprised.

The first quarter, which had begun with so much promise, turned out to be devastating to IBM. Profits dipped sharply and IBM's stock price plunged. Worse, the second quarter wasn't looking any better. It was frustrating for Akers and his top team. They had been taken totally off guard at a time when they were finally supposed to be getting close to their customers so they would be able to anticipate customers' needs, expectations and future plans. "By the spring," recalled Schwartz, "a lot of us were asking the question 'How could we not have seen this coming?' "

Scathing Words

It took a while, but word finally leaked out that John Akers was even more unhappy and frustrated with IBM's performance than anyone suspected. Unfortunately for Akers and IBM, the leak, at least temporarily, added to their problems.

Following the lead of several articles that had appeared in the media the prior week, *Newsweek* ran its version of the story in its June 10, 1991, issue. *Newsweek*'s article reported that Akers had complained, during a late April seminar for IBM managers, that his messages were getting muddled in the bureaucracy. *Newsweek* went on to summarize Akers's key points, as they had been leaked to the media:

> [IBM workers are] too damn comfortable at a time when the business is in crisis ... standing around the water cooler waiting to be told what to do.

> The fact that we're losing [market] share makes me———mad. I used to think my job as a rep was at risk if I lost a sale. Tell them theirs is at risk if they lose.

> I'm sick and tired of visiting plants to hear nothing but great things about quality and cycle time—and then to visit customers who tell me of problems.

> We get A's for being a company with an ability to change ... but with our current structure ... A is not good enough.

Interestingly, the immediate press and public reaction was to criticize Akers for making such statements. *Newsweek* asked, "Is this any way to run a $69 billion-a-year company renowned for its paternalistic management style?" And yet, the *Newsweek* article, the trade press and the public in general agreed with virtually everything Akers had said. In fact, *Newsweek* questioned whether Akers had gone far enough to shake up his company.

Business Week ran a similar story in its June 17 issue. In essence, the stories were all true. Akers had spoken to a management development class and had said basically what had been reported. What the media didn't report was that this class wasn't the only one at which Akers had made such remarks. Akers's remarks were not a spontaneous outburst as the media implied. Steve Schwartz recalled the incident:

> The facts are slightly different from the media reports. I know some people will be disappointed at that, but it's true. First of all, John wasn't the only one saying these kinds of things. One of the things I started in the spring of 1991 was talking to every management development class in Armonk. I wanted to do it because I thought it was a good way to gauge progress. I could talk to people in the classes, and in ten minutes I could figure out who was with it [MDQ] and who wasn't with it. That gave me insight into which organizations I needed to work with more closely. So it was really a sanity check for me. John wanted the two-way communication opportunity, as well as personally emphasizing the importance of these classes. We were the only two executives who met and spoke with every one of these classes.
>
> One of the questions John and every executive who met with the classes asked was, "How the hell could you not see this [decline] coming? Here it is the spring. The first quarter was not what we expected. The second quarter is going to be a disaster. What the hell's going on out there? Does everyone understand how serious this is? Do you people believe everyone's working hard and understands how serious the problem is? I'm not so sure everyone does."
>
> What John, the others and I were saying was, "We've been doing a lot of things. Our business results have suddenly turned from good to terrible, and we didn't have any notice that was about to happen. What's happened? What's working? What's not working? We've been at this transformation since the fall of 1986. We've been on Market-Driven Quality now for eighteen months. What's really going on out there?"
>
> The sad point about the whole situation is that, as reported in the media, it came out so negatively. As it turned out, I was there after he [Akers] spoke and saw the reaction was very positive. Everyone felt it was terrific that John was that open in discussing the prob-

lems we were having, and they appreciated the fact that he wanted *their* ideas and *their* thoughts.

While the facts of the "scathing words" may have been somewhat different from those reported in the media, the reality of the situation was the same. If the message about the need for fundamental change was getting out, and every effort had been made to get it out, it wasn't being acted upon fast enough or with enough consistency throughout IBM. A sense of impending crisis, of sailing toward an iceberg, had been essential for Rochester to cast off old ways of doing things and undertake fundamental change. Too many IBMers were still denying the need for sweeping changes. For them, the old IBM was still viable. It might be sick but it wasn't dead yet. IBM was "one big safety net" to them, as an IBM programmer reportedly said in 1991. It was a place where you didn't have to worry about taking risks or being out on the street, shining shoes, if you made a wrong move.

It became increasingly obvious to IBM's leadership that they were not going to be able to change this culture and fully implement Market-Driven Quality until they made two other very important changes. IBM was still too big, both in number of employees and in structure.

Slimming Down

By the summer of 1991, IBM had already been through nearly five years of downsizing. The company peaked at 407,000 employees in 1986 and since then had been steadily trimming its work force. For most U.S. companies facing the reality of too many people, the process of streamlining the work force is, if not easy, at least straightforward. They simply lay off workers. Layoffs were a common practice even by 1986. For example, between 1979 and 1984, over 10 million U.S. workers had been permanently laid off by their employers. But layoffs weren't a common practice at IBM. In fact, for almost fifty years, IBM had not laid off a single employee. While IBM was not the only U.S. company with a full-employment or no-layoff practice, it was the largest and most visible. Full-employment was a cherished part of IBM tradition and culture. It wasn't something Akers or anyone else wanted to abandon lightly. So, as Schwartz recalled, IBM sought a different way to trim its work force:

> By the spring of 1987, it was clear that we had too many people. We knew we had to do some trimming, so we had our personnel people take a look at our options. When they ran an analysis of our population, they came back with some interesting findings. We had a lot of people age fifty-five and older. We were also overfunded in our pension fund by almost $1 billion. We had heard about a technique that had been used by other companies called a five-by-five. The way it worked was that you add five years of service and five years of age to everyone for their retirement calculation. What that means is that with a stroke of a pen your fifty-five-year-olds are sixty and your sixty-year-olds are sixty-five. Then, you could offer them early retirement and fund it out of your excess pension funds.

IBM had begun using this early retirement option in 1987. Some sixteen thousand IBMers took the offer in the first year. IBM had accomplished its reduction without layoffs. That was the good news. The bad news was that they had no control over who left, as Schwartz explained:

> The earlier programs had worked for us in that we got reductions in the work force that we needed. But, by law, the programs could not be selective. Anyone who wanted to take advantage of them could. The result was that we had no control over who left and we ended up losing too many good people. We decided that we would have no more of that. We needed "selective" voluntary programs. There would still be incentives for people to leave, but they would be by location or job skill or whatever. We would manage the process.

IBM did manage the process and by 1991 had launched thirty-eight such plans. It had cut its work force by nearly thirty-three thousand people, including over seventy-five hundred managers. Yet it was clear that much more was needed. IBM had to cut its work force faster and deeper. It had to become more aggressive in persuading people to leave, and it could not continue to "manage" who left.

In March 1991, IBM announced what it called its Individual Transition Options (ITO) program. It also made its pension plan more attractive and loosened age requirements for employees with thirty years of service to make it easier for them to retire with full benefits. Under ITO, employees who retired or voluntarily resigned were offered a severance package of a one-time, lump-sum, cash payment equal to two weeks' salary for every year they had worked with IBM, with a minimum of two months' salary and maximum of one year's salary. Employees taking advantage of ITO also got extended medical insurance coverage and "transitional" consulting services to help them make the transition to a new career and a new life. It was an attractive offer, better than most IBMers had seen before and, many felt, they were ever likely to see again.

In addition to being more attractive, ITO was different from previous voluntary departure programs in two other respects. First, the program wouldn't be targeted just to employees in specific locations or positions. While the program was still somewhat selective, virtually any employee could participate. The resulting work-force reduction made it even more crucial that IBM achieve its quality improvements and employee empowerment, since there would be fewer people around to fix things that weren't done right the first time.

Second, for the first time, IBM managers would be allowed and even encouraged to approach specific employees and suggest that they take advantage of the voluntary resignation or retirement option. Employees with a skills "mismatch," employees located at facilities which might have their mission redefined, and "marginal" performers would be targeted for such encouragement. Once approached, they could take advantage of the resignation/retirement opportunity, or they could choose to remain. Those who chose to remain would have no guarantee that they might get a better resignation/retirement offer in the future. Neither would they be guaranteed that they would *like* the conditions of their continued "full employment," which might include transfers and/or job reassignment. Furthermore, IBM would not guarantee that it would be able to avoid involuntary actions sometime in the future.

The message was clear. IBM continued to be serious about getting the size of its work force under control. ITO would be another effort by IBM to accomplish the reduction of its work force through a voluntary program and preserve its tradition of no layoffs. IBM was also getting serious about a fundamental change in its structure.

New Baby Blues

The idea of restructuring IBM to push decision making farther down in the organization, provide senior executives with more autonomy, and thereby make the company more responsive to customers wasn't new to IBM. In 1988, in what was called, at that time, one of the biggest reorganizations in its history, IBM created seven lines of business (LOBs). The intention had been to push accountability and responsibility down to line-of-business executives as one step in getting closer to customers. As the line-of-business executives assumed their new responsibilities, there had been occasional clashes and infighting, such as a dispute about the potential overlap between the low-end AS/400 mid-range computer developed by Application Business Systems and the RT workstation line developed by the Personal Systems LOB. These disagreements often required mediation by Terry Lautenbach, who had been given the responsibility for overseeing the seven LOBs and making sure that they didn't work at cross-purposes. Yet, in spite of some conflicts, there had been some successes, particularly in speeding decision making among LOBs. Application Business Systems, for example, had truly exercised the full limits of the autonomy it had been given, as evidenced by Rochester's success with the AS/400.

By the summer and early fall of 1991, Akers and his top team were engaged in a series of discussions that kept returning to the LOB concept and whether they had gone far enough. Schwartz recalled the discussions:

> John [Akers] looked longingly at ABS [the Application Business Systems]. They had control over most of their development and manufacturing, and ABS was being run like a business. Decisions were made like a business. ABS had also been very successful. On the marketing and services side, the country organizations [IBM Japan, for example] that were measured on profit, as opposed to the United States organization that had traditionally been a cost center, always seemed to be more responsive to their customers and better

able to do things on a long-term basis, because they were managers of their own financial destiny. John decided that we had to make people more accountable, reward them for success, be able to identify those who weren't successful, and, most importantly, get more people to feel ownership of their piece of the business. Plus, it had become clear that the business had just gotten too complex to manage centrally, and the competition had changed significantly. We still had a few large, vertically integrated, global competitors such as Hewlett-Packard, Digital and Fujitsu, for example, although none were nearly as large as IBM. But, we also had specialty companies like Apple, Compaq, and Sun Microsystems. Then, there were fifty thousand or more niche players out there. Many of them could move faster, exploit opportunities faster than we could.

By November of 1991, Akers and his team were moving closer to a decision about IBM's future, and word began to leak out to the media. Since the spring, it had been obvious that a dress rehearsal for major change was under way. IBM had sold off its typewriter and printer division in March. It had converted its Systems Integration division into a wholly owned subsidiary in May. September had brought the disbanding of the desktop software unit. Finally, by November, Akers was admitting to the business press that "an extraordinary transformation" was being planned.

On November 26, Akers made the announcement that by now was expected. IBM would be restructured into a group of wholly owned but autonomous marketing, service, product development and manufacturing companies. Each company would be managed independently. IBM would also continue its work force reduction, targeting about twenty thousand jobs during 1992 with perhaps more to come. While details were sketchy about the new organization, it was clear that this reorganization, although a logical extension of its actions to date, would be very significant— possibly even a revolution.

In December, Akers assembled his senior executives for the annual senior managers' meeting, a meeting that had never before been held prior to the beginning of the calendar year. This year, however, the messages he had for his managers could not wait even a few weeks. He told the executives that IBM would be decentralized, and even more decision-making authority would be passed to the leadership of its various units. Each of these units would have their own profit-and-loss responsibility and be freed from much of the corporate overhead expense. Then, he went on to tell them:

> The new IBM is a seventy-eight-year-old company—the most successful enterprise of its kind in the world—determined to harness a legacy of hard-won business and human ethics to the promise and potential of our future.
>
> We have one common denominator for accomplishing this, one stock in trade, and that is *value*. Increasingly, in our customers' eyes, the value of IBM is you and me. In the new IBM, we define ourselves by the value we create and the values we live by.
>
> [Figure 12.1] maps the connection of IBM's immutable beliefs of respect for the individual, excellence, and service with the value we create for our customers, our shareholders, and, ultimately, for ourselves.
>
> We have one common goal: to bring our values to bear to help our customers succeed and prosper.

Negotiations would begin soon between Akers and the unit heads about contracts each unit would have with the IBM Corporation to deliver results, based upon seven measures of performance. Four of these would be financial (VALUE) measures: improvement in revenue, profit, return on assets, and free cash flow. The remaining three measures would be VALUES measures: customer satisfaction, employee morale, and quality improvement. The success and pay of executives running these independent businesses would be heavily dependent upon not only their business success but their ability to maintain and improve customer satisfaction, employee satisfaction, and quality.

By spring 1992, contracts for the thirteen new independent businesses had been negotiated. The units would be positioned so IBM could utilize different financing and/or ownership models, even to issuing separate stock in at least some of them, if that made sense. There would be nine manufacturing and development businesses and four marketing and service companies:

- *Enterprise Systems:* responsible for manufacturing mainframes and related processors and software;
- *Adstar:* responsible for manufacturing storage devices (tape and disk drives) and related software;

- *Personal Systems:* responsible for making personal computers, workstations and related software;
- *Application Business Systems:* responsible for making minicomputers such as the AS/400 and related software;
- *Programming Systems:* responsible for developing software for data management and office systems;
- *Pennant Systems:* responsible for making printers and related software;
- *Applications Systems:* responsible for developing software for a wide range of industries and expected to shift its focus more toward services;
- *Networking Systems:* responsible for products and services for operating and managing information;
- *Technology Products:* responsible for manufacturing chips and electronic circuits; and
- *Four geographic marketing and service companies:* IBM Europe/Middle East/Africa, IBM North America, IBM Asia Pacific, and IBM Latin America.

How the Federation Will Work

With the creation of thirteen increasingly independent businesses, the natural question was how could IBM make this federation of businesses work. To answer that question, IBM spelled out certain roles and relationships in a 1992 *Think* magazine article. The nine manufacturing and development units would supply products and manage profits at the wholesale price level. They would be free to decide where the best business opportunities were and to tailor existing products and develop new products to meet those markets.

While the biggest customers of the manufacturing and development units would be the four IBM geographic marketing and service units, those would not be their only customers. If they wished, each manufacturing and development unit could become a supplier to other companies who would sell IBM products and technologies under their own logos, as shown in Figure 12.2.

The four geographic marketing and service units would be re-

Figure 12.1
CREATING VALUE

"IBM is about two simple propositions," IBM Chairman John Akers has said. "They are the value we create and the values we live by." These two propositions together will largely define the future of the family of companies IBM is becoming.

THE VALUE

Value for Customers. . .

Value for Employees. . .

Through its worldwide marketing and services units, business partners, and strategic alliances, IBM offers superior skills and creates tailored solutions for each customer's unique needs.

From its manufacturing and development businesses and their key alliances come the timely and competitive offerings to meet the demands of the markets IBM serves.

Unifying all of IBM's efforts is its continuing pursuit of Market-Driven Quality—a process for achieving world-class quality in everything it does.

through personal and professional fulfillment from the pride they feel in their performance and the opportunities they create for rewards and growth.

Key measurements for the value that IBM creates are contributions by each of its businesses to revenue, profit, cash flow, and return on assets.

THE VALUES

Respect for the Individual—Integrity, ethical conduct, personal dignity, recognition, appeal and grievance procedure.
Service—Setting and sustaining the highest standards for customer satisfaction; measuring performance against goals.

A SPECTRUM OF

WE CREATE

Value for
Shareholders. . .

Value for Business
Partners. . .

Value for the
Community. . .

through returns on
investment that are
commensurate with their
investments in IBM's
businesses.

through mutually
beneficial relationships
that are based on a
shared sense of
innovation and the
achievement of goals.

through the benefits and
progress that stem from
the uses of IBM
technology and the
company's sense of
social responsibility
wherever it does
business.

WE LIVE BY

Excellence—Continuous improvement in skills, services and products;
dissatisfaction with status quo; entrepreneurial, empowered individuals and
teams.
All business units will be measured on morale (respect for the individual),
customer satisfaction (the best customer service), and quality (the pursuit of
excellence).

BUSINESSES

The value created by IBM is meant to
benefit all those with a stake in IBM's
success. It is realized through
imaginative and timely products and
services that help solve problems and
bring the benefits of technology to
people and businesses all over the
world.

The values IBM lives by are
represented by the three Basic Beliefs
that have guided the company
through decades of change. They are
as relevant as ever, and each of the
new businesses will establish specific
practices and programs that carry
these values forward.

tained as IBM's "single face to the customer." They would focus on identifying customers' needs and packaging products, software, and services to meet those needs. While the marketing and service units would have the exclusive franchise to introduce and market IBM-brand products in their geographic area, they wouldn't be limited to IBM products. Now they would be allowed to buy from other manufacturers or service providers if they felt that the non-IBM supplier offered something that would better meet the customers' needs for function, price and availability.

The new "federation" of IBM businesses would be a drastic departure from traditional IBM practices and wouldn't be limited to just the thirteen new autonomous businesses. Changes would also occur in the role, responsibilities and relationships of corporate and unit support staffs that handled such matters as patent administration, payroll, and personnel. Two categories of such service units would be created. One category, called basic service units, would provide services at cost to internal customers. These

FIGURE 12.2
The Relationship Between the Business Units

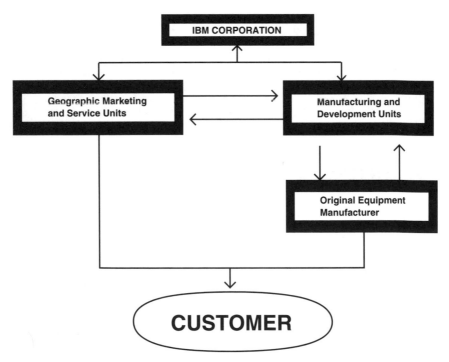

basic services would include functions like personnel, training and employee benefits administration.

A second category would be profit centers providing services for a profit to both IBM organizations and other companies, as shown in Figure 12.3. These would include, but not be limited to, such areas as translation services, manufacturing engineering and property management. During a transitional phase, these service units would have a "right of first refusal" over work to be performed in their areas of expertise. However, after an unspecified period of time, these units, like the rest of IBM, would have to compete with non-IBM providers. Every unit at every level of IBM would be measured on its financial performance. And every unit would have to add value.

Overseeing this new federation would be IBM's Management Committee located in Armonk, New York. Composed of IBM's top executives, the Management Committee would determine strategic opportunities to maximize IBM's financial results; establish company policies, practices and goals; negotiate performance contracts with the business and geographic units; assess unit performance; provide advice and counsel to unit managers; mediate disputes between units; and perform other missions that, for legal or company policy reasons, could not be delegated to the operating units.

FIGURE 12.3
Selling Support Services

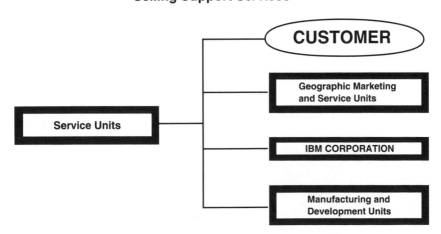

This new federation of companies was one of the two key components of IBM's new business strategy. The other key component was Market-Driven Quality. The link between the two components was the customer. The objective was to be the best at meeting the needs and wants of the customers in those markets IBM chose to serve.

Postscript: The Other IBM

By the summer of 1992, the key elements for successfully remaking IBM were in place. The autonomous businesses had negotiated their contracts. The Individual Transition Options (ITO) program was, if anything, working almost too well, with nearly twice as many IBMers taking advantage of the program as anticipated. MDQ had progressed beyond the implementation stage and, after two years, was becoming a way of life for many IBMers. The elements for real transformation were in place. Even Wall Street was responding positively. IBM's stock, which had plummeted from a 1991 high of $137 per share to a low of $82 in April 1992, had climbed back to $110 by midsummer. *Business Week* was trumpeting IBM's revival. "Yes, indeed," it said in the July 13, 1992, issue, "IBM is back—at least, as far as Wall Street is concerned." All IBM needed was continuing commitment to its strategy and, most important, time. But, time was a problem.

As 1992 progressed, anticipated improvements in the world economy failed to materialize and actually became worse in Europe and Japan. IBM's business results were seriously impacted and it became obvious that in spite of MDQ, the restructuring, and the downsizing there would be no magical short-term turnaround in IBM's overall revenues and profits. In response, by late summer of 1992, IBM's stock started to slide. Seeing the value of their stock dwindle overnight, stockholder groups became restless. Some began threatening to wrest control of the company from the board and management. Akers, in particular, became the target for those who sought someone to blame.

Finally, in January 1993, Akers went before the board and, in a surprise move, recommended they accept his resignation as CEO. IBM's president, Jack Kuehler relinquished that title and became a vice chairman of the board. Frank Metz, the chief financial officer, announced his retirement. The business press was filled with reports of IBM's troubles and speculation about the company's future. To the casual and not-so-casual business press reader, it seemed there was little right about IBM. But that wasn't true.

There were, in reality, two IBMs. There were those business units that were just beginning the transformation to an MDQ culture being described by the business press. Then there was cadre of IBM business units that had progressed much further with MDQ. They weren't getting much attention from the business press, although they should have been. Compared to IBM as a whole, these units of IBM were doing quite well. Rochester was a leading example.

IBM Rochester

IBM Rochester began the journey to its own future in the mid-1980s when, in order to survive, it was forced to rethink who and what it was. The resulting changes and improvements made at Rochester positioned the site to compete for and ultimately win the 1990 Malcolm Baldrige National Quality Award. More important, those changes positioned Rochester not only to survive, but to prosper. In spite of what was happening to IBM as a corporation, and in spite of doubts about their ability to sustain improved levels of performance, Rochester continued to post impressive results during the two years after winning the Baldrige Award. For example, Rochester

- Increased revenues from computer and operating system sales by an additional 7 percent

- Increased market share by an additional 2 percent
- Improved customer satisfaction by an additional 1 percent, a 9 percent improvement over 1988
- Increased total installments by an additional 7 percent
- Cut inventory by an additional 16 percent
- Improved total inventory turns by an additional 13 percent
- Improved new inventory turns by an additional 18 percent
- Reduced engineering change scrap by an additional 25 percent
- Reduced obsolete inventory scrap by an additional 41 percent
- Reduced warranty scrap by an additional 32 percent

The MDQ Leaders

If Rochester had been the only unit within IBM showing improvement, it might have been dismissed as an anomaly. But Rochester *wasn't* alone. The "other IBM" was much bigger.

Part of the MDQ implementation was the creation of an MDQ Achievement Award program to recognize IBM units which scored high on Baldrige-based MDQ assessments, and by end of 1992, IBM had awarded over fifty of these awards. In total, the units receiving awards employed over one third of the IBM workforce. Like IBM Rochester, these MDQ award winners were doing quite well. For example,

- Customer satisfaction, from 1989 to 1992, increased 4 percent more for the achievers than for IBM in total and was 6 percent higher than the rest of IBM
- Market share was 6 percent higher for the achievers than for IBM in total
- Revenue, from 1989 to 1992, increased 19 percent more for the achievers
- Operating profit, from 1989 to 1992, increased 31 percent more for the achievers than for the rest of IBM
- Based upon the most recent surveys, morale among MDQ award winners was 9 points higher for

nonmanagers and 13 points higher for managers, compared with IBM overall

These units have made significant progress on the continuing journey to their future and have set their course to survive and prosper. Only time will tell whether they succeed, but they have started their journey with all the right tools. By 1993, the rest of IBM was following their lead.

The Future of IBM

Will there ever again be an all-powerful, invincible Big Blue that will dominate all sectors of the computer industry? Of course not. The industry has changed. Such dominance by any single company is impossible. Will there be a collection of smaller IBMs that will become strong and, in some cases, even dominant players in their chosen market niches? We have no doubt about that. IBM Rochester and the MDQ Award winners have already shown the way.

IBM Rochester's Winning Baldrige Application

This appendix contains the complete text of IBM Rochester's application for the Malcolm Baldrige National Quality Award, as it was submitted to the National Institute of Standards and Technology in the spring of 1990. The only difference between the application reprinted here and the one submitted to NIST in 1990 is the deletion of certain confidential information.

To our knowledge, this is the first time any winning Baldrige application has been reprinted in its entirety for general distribution. The authors would like to thank the IBM Corporation for their permission to reprint Rochester's application in this book.

We hope that our readers will find this reprint of Rochester's winning application instructive, with respect to both the Baldrige award and the depth and scope of activities that are required to achieve world-class standards of product and service quality.

IBM Rochester's 1990 Malcolm Baldrige National Quality Award Application

Contents

Overview

IBM* Rochester, Minnesota, is the main site for the Application Business Systems (ABS) line of business, one of seven units of IBM U.S. (fig. 0-1). Rochester is responsible for worldwide development and U.S. manufacturing of IBM's:

- Application System/400* (AS/400*), and AS/Entry Systems (fig. 0-3)
- Hard disk storage devices for IBM's midrange and Personal System/2* (PS/2*) products (fig. 0-4)

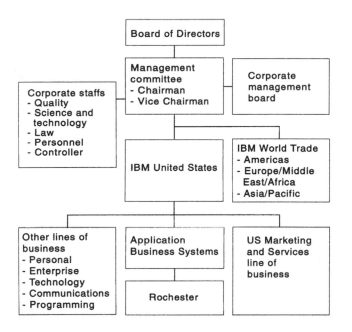

Figure 0-1. Rochester within the IBM Corporation.

Our 6750 Rochester employees who develop, manufacture, and support midrange products include 66% engineers, programmers, and other professionals. This represents 2.4% of IBM U.S. and 1.8% of IBM worldwide. We are not unionized and every employee has the opportunity to discuss anything with any level of management including our chairman, John Akers. IBM Rochester, ABS, and our Marketing and Service line of business form a highly motivated, cohesive team with a total quality system that has over 400,000 customers worldwide. 1989 ABS revenue was $X.X billion, XX% of IBM worldwide.

* IBM, Application System/400, AS/400, Personal System/2, and PS/2 are trademarks of the International Business Machines Corporation.

Fig. 0-2 shows that our people, our products, and IBM enjoy outstanding reputations for quality in industry, government, academia, and the general public. Our 3.6 million square foot development and

Segment	Quality Indicator
Consumers: 1990	Sierra Group *Sierra 5000 Database* rates AS/400 satisfaction highest compared to eight major competitors in all major mainframe indicators
Academia: 1990	IBM receives the Danforth-Westinghouse Award for Quality in Manufacturing from Syracuse University.
IBM: 1989	IBM Rochester receives IBM U.S. first annual quality award for best site.
Government: 1980-1989	IBM Rochester receives Minnesota Safety Council Award for the 10th consecutive year.
1989	IBM Rochester receives Minnesota Energy Award.
1988	IBM receives U.S. Department of Labor Opportunity 2000 Award for outstanding achievement in human resources and social responsibility.
1990	President Bush awards IBM Rochester employee Dave Schwartzkopf the President's Trophy as National Disabled American of The Year.

Figure 0-2. IBM's Strong Reputation for Quality.

manufacturing facility produces technology such as magnetic disks and heads, circuit boards, disk drives and systems in short cycle time with competitive cost/performance. We assemble light electronics, have base manufacturing technologies such as machining and plastics, and our tool and model makers produce most of our test and process equipment. Computer networks provide timely, worldwide communication to other IBM locations, to support product development, manufacturing process control, and service support. Our sister manufacturing facilities are in Mexico, Japan, the United Kingdom, and Italy. Customer relationships are managed through our local branch offices around the world.

Midrange computer technologies use leading-edge electronic circuitry and programming, including operating systems that control the computer, and application programs that help customers run their businesses. Key quality and service characteristics of computer systems are reliability, cost of ownership, service and support. Midrange computers, priced from $10,000 to $1 million, are a $26-billion worldwide market, encompassing an estimated 13 million potential customers. In this extremely competitive market, a dozen worldwide companies, including IBM, DEC, Fujitsu, Nixdorf, and Hewlett-Packard, generate 60% of the midrange market revenue. They offer a full range of systems serving virtually all markets. The rest is comprised of over 200 other companies, called niche competitors, who offer products for specific segments. Our products serve small, medium, and large businesses ranging from 10 to 1000 employees. Sixty percent of our customer installation base is in Europe and the Pacific Rim.

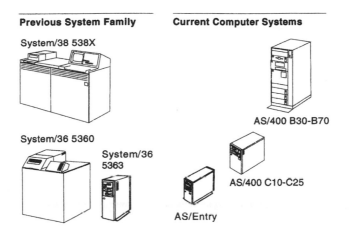

Figure 0-3. Rochester's Midrange Computer Family.

Hard disk drives are advanced electro-mechanical devices that use magnetic disks and heads to store and retrieve information. Heads *fly* within micro-inch tolerances while reading and writing information on rotating disks. They are designed in industry-standard sizes such as 3.5, 5.25, and 8-inch diameter disks.

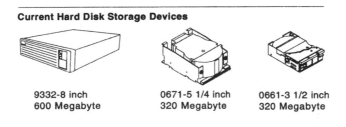

Figure 0-4. Rochester's Hard Disk Storage Products.

We use clean rooms to assemble parts with extremely critical tolerances. Key quality requirements are reliability, warranty, and price. In 1982, we responded to customer demand and entered the market for small, hard disk drives. These devices are used in our systems and also sold to Other Equipment Manufacturers (OEM). In this extremely competitive, $23 billion industry, Seagate, Maxtor, and Micropolis are the major competitors. Many companies have manufactured their U.S. developed products offshore for cost advantages. We have been able to gain industry leadership because of our quality culture. Our revenue has increased at a 33% compound growth rate since 1986.

Our quality improvement initiatives have made us global leaders in business and customer satisfaction. We have integrated our customers and suppliers into our prevention-based planning and product development process. This has doubled the reliability of our products and reduced our maintenance prices by over 50%, improving warranty duration from 3 to 12 months. We have reduced our total cycle time by over 60% and our break-even time for recovering development and introduction costs by 62% since 1983. These quality improvements have made our products the benchmarks for competitors in customer satisfaction and cost of ownership. Worldwide customer acceptance of our products has enabled us to increase the number of our installed systems by 50% in the last three years and to increase our market share in each of the last two years. ABS revenue growth was 24% last year, compared to 9% growth in the industry, and revenue per employee has increased 35% since 1985.

Our 7000 business partners worldwide help sell, install, and service AS/400 systems. They develop application programs concurrently with our development and manufacturing teams. Over 1000 application programs for solving major customer needs, such as banking and transportation, were available on the day we announced the AS/400 system in June 1988. Over 2500 application programs provide solutions today—a number that is growing daily worldwide. By incorporating our suppliers in our design phase and prevention initiatives, we improve the quality and timeliness of their processes and ours. As a result of our supplier quality improvements, we use their products without incoming inspections.

Customer responses and trade press assessments of the AS/400 system and our hard disk products have been outstanding. Within 18 months after initial shipment, more than 100,000 AS/400 and AS/Entry systems had been installed worldwide. Rochester's successful market-driven process is now being adopted throughout IBM. Because we openly share our quality concepts with our business partners, many of our techniques are being applied outside IBM as well. We work with other hard disk suppliers to qualify their devices even though they compete with us for personal computer business. We believe that the lessons learned in Rochester have wide applicability for all U.S. businesses.

In the following application, we believe we have demonstrated the leadership, innovation, and achievement sought by the Malcolm Baldrige National Quality Award Consortium, Inc. Our quality initiatives are the basis for our worldwide competitive strength today and the foundation for our strength in years to come.

1. Leadership

"Quality improvement results from management actions. It must begin at the top; it will not happen any other way."

—John Akers, IBM Chairman of the Board

1.1. Senior Executive Leadership

1.1.a. Leadership and Personal Involvement: Following a tradition of leadership based on continuous improvement, Rochester senior executives focus on quality improvement initiatives. Rochester General Manager Larry Osterwise and his executives have created and communicated to all employees their vision for the site:

- Customer—The Final Arbiter
- Quality—Excellence in Execution
- Products and Services—First with the Best
- People—Enabled, Empowered, Excited, Rewarded

and a simple but powerful quality policy:

Rochester Excellence . . . Customer Satisfaction.

Goal Setting and Initiatives: Figure 1-1 depicts our quality journey. Executives set quality goals based on their vision, benchmarks, and input from customers, managers, and employees.

	1981	1984	1986	1989 →
Focus	Product and process reliability	Process effectiveness and efficiency	Competitive and functional benchmarks	Market-driven customer satisfaction
Goals	Zero defects	All processes rated 1	World-class	100% customer satisfaction
Initiatives	PRIDE	QFBP	You Make It Happen	Rochester Excellence... Customer Satisfaction
Execs	WC Lowe	CA Haggerty LL Osterwise	LL Osterwise	LL Osterwise CH Bajorek

Figure 1-1. Rochester Quality Journey.

213

Working with their teams, executives establish initiatives, building on previous experiences, to meet the quality goals. They own and review progress toward the goals. As a result of these reviews, we refine our initiatives, following the plan-do-check-act cycle. Examples of these initiatives are People Responsibly Involved Developing Excellence (PRIDE) and Quality Focus on the Business Process (QFBP).

Planning and Reviewing: Knowing the strategic value of quality and demonstrating their commitment, the executives have established and are members of the Site Quality Steering Committee (SQSC). This team formulates the site quality plan and, through regular progress reviews, ensures that goals are met.

Teams: Cross-functional teamwork is a quality improvement strategy across the site and is extended worldwide to include all partners. Executives not only encourage and establish teams within and across their areas but also participate in teams that play a key role in the leadership process. The SQSC is an example of cross-functional teamwork.

Education and Training: To be more effective, efficient role models for quality (item 1.3.a.), each Rochester executive received and provided over 60 hours of market-driven quality education in the past year. Executives train and coach their teams. Our executives learn from every meeting with customers, suppliers, business partners, competitors, other industry leaders, consultants, and educators. For example, Xerox CEO David Kearns spoke at our 1990 annual management kickoff meeting.

Recognition: Rochester executives personally recognize employee contributions to quality in many ways, such as thank yous, time off, and monetary awards. In 1989, our executives reinforced their commitment to quality by participating in over 200 awards, totaling over $1.5 million. For example, Rochester Engineering Lab Director Keith Slack awarded $38,500 to an 11-member team that improved a key development process.

Competition: To understand competition (processes, approaches, and capabilities) and to establish competitive benchmarks, one of our senior managers, Jim Flynn, analyzes worldwide competition. Midrange competitive evaluations are conducted in Rochester and the Tokyo Systems Evaluation Lab (TSEL), which is partially staffed by Rochester employees. We partially fund the *Marketplace News and Analysis Digest,* which provides online access to competitive information. This Digest was issued 82 times in 1989 to 30,000 IBM employees.

Suppliers and Customers: Because suppliers are vital in producing high-quality products, we view them as extensions of our processes. Our executives establish close partnerships with our suppliers (such as Motorola, Seagate, IBM Burlington, and IBM Lexington), communicating quality as our prime business strategy, improving their quality processes and ours. Site executives frequently contact customers to obtain input and feedback for product requirements, satisfaction assessments, and assistance. Customer councils (item 3.1.d.), customer partnership calls (item 7.2.c.), the executive assistance program, and one-on-one meetings are but a few of the input and feedback approaches we use.

Rochester has played a major role in setting IBM's quality direction. At the October 1989 IBM Corporate Management Committee meeting, Larry Osterwise described Rochester's quality management system. IBM U.S. General Manager Terry Lautenbach set the direction for each line of business to follow "the Baldrige discipline, the Rochester quality management system." At the February 1990 IBM U.S. senior executive meeting, Larry was the featured speaker, again presenting Rochester's quality management system to the 400 top executives. A videotape summary of the meeting was distributed throughout the corporation. Larry and the Rochester senior management team have provided quality direction to and learned from numerous IBM sites and management teams.

1.1.b. Approach to Building Quality Values into Leadership Process: The cornerstone of our successful quality process is executive leadership, embodied in seven actions:

- Create an exciting vision and establish a policy and management system based on quality values
- Make quality the foundation of our business
- Communicate often with inspiration
- Educate, educate, educate
- Foster ownership and commitment by each employee
- Measure and continuously improve
- Demonstrate personal commitment daily

The process in figure 1-2 shows how quality values are integrated into our leadership process. Strong, direct feedback channels are key parts of this closed-loop system, achieving employees' ownership and understanding and a solid quality culture. Our approach has been adopted by the IBM Corporation (item 1.1.a.).

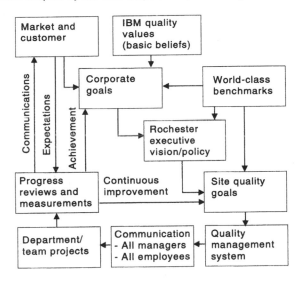

Figure 1-2. Integrating Quality Values in the Leadership Process.

1.1.c. Internal Communication: John Akers visits Rochester frequently, reviewing our quality achievements and understanding our quality processes. He speaks to all employees, reinforcing the strategic importance of market-driven quality and customer satisfaction.

At the 1990 IBM U.S. senior executive meeting (item 1.1.a.), Terry Lautenbach presented the IBM U.S. Best Site Market-Driven Quality Award to Rochester. In Rochester, he spoke to all employees about the strategic value of quality.

To foster an environment of cooperation and commitment, our ABS and site executives discuss our quality vision regularly and solicit vital feedback from employees. In 1988–90, 3000 employees attended executive roundtables, hosted by ABS General Manager Steve Schwartz and other key ABS executives. In addition, Larry Osterwise holds all-employee meetings twice a year, focusing on communicating future challenges and aggressive goals. To reinforce these goals, brochures, posters, and pocket cards are distributed to maintain a constant awareness of our quality policy. Larry encourages all employees to send him direct, online messages and speak freely to him on any issue. He accepts all messages, and personally responds to each one. For example, in 1989, he responded to all Speak Ups (item 4.2.b.). Site executives regularly speak at all management classes, new employee orientations, and employee symposiums. They attend area and department meetings and hold employee roundtables, discussing the importance of quality and every employee's involvement and commitment.

1.1.d. External Communication: To foster quality understanding and improvement outside IBM and to learn from others, Rochester executives share our vision and expertise with external groups through speeches, interviews, and published papers. For example, Larry Osterwise shares our quality management system and our knowledge from the Baldrige Award discipline. In the past six months, he spoke to the top 300 managers of the Emerson Corporation, to APICS (Twin Cities), and to the Chairman's Council of PP&G Industries, and was interviewed by *Business Month* magazine. Raul Cosio, Systems Plant Manager, presented computer-integrated manufacturing to the University of Minnesota School of Mechanical Engineering and has worked with Rochester schools to improve their student guidance processes. Rochester Programming Lab Director Bill Warner speaks on software quality at COMMON (item 7.6.a.). Rochester Storage Products Director Chris Bajorek regularly speaks on magnetic recording processes and trends. Our executives have published papers on these topics in periodicals such as *Electronic Design News* and *CompEuro.*

1.2. Quality Values

1.2.a. Content of Quality Directives: The quality values that are the foundation of IBM's traditions and quality culture are the three basic beliefs expressed 75 years ago by IBM founder Thomas J. Watson.

- Best customer service in the world
- Pursuit of excellence
- Respect for the individual

This commitment is recorded in Corporate Policy Letters (CPL) and expanded into formal quality directives, known as Corporate Instructions (CI).

IBM's quality policy, described in CPL 132A (Quality), issued in 1981, updated in 1988, is that it is everyone's job to deliver defect-free total solutions, on time, every time, to enhance customer partnerships. CI 105 states that each new product must be superior in quality to previous IBM and competitive products. We must demonstrate our compliance with CI 105 to the corporate director of quality and other line executives before introducing a product. CI 101 requires continuous improvement of all our business processes, product and nonproduct, to make them more efficient, effective, and adaptable.

Our site vision (item 1.1.a.) and quality policy, developed with employee participation, is based on these directives.

1.2.b. Projection of Values: To ensure that everyone understands and personally adopts quality as a primary business strategy, we use many activities and vehicles for communicating, projecting, and reinforcing quality values. These activities include all-employee meetings, regular department meetings, ABS senior executive roundtables, IBM U.S. and ABS quality awards, and the performance planning, counseling, and evaluation process. The key communication vehicles are *Rochester Today* (daily bulletin board notices), *IBM Rochester News* (a home-delivered monthly newspaper), and *ABS Horizons* (a quarterly newspaper), all of which highlight quality success stories and publicize quality awards.

Figure 1-3 depicts how quality values, the foundation for customer satisfaction, are deployed through our site and corporation.

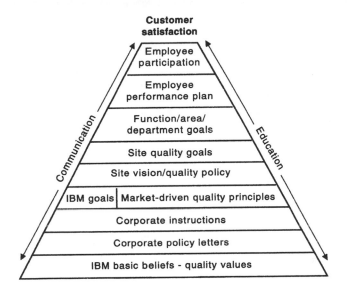

Figure 1-3.   IBM Quality Value Deployment.

In addition to the previous activities, senior management demonstrates their commitment by enhancing quality education and setting very aggressive improvement goals (10x by 1991, 100x by 1993).

1.2.c. Importance of Quality Values: In IBM, there is no tradeoff for our basic beliefs, our quality values. We firmly believe that putting our quality values ahead of short-term business results is the right thing to do for our customers, our business partners, and ourselves.

Best Customer Service in the World: By "being the best," as John Akers says, "at satisfying the needs and wants of our customers, everything else important will follow." In a recent example, a supplier's hard disk met the original quality specifications, but quality improvement in our own hard disk exceeded the specifications. We did not ship the supplier's product until our internal knowledge was transferred and applied to the supplier's product and until its specifications equaled that of our own hard disk.

Pursuit of Excellence: The Rochester team is committed to improvement. Individually and collectively, we take pride in leading the IBM Corporation and our industry. We know that the bar of excellence is always rising, and to be the world leader, we must improve continually and by leaps and bounds. In another example, a major AS/400 software shipment was delayed when analysis demonstrated that additional customer environment simulation would improve software quality, resulting in higher customer satisfaction and shorter future product cycles.

Respect for the Individual: This is our most important basic belief. Providing the necessary training and tools enables people to achieve their goals. The amount allocated for education is equivalent to 5% of our payroll; the industry average is 1%. From 1986 to 1989, we committed over $300 million in capital to enhance our processes and our data collection systems.

Taking proactive, preventive actions, and placing quality first, may adversely affect short-term revenue and profit to IBM. However, these actions reinforce to our employees, suppliers, and customers that quality is our primary business strategy. Our business results demonstrate that the long-term gain clearly outweighs a short-term loss.

1.2.d. Extent to Which Quality Values Are Adopted and Reinforced: The extent to which the quality values have been adopted across the site is evaluated by several means, such as the yearly opinion survey, manager (skip level) interviews, Speak Ups, employee suggestions, one-on-one employee-manager discussions, and roundtable feedback. In addition to specific opinion survey quality questions, such as "How would you rate your department on providing high-quality service and/or products?," employees are also encouraged to submit written recommendations for quality improvement. We use information obtained from these feedback methods to adjust and improve our quality initiatives, such as providing more education, clearer communication, and greater empowerment. Acceptance of our quality values by our people can best be reflected by a comment made by Deb Timm, an AS/400 systems employee: "My key objective is to help produce a product in the shortest cycle time with no defects, ensuring quality systems for our customers."

Employee acceptance is reinforced by sharing internal and independent customer satisfaction survey data and by working in teams to develop quality improvement action plans. Employee acceptance is also reinforced by recognition and reward. For example, employee Tom Thompson received $70,553 for his suggestion to improve the engineering design process. Most important, employee acceptance is reinforced by managers' actions.

1.3. Management for Quality

1.3.a. Key Strategies for Involving All Managers: To ensure focus on continuous quality improvement and customer satisfaction, all levels of management are involved and become role models. Our key management involvement strategies are:

Education: All managers receive (minimum of 40 hours per year) and then provide quality education to their teams in quality fundamentals, Baldrige quality guidelines, tools, and techniques.

Process Ownership and Improvement: Managers own processes and subprocesses, establish improvement teams, define goals, guide improvement actions, and review progress.

Cross-functional Teams: Managers together with employees from across the site meet to address specific opportunities. We also have *standing* teams like the Site Resource Management Board. In a support process example, a 10-member customer-supplier cross-functional team reviewed our capital equipment request process. They identified quality improvements that reduced the cycle time and approvals required by 50% each.

Customer Involvement: Our managers recognize that delighted customers (external and internal) are the key to their success—Rochester Excellence . . . Customer Satisfaction. Managers and employees have identified their customers and interact regularly with them to understand needs, formulate actions, and measure progress. Examples of external customer contacts are customer partnership calls, customer briefings, and customer councils. For internal customer-supplier partnerships, see item 1.3.b.

Level	Roles	Responsibilities
Executives	Quality leadership and quality system management	Establish policy, set strategy and goals for site
Area managers	Functional strategy, operating plan implementation, cross-functional teamwork	Implement goals, cross-functional integration
Middle managers	Plan implementation, consistency across organizations	Weekly/monthly implementation, functional integration
1st-line managers	Plan implementation, employee morale, team building	Daily implementation, employee understanding, encourage ownership, commitment, idea generation

Figure 1-4. Principal Roles and Responsibilities by Level.

Roles and Responsibilities: All levels of managers have clearly defined roles and responsibilities (fig. 1-4).

Coaching and Measurement: Managers' commitment, involvement, and cooperation are continually reviewed and improved through the performance planning, counseling, and evaluation process (item 4.4.b.).

1.3.b. Strategies to Promote Cooperation among Managers: To increase the effectiveness and efficiency of our quality management system, we promote management cooperation. The following strategies are key:

Have a Common Understanding of and Commitment to Our Vision, Policy, Goals, and Quality Management System: Education addressed in items 1.1.a. and 1.3.a. and communication addressed in item 1.1.c. support this strategy. Real-time tools such as fax, videoconferencing, and PROFS (item 2.1.b.) connect employees so everyone can work together easily, sharing ideas, information, and data.

Devise a Consistent Set of Goals and Measures: This is accomplished in a top-down manner, each goal supporting a higher level goal.

Develop a Management Structure of Well-Understood Interdependencies: To support this strategy, we hold regular cross-functional meetings and assign people from various functions to work as a team in a single location.

Use Internal Customer-Supplier Councils Extensively: Internal suppliers hold regular meetings with their customers to obtain feedback, including satisfaction, needs, and wants, and to present their plans.

1.3.c. Reviews of Status and Actions Taken: We check the status of our quality plans to understand where preventive and corrective actions are required. Our quality process is a participative one, with reviews and opportunity for feedback taking place continuously at all levels of management and employees.

Beginning at the executive and senior management level, the Rochester Management Committee (RMC) and the Site Quality Steering Committee (SQSC) each meets twice monthly. The RMC reviews status in key areas and initiates action, with quality being the first topic on the agenda. The SQSC reviews our quality management system, goals, processes, strengths, and opportunities for improvement. Cross-functional teams bring topics to these committees and own resulting actions. Our worldwide marketing and service team meets monthly with Rochester development and manufacturing. They review process and product quality and customer satisfaction.

In addition, manufacturing readiness reviews and development self-assessments are held at specified key points in the product cycle. At these quality action meetings, progress in achieving goals, nonconformance issues, detailed analyses of root causes, new improvement opportunities, and action plans are presented and discussed. Checkpoints are set for future management reviews.

Types of actions taken include allocating resources (people, money, time), approving recommendations, and assigning owners. A recent review showed that IBM Japan was experiencing problems in manufacturing hard disks. Rochester engineers and managers worked with their Japanese counterparts to determine the root causes and correct the process to prevent reoccurrence. The team continued reviewing the results, making refinements.

1.3.d. Assessing Effectiveness: Results of our processes are the prime indicators of effectiveness. Increasing employee suggestions, opinion survey comments, and functional and cross-functional teamwork demonstrate that our approach is effective and improving.

First, we review process results via key measurements, such as, external and internal customer satisfaction. Second, we review progress on key process improvement activities, such as, hardware simulation and error prevention. Third, we review the feedback from participants in the processes (item 1.2.d.). In every case, the results are compared to specific goals and checkpoints. Whenever plans are not achieved, teams reevaluate, recommend, and implement required changes.

To increase the effectiveness and efficiency of our market-driven quality education, a cross-functional team developed the Rochester Management College. The college brought all managers together twice in 1989, each time for two days, to learn from experts. Evaluation forms indicated this was a very successful approach.

1.3.e. Key Indicators of Involvement: Our opinion survey contains key indicators of management involvement and cooperation. First, an opinion survey question asks how well "the people I work with cooperate to get the job done." To this question, 88% of managers responded positively and only 4% negatively. To address involvement, a question asks, "Have you participated in a quality improvement activity?" To this question, 89% of managers responded positively and 5% negatively. These responses plus the write-in comments are used to improve effectiveness, involvement, and cooperation.

Other major indicators are how resources are deployed and the results of that deployment. For example, to prevent defects and shorten cycles we implemented a strategy of Early Manufacturing Involvement (EMI) with development. EMI spending has increased three times since 1983 to over 6% of manufacturing output. Since 1985, we reduced our development expense break-even point by 62% and in-plant manufacturing cycles by 74%.

1.4. Public Responsibility

"IBM should be a good corporate citizen."
  —IBM principle

1.4.a. Promoting Awareness and Sharing: In order to advance society in general and help the U.S. become more competitive, we promote quality awareness and share our successful quality strategies with outside groups, including community, business, trade, schools, and government.

Reviewing our strengths led us to establish numerous initiatives in a variety of areas. Our Teach the Teachers, Visiting Scientists, mentor, and pre-professional programs not only improve teaching and teachers, but also excite and involve students. Since 1982, these programs have reached over 3000 teachers and administrators and countless students. We fund National Technological University's leading-edge courses and seminars (many quality focused) broadcast to Rochester Community College. We provide access to the community as well as to IBM. For nonprofit agencies, we share our human resource and managerial skills by offering a series of management development courses. The State of Minnesota's Striving Toward Excellence Program (STEP), which promotes increased effectiveness and efficiency in state government agencies, was developed with the support of IBM Rochester.

IBM Rochester has actively supported and participated in the early development of the Minnesota Quality Council. We hold leadership positions in virtually every major educational, community, and business organization in the state.

These activities have resulted in numerous awards given to our site and our executives. Two examples are the 1986 Minnesota Chamber of Commerce Keystone Award presented to IBM Rochester for contributions to job growth and economic development, and the 1989 Rochester Mayor's Medal of Honor Award presented to Larry Osterwise for personal leadership in the community.

1.4.b. Encouraging Employee Involvement: Employee leadership and involvement are encouraged in many ways, with our executives leading by example (item 1.1.d.). We support their full-time involvement through our loaned executive program. Dave Schwartzkopf is on executive loan to the Minnesota Department of Jobs and Services, Division of Rehabilitation Services and is responsible for developing employment opportunities for people with disabilities. President Bush awarded Dave the President's Trophy as the national 1990 Disabled American of the Year. Involvement also extends to the education community. Each year since 1982, we have loaned employees as full-time faculty members to high schools, colleges, and universities. Since 1984, employees have taught continuous flow manufacturing, statistical process control, and design of experiments to over 1000 non-IBM employees.

We enable our employees through technical partnerships. Our IBM Fellow, Al Cutaia, is working with Rochester's Mayo Clinic researcher Dr. Glen Forbes. They are leading a Mayo-IBM team of physicians and researchers to dramatically improve medical image processing, enabling physicians to more effectively and efficiently diagnose illnesses. When complete, this technology will be made available internationally.

We encourage employees to participate in and share their expertise with technical professional societies and national and international standards committees. Dan Rapp along with four other Rochester IBMers founded the local chapter of the Association for Computing Machinery. Dan Rand is the Rochester representative to the SE Minnesota section of ASQC. Larry Saunders was recognized when he led the design of a very high-level design language (VHDL) subset standard, which was accepted by IEEE. The application of this standard provides an excellent basis for design quality and faster development across the industry. One of our executives, Chris Bajorek, has set an example by being named an IEEE Fellow. John Trnka is program chairman of the 1991 IEEE International Solid-State Circuits Conference.

We encourage employee involvement in community activities through financial assistance. Our Fund for Community Service provides grants to nonprofit organizations in which our employees volunteer their time and skills.

We have developed effective recognition vehicles. For example, an author recognition program was initiated in 1987 to encourage employees to publish. The response has been dramatic; the number of publications has risen from 279 in 1986 to 907 in 1989.

In all, we have over 500 employees actively engaged in local, state, and national activities.

1.4.c. Full Integration: To ensure that we fulfill our commitment to be a good corporate citizen and to effectively and efficiently integrate our initiatives and activities with the external community, our Site Services Director, Dick Lueck, develops an annual plan to apply our strengths to meet the needs of our community (local, state, regional, and national). The Rochester Management Committee periodically reviews the plan, progress, recommended changes, and new initiatives.

Quality leadership is provided to local and national safety, health, and environmental organizations, including:

- American Society of Safety Engineers
- Water Quality Board
- Minnesota Safety Council
- Olmsted County Safety Council

IBM Rochester fully complies with all local, state, and federal regulations. We set a quality example with quality action teams and programs such as:

- The IBM emergency response team, which is integrated into the local emergency planning commission (participated in 14 drills and 55 hours of training with the Rochester Fire Department)
- Programs to review 210 major suppliers for environmental awareness and compliance
- Programs to address global issues such as chlorofluorocarbon elimination, waste reduction, recycling, air emission control, and groundwater protection
- The IBM Rochester chemical distribution and chemical waste center program

These leadership activities have resulted in the following recognition:

- Governor's Award for Excellence in hazardous waste management in 1985 and 1986
- Minnesota Safety Council Award, 1980–1989
- 1989 Minnesota Energy Saver's Award

Ethics: To encourage the highest ethical and legal standards in the workplace, the IBM *Business Conduct Guidelines* are required reading annually for all IBM professionals. This booklet is regularly updated and provides guidance for personal conduct and protection of IBM assets, obligations to others when conducting IBM business, considerations and possible conflicts of interest that may arise on an employee's own time, and competition law as it relates to individual employees and IBM.

Summary: We earn our reputation for quality every day, every year. Outstanding leaders and dedicated employees work together to develop, revise, and maintain quality values that work: for our customers, our suppliers, our community, and ourselves.

2. Information and Analysis

To support our quality priorities of total cycle time reduction, expand customer and supplier partnerships, improve product and service quality, and increase ownership (item 3.3.a.), we provide timely, accurate, easy-to-interpret, meaningful information.

2.1. Scope and Management of Quality Data and Information

2.1.a. Criteria for Quality Related Data: Our data is consolidated and integrated into information bases that enable our empowered employees to gain and transfer knowledge, identify opportunities, and improve our overall quality management system. Our goal is to provide information online to ensure that employees have easy access to integrated databases that link us with our customers, to other IBM manufacturing and development sites, suppliers, our marketing and service team, and our business partners (fig. 2-1).

Information included in quality-related databases meets the following criteria:

- Supports our quality priorities (fig. 3-6)
- Increases our knowledge of customer needs and expectations
- Contributes improved quality to customers through defect prevention and service
- Increases our competitiveness in product cost, quality, and delivery
- Encourages employee participation
- Integrates or eliminates redundant data

2.1.b. Scope and Types of Data: Figure 2-2 shows the depth and breadth of quality data we use to assess customer requirements. The scope of data extends to all parts of our business and to every manager and employee. For example, we collect data on customers, our engineering team, our manufacturing team, suppliers, and our service team, among others. Data is collected from user groups, business partners, and competitive analyses to generate requirements, validate designs, establish benchmarks, and improve service support. Our Engineering Design System (EDS) and our software development system, IDSS, automatically translate design data to process data, and transmit information to IBM development and manufacturing locations worldwide. Our materials and documentation logistics systems, EMLS and DPRS, provide the same capability for controlling customer orders and the manufacturing process. Electronic Data Interchange (EDI) links suppliers to us; and Electronic Customer Support (ECS) links our customers to our business partners and us. The Professional Office System (PROFS) links employees worldwide allowing them to communicate and share data.

2.1.c. Processes and Technologies Used: All professional employees have their own workstations and, where appropriate, production employees have access to workstations. To ensure consistency, employees are given standardized workstation tools based on their discipline and skill. Each employee has access to many databases including those in figure 2-2. Information is available for quality problem and opportunity analysis. Employees are trained in procedures and equipment usage through on-the-job and classroom training (item 4.3.a.). This training ensures the validity, timeliness, consistency, and effective delivery of information to improve the quality of our products and processes. We

224

Figure 2-1. Required Information/Data Flow in Support of Quality Priorities. Fig. 2-2 lists the types of databases.

Area (fig. 2-1)	Ext.	Int.	Description / Data Type	Ref
Market and Competitor	X		Advisory councils - Customer product requirements	3.1.d.
	X		Sierra Group, InfoCorp, Etc.., - Industry research	7.8.b.
	X		Consultant data - Competitive performance / profiles	7.8.b.
		X	Market Place News and Analysis Digest - Competitive information	1.1.a.
		X	TSEL: Tokyo competitive performance / Cost benchmarking	1.1.a.
Planning		X	Business plans, functional strategies, quality priorities	3.1.a.
	X		AHP: Analytical Hierarchical Process - Prioritization modelling	3.1.a.
		X	QFD: Quality Functional Deployment - Requirements matrix	5.1.a.
		X	ESS: Executive Support System - Competitions, product performance, demographics	2.2.d.
		X	Comprehensive product plan - Development and quality specs	5.1.b.
Support Services		X	PROFS: Professional Office System - Messages, documents, calendar, data	2.1.b.
		X	MSE, TECHED: Technical Education - Course content, requirements, enrollment	4.3.a.
		X	EOS: Opinion Survey - Indicators of morale and empowerment	4.2.b.
		X	PDMS, CERIS: Employee data systems - Skills, history, salary, etc.	2.2.b.
		X	FAIRS: Fixed Asset Inventory Records System - Asset control	2.2.d.
		X	Conferencing disks - Electronic information/conversations	5.5.c.

Group		System & Data	Ref.
Worldwide Development	X	EDS: Engineering Design Systems - Automated circuit specs, layout, test data, EVE	5.1.d.
Suppliers	X	CATIA, CADAM: Mechanical engineering design, predictive, analysis tools	5.1.d.
	X	IDSS: Integrated Development Support System - Program design, tracking data	2.1.b.
Rochester Development	X	PTR: Problem Tracking Resolution - Quality field support, audit data	4.2.c.
	X	DPRS: Development Production Records System - Bill of materials control data	5.1.d.
Worldwide Manufacturing	X	MCS: Manufacturing Control System - Quality and process control data	5.2.a.
	X	EMLS: Enterprise Materials Logistics System - Parts planning, inventory control, volumes	5.1.d.
	X	Manufacturing cost systems - Cost performance, control, benchmarking	3.2.a.
Suppliers	X	EDI: Electronic Data Interchange - Specifications, billing, supplier data exchange	5.7.b.
	X	Supplier surveys - Quality guidelines and performance	5.7.a.
Rochester Manufacturing	X	Quality component measuring system - Supplier quality training data	6.4.b.
	X	Environment impact / Chemical control system - Safety, movement, acoustics, health	1.4.c.
Customer	X	COMMON: Independent user group - Customer product requirements	7.6.a.
	X	Customer surveys - Requirements, quality, satisfaction	7.8.a,b.
	X	Critical customer situations - Customer complaint avoidance	7.7.b.
	X	CPC: Customer partnership calls - Product satisfaction, prospecting	7.7.a.
Market, Service, and Business Partners	X	ECS: Electronic Customer Support - Customer response and service	2.2.c.
	X	AAS: Advanced Administrative System - Order configuration / processing	2.1.c.
	X	SDMS: Service Data Management System - Reporting parts failure field data	2.2.c.
	X	RETAIN: Technical Assistance Information Network - Field problems / solutions	7.2.f.
	X	EQUAL: Electronic Quick Answer Library - IBM product information	7.2.b.
	X	HONE: Hands On Networking Environment - Quick service reference and product information	7.2.b.
	X	SCE: Service Cost Estimates - Customer support requirements	5.1.c.(2).

Figure 2-2. Scope of Data. Quality improvement achieved through availability and use of relevant data.

automate manual processes and integrate data to achieve consistency and standardization of information. Each database has a designated owner who controls the validity of data and system security. This owner also establishes update requirements and periodic independent data reviews.

Figure 2-3 shows the process for determining and managing data to ensure validity, standardization, consistency, and timeliness. Customer requirements, plans, standards, and product specifications determine the information to be included in the database. The owner of the data forms a team. The team creates specifications, defines content, and validates database design and contents. Teams (for example, System Products Assurance) verify, audit, and measure systems and data prior to availability. Quarterly business self-assessments review the update frequency, consistency, and accuracy of data.

Independent organizations verify standardization of information and consistency across functions through controls, reviews, and audits.

To validate our information, we use our own technology such as bar coding and computer field/range checking (computer validates input data based on what is expected), extensively reducing data entry errors. Most manufacturing equipment is computer-integrated, thereby automatically collecting production information and eliminating manual input errors. Database structures with online prompting and input validation govern standardization of content and format. For example, EDS rules govern data entry and automatic translation of data to manufacturing information transmitted worldwide.

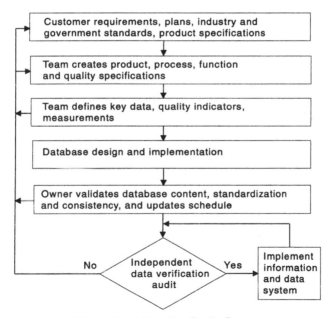

Figure 2-3.   Information Quality Process.

The following are key examples of technology and processes used to ensure standardization, consistency, reliability, and timeliness.

Integrated Development Support System (IDSS): IDSS is a tool used to control software development across many sites worldwide. It is used to manage our software libraries, to control change, and to create and distribute multiple software products. The consistency and standardization provided by IDSS for thousands of programmers improves the quality of software development and production and gives the customer a higher quality product. IDSS was developed in Rochester and is now a corporate system used by 14,000 programmers at 35 sites.

Order Configurator: With the AS/400 Order Configurator, we have eliminated inconsistencies in ordering that could cause problems during installation. Figure 2-4 shows the process from customer order to customer delivery. Order placement (Advanced Administrative System) is assisted by the Artificial Intelligence (AI)-based configurator. It uses its rules-driven knowledge database to determine the cause of any configuration inconsistencies and then prompts for the correct input. The configurator verifies that all order detail is correct, validates prices, and transmits the order to the manufacturing plant. This order to build and test the product is then processed through our Manufacturing Control System (MCS), which automatically controls the assembly sequence and build process. Customer ordered software is automatically loaded onto the system, documentation is added, and the loop is completed when the ordering system addresses the shipment to the customer's location. Our defect free installation measurements and delivery time improvements verify the effectiveness of the configurator (fig. 6-6).

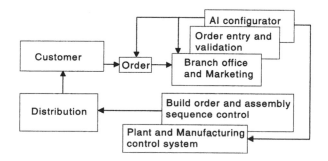

Figure 2-4.   AI-Based Order Configurator.

2.2. Analysis of Quality Data and Information

2.2.a. Principal Types of Analysis: We use data and information analysis throughout our organization to support our leadership objectives. Key processes and operations are continuously monitored using statistical process control techniques (item 5.2.a.) to ensure defect prevention. Trends in customer satisfaction, our business processes performance, product performance, administrative services performance, employee morale, and safety are monitored and compared to goals for improvement. Based on this analysis, product and service objectives are continually improved. Our site managers respond to quality variances or adverse trends by evaluating the performance of our key systems and processes. To verify the performance and quality improvement, we use our own products and technology (use what we sell) in customer support, product design, manufacturing, and service. Examples of key analysis techniques and their applications are shown in figure 2-5.

Applications and (Techniques)	Reference
Key measurements (variance, root cause)	1.3.d, 5.2.f.
Employee empowerment/morale surveys (trend)	1.3.c., 4.2.b,c,d.
Benchmarking (variance, comparative)	3.2.a.
Safety/environmental impact analysis (trend)	4.5.a.
Design simulation analysis (predictive)	5.1.d.
Process reviews and performance (trend)	5.1.b.
Product performance (trend, Pareto, root cause)	5.2.d.
Component/product life (statistical)	fig.6-3
Competitive product analysis (comparative)	6.2.b., 7.8.a.
Market segmentation (statistical)	7.1.a.
Customer requirements preference (conjoint)	7.1.a.
Analysis of customer satisfaction (variance)	7.7.a,b., 7.8.a,b.
Internal/independent customer surveys (pro forma)	7.7.a., 7.8.a.

Figure 2-5. Key Analysis Techniques and Their Applications.

2.2.b. Supporting Key Objectives: Analysis is used to support our vision, quality objectives, and priorities (fig. 3-6). Key measurement data and information from our planning processes (item 3.1.a.) is analyzed to determine resource deployment, strategic goals, and to establish operational plans. Managers use personnel data systems (PDMS/CERIS) to implement and analyze the effectiveness of human resource policies. Skill levels and demographics are determined and analyzed for use in long-term skill forecasting and future education requirements, using the Management System for Education (MSE) (item 4.3.a.).

Market segmentation, customer preference, and customer satisfaction analysis is used to effectively plan product strategies to meet current and future customer requirements. Design simulation, life expectancy, product performance, and process yield data are analyzed during a product cycle to isolate potential problems affecting quality and to influence the design and development of future products.

Through our investment in data processing equipment, we reduce our total cycle time. We continue to improve simulation in design logic, benchmarking, and computer models to prevent defects and remove steps in our development process. For example, to prevent hardware defects, we use the Engineering Verification Engine tool (item 5.1.d.) to simulate design logic. With the use of benchmarks and models in this simulation tool, we continue to remove steps in our product development process. Through the use of this and other tools, we have redirected the efforts of 50 engineers, 80 programmers, 20 support personnel, and reduced the development cycle time by six months ($7–8 million in savings).

Computer systems are programmed to perform prevention-based analyses that control product quality. A process called *condition notification* electronically warns of potential out-of-specification situations before they occur. Production statistics and quality performance data is reviewed by management in daily production status meetings to improve product quality and production line performance.

2.2.c. Gathering and Analyzing Data: Our approach is to provide information online, invest in advanced system tools, and use automatic data collection methods that improve information reliability, data accessibility, and analysis. We have established a site statistics center whose responsibility is to provide education and consulting services to the entire site for improved analysis techniques. We continue to take steps to improve data availability and accessibility by making significant investments in information and data processing systems and tools. For example in 1988 and 1989, we invested over $50 million in data processing equipment and we continue that commitment in 1990. To shorten the time to resolve problems, we trace and correlate field performance problems back to parameters within the manufacturing process (i.e. serial number, production date or lot, and operational parameters). We then take immediate and appropriate action to eliminate performance problems at the source.

An important step taken to shorten our data gathering and analysis cycle and improve customer support is our Electronic Customer Support (ECS) system.

Electronic Customer Support: ECS integrates support functions for our customers. Electronic self-diagnosis is used to analyze problems and report them. The system automatically analyzes the problems it detects, but problem analysis can also be initiated and diagnosed by the customer. Component information and symptoms of a problem are checked against tables of information on system failures. The information about failures and their causes is gathered during product development using simulation and failure modeling. Tables indicate where additional diagnosis or data analysis is required to determine the cause of the failure. When the problem is diagnosed, ECS reports it to our Remote Technical Assistance Information Network (item 7.2.f. RETAIN), where additional system failure information exists. To determine if the reported problem is known or new, symptom and fix information is reviewed. A repair call is initiated for known hardware problems and required parts are identified. Corrections are provided electronically for known software problems. New problems are directed to support personnel who contact the customer and provide direct support (fig. 2-6). Once solutions are determined, the system RETAIN database and the fix database are updated.

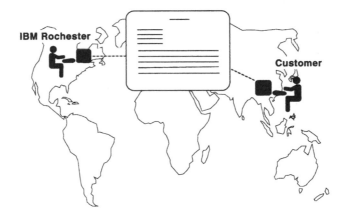

Figure 2-6.   ECS Copy Screen Image. By viewing the same screen simultaneously, a Rochester programmer and a customer in Taiwan can resolve a problem interactively.

All software fixes are included in the next release to improve our quality. Hardware problem and cause information gathered in RETAIN is analyzed for design changes and is used for system quality improvements. Returned parts are analyzed by design teams to

determine the cause of the failure and the corrective action needed. The RETAIN knowledge base is electronically updated as new data on problems and resolutions is collected
to improve the accuracy of the problem analysis process. Defects are tracked and data
is analyzed to ensure that reported problems are corrected without inducing new problems. This approach ensures that corrections are validated before being included in future product releases. We use a service database called Service Data Management
System (SDMS) to monitor service calls and to verify that our design changes have resolved problems. ECS problem analysis has shortened the feedback cycle, increased the
defect removal rate, and significantly enhanced the level of customer support. ECS is
cited by our customers as one of our most important product improvements.

2.2.d. Analysis Leading to Change: Our approach is to provide effective, reliable, and
flexible systems and databases that can be analyzed to continually improve our quality
priorities. We continually review our processes through self assessments and key measurement analysis that lead us to change the data we collect and to analyze data more
reliably. Where there is contradictory information, adverse trends, or inconsistencies in
data, quality teams assess the information and perform an in-depth audit of the process
and data collected. With this assessment, the data owner, along with the teams, establishes quality improvement actions to ensure the reliability of data for improved analysis
using the process described in figure 2-3. An example of changes we made in collecting
data that improved the reliability and analysis of information is our Fixed Asset Inventory
Records System (FAIRS). Teams analyzed asset management data history and suggested changes to systems and information that resulted in quality improvement plans.
Installed in 1987, FAIRS has improved the accuracy of asset management records by
100%, while also improving asset accountability and utilization.

An example of a data management system that provides managers and planners with reliable and very flexible information is the Executive Support System (ESS).

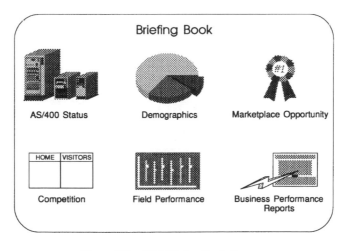

Figure 2-7.   ESS Briefing Book Screen.

Executive Support System: Figure 2-7 shows the scope of data available in ESS through
its icon-based operation. Competitive information, market research data, our installation
base demographics, customer satisfaction data, market segmentation, and sales projec-

tions are examples of information available on ESS. Our market research team continues to expand the capability of ESS based on data analysis and customer requirements by adding access to IBM and industry-wide information. ESS provides benchmark information to assess opportunities for improving business quality, preventing defects, and responding to changes in market conditions and our products.

3. Strategic Quality Planning

Our customers' success is our success. We make our customers successful by providing them with solutions that give them a competitive advantage. Our market-driven quality strategy is our road map to achieve worldwide industry leadership.

3.1. Strategic Quality Planning Process

3.1.a. How Strategic Quality Plans Are Developed and Integrated: Corporate, IBM US, and ABS headquarters shape our five-year strategy (**1** in fig. 3-1) by setting policies, goals, and formulating corporate quality instructions (item 1.2.a.). In response to these goals, we develop five-year business and quality strategies to achieve worldwide industry leadership.

Integrating Quality into the Business Strategy: Our business strategy **2** describes the long-term plans necessary to achieve leadership market share and revenue goals. Strategic benchmarks set from the analysis of leading competitors and other companies form the basis of our quality improvement plans. These benchmarks **3** take into consideration historic and technology improvement trends. Each organization then develops a functional strategy **4** that identifies the resources to achieve our quality priorities **5** and business goals. Cross-functional teams meet weekly during the first quarter of each year and have regular management reviews as the strategy is developed.

We use advanced tools in our planning process. Conjoint analysis is used to highlight trade-offs between customer preference and product functions. The Analytical Hierarchical Process (AHP), a mathematical decision support tool, is used to determine the priority of our plans to achieve optimum business results. Our financial planning model uses industry benchmarks to assess the balance between the investment required to achieve our quality objectives and our business revenue and profit goals.

Annual Plan with Two-Year Horizon: Each year in the Operating Plan cycle **6**, we develop plans to commit resources (people, dollars, and facilities) to execute our business and quality strategies. Information about current market and industry environments, competitive announcements, and customer satisfaction is disseminated throughout our organization by our market research group in order to establish benchmarks and identify areas for improvement. We set new quality objectives to ensure leadership. Employees **7** provide managers with resource and schedule plans that will achieve our business targets, and quality objectives and priorities (item 3.3.a.).

The Rochester Management Committee (RMC) approves our operating plan when short-term targets support our strategic goals.

3.1.b. Data, Information, and Analysis: The principal types of data and information (fig. 2-2) that we use in planning are:

- Market research databases
- Feedback from our customer advisory councils
- Customer satisfaction surveys

233

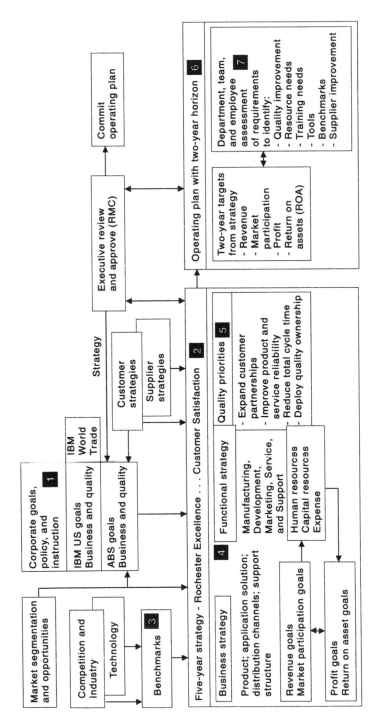

Figure 3-1. Integration of Quality Planning and Overall Business Planning. Short- and long-term quality improvement priorities are the key strategies to achieve our business leadership goals.

Customer success,
delighted customers,
satisfied customer
needs, new
opportunities

More satisfied
customers, more
timely solutions

Stable
requirements

Faster market response,
increased competitive
advantage

Prevent development,
manufacturing, and
service defects

Increased
productivity,
reduced cycle time

Figure 3-2. Market-Driven Quality Strategy.

- Competitive analysis reports
- Consultant quality studies
- Key supplier capabilities

We identify trends and develop criteria to establish quality benchmarks.

Through the comprehensive analysis techniques described in figure 2-5, we assess worldwide markets, competition, and customer feedback. Using our databases, we identify long-term business opportunities by industry segment. Targeting high-growth industries worldwide, we further segment these industries to characterize customer needs and wants, competition, and new market opportunities. We use manufacturing process control history and test results to define our current process capability, and assess the feasibility of improvements to products and processes. Both the business strategy and functional strategies are evaluated and updated annually using this new information.

We share technology information with our suppliers to improve cycle times, process capabilities, controls, and cost. Comparisons with suppliers, other IBM technology providers, industry, and competitors are done to search for new, innovative ideas, and to evaluate the feasibility of our plans.

3.1.c. Benchmarking to Determine Our Quality Position: **3** Our approach is to collect data to understand our current and projected quality position, set benchmarks, and identify opportunities. Our competitive analysis teams gather data to compare over 200 competitors.

We compare product performance, reliability, cost, and function data, as well as competitors' development processes, tools, and techniques to identify gaps or opportunities for improvement. We also investigate companies that are leaders in delivering products and services outside of the computer industry. Support service parameters, such as data processing system reliability and response time, and the quality and efficiency of administrative services are also compared. Since no one company is the world leader in all quality aspects, we establish *composite best of breed* benchmarks. These benchmarks for products and services are established using the best elements of the leading companies. Our goal is to be better than this benchmark.

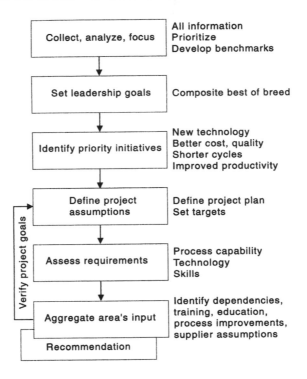

Figure 3-3. Determining Key Quality Requirements.

3.1.d. Customers, Suppliers, and Employees

Customers: Our market-driven quality strategy (fig. 3-2) makes customers full partners in our development process. This quality circle illustrates how we achieve customer loyalty and satisfaction by involving them in planning, product development and introduction, and validation of our decisions.

Customers participate with us in setting our strategic quality plans through worldwide customer advisory councils, lab consultant programs, and cooperative improvement projects. Through this participative process, customers prioritize product and service features, and validate that our plans and strategies meet their needs. This involvement reduces development and manufacturing rework and improves service offerings. As we improve productivity, reduce cycle time, and respond more quickly to market needs, we increase our customers' competitive advantage.

Supplier Partnerships: Our business success depends on the quality leadership of our suppliers. We purchase technology, major assemblies, and critical supplies from them. These suppliers are integrated into the total quality planning cycle to enable us to reduce the time required to develop and produce a product, reduce costs, and become leaders in delivering defect free products. With our suppliers, we exchange information on process and technology, decide what to produce and purchase, and jointly plan new quality improvement priorities to achieve business goals.

Employees: 7 Our employee involvement is fundamental to successful planning. Most new improvement plans originate from employee ideas. Employee teams identify needs for capital equipment, staffing, education, and process development. Management and peer review teams ensure that all area marketing, service, and product plans are synchronized.

3.1.e. Determining Key Requirements: Figure 3-3 illustrates our process for determining key quality requirements. Our Corporate Instruction 105 defines our criteria for exceeding the quality of our previous products and of competitive offerings. Information from industry and competitive sources is collected and analyzed. From this analysis, we establish benchmarks. We evaluate our data against benchmarks to identify gaps and set new leadership goals.

Based on these goals, we propose initiatives to close performance gaps and establish leadership. We establish key assumptions necessary to execute these initiatives, define a project plan, and establish targets for quality, schedule, cost, functional content, and service. We communicate the project plan to cross-functional teams. To assess the feasibility of the project within each function, these teams evaluate internal and supplier process capabilities, technology availability, and skill requirements. They develop the implementation plans required for areas such as education, training, capital, people, expense levels, and supplier needs. The assessment team aggregates input from all functions, calculates the total investment, and determines the payback and measurement system. Any external dependencies are identified. With the original project targets and quality goals as criteria, trade-offs are made among schedule, resources, and investment. Peer reviews verify that the project as defined will meet the goals. The project recommendation is taken to the System Management Board (fig. 5-2, SMB) for acceptance.

3.1.f. Plans Implemented, Resources Committed, and Requirements Deployed: Upon SMB approval, we implement the project plan and deploy the requirements using project management techniques. Any external dependencies are committed. The project has an owner responsible for obtaining commitments on critical skills, staffing, and capital. Functional organizations compare the project with other projects and decide its priority based on the quality priorities (item 3.3.a.). We deploy project requirements as follows:

The project is communicated to all people involved through area meetings. Key suppliers and customers involved in the project are included in the meetings, or in special meetings held at their locations. A measurement system is established to monitor progress toward goals.

Specific quantified requirements and measurements are deployed to each individual area involved. These are documented in the area manager's performance plan. In turn, they further deploy the requirements within their organizations to each employee. Once the project is communicated, and goals understood, managers work with employees to develop individual performance expectations for the project. Performance results are reviewed quarterly.

3.1.g. Improvements in the Planning Process: Our planning process is evaluated twice a year through self-assessments, and monthly comparisons of actual performance to the goals we set in our strategic and operating plans. Cross-functional review teams evaluate the plan process with the following measures:

- Planning cycle—keeping it short
- Plan modifications—minimizing change
- Process steps—simplifying them

Information gained through studies of competitors and other companies' planning processes is used to establish benchmarks. Comparisons of benchmark data to our own plan process assists us in identifying opportunities for improvement and in establishing goals. Market planning experts from leading universities help us evaluate and implement innovative approaches to improve our planning process.

The owner of the plan process communicates goals and changes, and collects feedback from all organizations to ensure understanding and ownership. The new process is then documented.

IBM Rochester's planning process has been established as a model that will be used across the corporation and has received accolades from the academic community. Future initiatives for our market-driven quality strategy (fig. 3-1) are:

- Improving decision support tools to improve the accuracy and simplicity of the process
- Further integrating customers, suppliers, marketing, and service into the product planning, design, and development process to get continuous feedback and confirmation of our decisions

3.2. Quality Leadership Indicators in Planning

3.2.a. Criteria for Selecting Benchmarks: Figure 3-4 depicts our process for selecting and establishing leadership benchmarks and goals, and figure 3-5 shows our sources of data. Corporate Instruction (CI) 105 (better quality than previous products and competitors' products) and CI 101 (offering more effective, efficient, and adaptable business processes) define our criteria for competitive comparisons and industry benchmarks. We compare ourselves to the best product competition worldwide, perform process comparisons with other IBM locations, and evaluate nonproduct processes of competitors and other companies.

We develop benchmarks by analyzing over 200 competitors and other industry leaders. Through our segmentation process (fig. 7-2), we categorize leaders in each of the major worldwide market segments by geography. We determine the strategies of competitors, both full range and niche, from industry consultant information and other detailed analyses. Our criteria for benchmarks are:

- Quality leadership in high priority areas
- Superior tactical and strategic business results
- Technological leadership introduction, and use
- Nonproduct service excellence in support systems

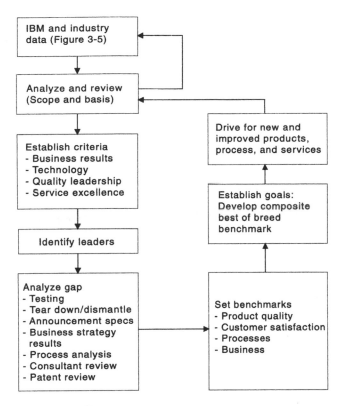

Figure 3-4.   Process for Benchmarking.

Our key benchmark areas are:

- Business—worldwide tactical and strategic market share by revenue, volume, and profit
- Products—mean time to failure, cost, safety
- Processes—cycle time, order and delivery
- Service and support—warranty, service cost, nonproduct service, administration
- Customer satisfaction—cost of ownership and satisfaction indicators

3.2.b. Sources of Data: The table in figure 3-5 indicates the depth and breadth of our internal and external sources for benchmark data.

3.2.c. Changing the Scope of Comparisons: While our current benchmark criteria is comprehensive (item 3.2.a.), we are expanding the scope of the composite best of breed to select the best element of the best company, competitor or not. In this way our goal becomes the best in all aspects of our business worldwide. We have begun to benchmark other companies' quality management systems, and apply what we learn to strengthen our system. Incorporating Motorola's Six-Sigma[1] approach will improve our

---

[1] Six Sigma and design is a trademark of Motorola, Inc.

Scope	Source	IBM	Independent	Type of Information
Customer	Customer Partnership Calls	X		Satisfaction with IBM vs. competitive equipment
	Booze/Allen Research Consultant	X	X	Mission critical customer strategy
	Customer Advisory Councils	X		View of our solutions vs. alternatives
Quality	Industry Quality Leaders		X	Quality management systems
Competi- tion	Industry Trade Magazines		X	New announcements, industry strategy, etc.
	Competitive Analysis Organization	X		Testing
	Tokyo Systems Evaluation Lab	X		Disassembly and analysis to study architecture, reliability, new design techniques, documentation, etc.
	Rochester Technical Evaluation	X		
	Dallas Performance Center	X		
	Business Analysis Group	X		Business projections, investment strategies
	Sierra Group		X	Cost of ownership comparisons, testing
	DataPro		X	Customer satisfaction surveys
	Competitive Analysis Newsletter	X		Monthly trade journals, new announcements
	Consultant Reports		X	Independent testing, comparisons, and strategy
Market	Marketplace News and Trends	X		Online monthly status of global market strategy
	University Consultant Studies		X	Long range industry strategies
	Industry Seminars	X	X	Long range industry strategic key solutions
	Executive Support System	X		Online market strategy and trends
Process	Competitive Analysis Teams	X		Evaluate process/tools used to design products
	Leaders in Key Processes in Non-Computer Related Industries		X	New strategies that can be applied to product or nonproduct processes

People

Personnel Opinion Surveys	X	IBM morale indicators compared to other sites
Mayflower Survey		X	Industry comparisons of employee morale indicators

Product

IBM Standards	X	Product design, safety standards, ergonometrics
U/L, FCC, CSA Standards		X	Independent testing laboratories
Worldwide Standards and Laws		X	National standards (safety, environmental)

Figure 3-5. Sources of Benchmark Data. Scope of internal and independent data sources.

Leadership Vision
(item 1.1.a.) ⟹ **Leadership Objectives from Market Driven Quality Strategy (fig. 3-2)** ⟹ **Quality Priorities**

Leadership Vision (item 1.1.a.)	Leadership Objectives from Market Driven Quality Strategy (fig. 3-2)	Quality Priorities
Customer-the final arbiter	Customer satisfaction	Enhancing customer partnerships
Quality-excellence in execution	Reliability	Continuous improvement in product and service reliability
Products and services-first with the best	Cycle time	Reduce total cycle time
People-enabled, empowered, excited, and rewarded	People productivity	Deploying quality ownership

Figure 3-6. Translating Visions to Leadership Objectives and to Priorities.

quality and our measurement systems. Our market research organization continually searches for new sources of data such as industry databases. As they become available, we procure them and integrate them into our ESS system (item 2.2.d.). We continually change and expand the selection base of companies that we benchmark in order to maintain leadership goals in a dynamic, competitive, global market.

3.3. Quality Priorities

3.3.a. Principal Priorities: Execution and delivery of superior products and services in the shortest possible time requires the best people, trained on the most productive tools, and focused on preventing defects in everything they do. We translate our vision into quality leadership objectives and then into quality priorities (fig. 3-6) which support our objectives. These quality priorities are described in figure 3-6.

Customer Partnerships: Our short-term priority is to form an independent organization dedicated to being a customer advocate in the product development process. In partnership with customers, this group will assess, at regular development checkpoints, how well our product and service plans meet customer expectations.

Our long-term priority is to extend the scope of our requirements planning into our customers' operations. By evaluating their most severe environments and the designs of their software application programs, we will be able to design more robust products and services. This will improve customer satisfaction and loyalty and will provide customers with superior solutions to improve their businesses.

Continually Improving Product and Service Reliability: We have made significant progress in the use of advanced techniques to isolate and prevent defects in design and protect our customers from disruptions. Powerful tools such as EVE (item 5.1.d.) simulate complex system designs before we build hardware. We are complementing EVE with advanced design languages that eliminate manual process steps, simplify our process, and remove opportunities for injecting defects in the design. Our long-term priority is to develop techniques that will automatically translate specifications into hardware models. Our strategy for the future is to design systems that never disrupt our customers' operations and can be maintained without having to turn their machine off. We also will use high availability technologies and techniques, such as predictive analysis, which will shield customers from interruptions and unexpected maintenance.

Reducing Total Cycle Times: Responding quickly to customer demand is key to leadership in customer satisfaction and business results. In the 1980s, we reduced our total cycle times by 60%. Our short-term priority is to share our Continuous Flow Manufacturing (CFM) principles with our suppliers, integrating them into a total cycle time reduction effort. To simplify processes and improve communications, we will link our suppliers to us through Electronic Data Interchange (EDI).

Our long-term priorities for reducing cycle times are to integrate all internal organizations, draw suppliers and customers into the early planning phases of new products, expand our computer integration throughout our entire system, and apply new design tools and techniques to prevent defects and to simplify and shorten processes.

Deploying Quality Ownership: Since 1985, the productivity of our development people has doubled. Our teams are designing and deploying advanced technology design tools.

They take responsibility for developing the techniques necessary to achieve our quality goals. Employees volunteer to transfer knowledge to their peers on quality topics such as SPC and design of experiments. They disassemble and analyze competitors' hardware and present their findings at site wide technical exchanges and at department meetings.

Our long-term priority is to benchmark the quality systems of leading companies. We will analyze this information to dramatically improve our deployment of quality responsibilities throughout our company. We will emphasize automated defect prevention and remove error-prone process steps to free our people to focus on further quality improvement initiatives.

3.3.b. Resources Committed to the Plan: Our people are committed to quality improvement in everything we do. Figure 3-7 illustrates our trends and projections in people and capital resources committed to achieve our quality priorities.

Quality Priorities	1985-89	1990-91	1992-94
People			
Customer partnership	4%	5%	increase
Improving reliability (tools)	6%	9%	increase
Reducing cycle time	4%	5%	increase
Deploying quality ownership	5%	6%	increase
% of total Person Years	19%	25%	
Capital (% of total)	22%	27%	stable

Figure 3-7.   Resource Investment.

As a result of our quality improvement initiatives, we reduced our staff by 15% since 1985, while increasing our volumes. In addition, we redeployed 6% of our people from detection to prevention and improvement based initiatives, increasing our quality competitiveness. To continue to compete in our dynamic industry, we keep our people technically educated and vital. Our investment in education has increased 21% over the last three years. Capital spending for quality improvement has increased 5%, while total capital has been flat or decreasing.

Our software quality improvement plan is to deploy Programmer Workbenches (PWB) throughout our development organization. We will invest over $50 million in new computers and object-oriented programming processes to prevent defects in our designs. From this investment, we project a savings of $190 million by 1994 due to improved quality.

Our trends throughout the 1980s show we continually reduced cost associated with defects. Capital spending to detect defects has declined 75%, write-offs as a percent of output have reduced 45%, and engineering changes as a percent of output have declined 60%, while quality has continually improved.

3.3.c. Supplier Partnership in Quality Improvement: Supplier partnerships are key to our reduced cycle time priority. In 1989, purchases from suppliers as a percent of total output was 27%. This will increase to 31% in 1990, and continue to increase. We view suppliers as an extension of our business. Their success is our success. Our strategy is to select capable, full-service suppliers who deliver high-quality major assemblies, requiring no incoming inspection, and who control the quality of their own subcontracted goods and services. Then, we establish long-term relationships, benefitting each other. We select suppliers based on Best of Breed (BOB) analysis identifying quality and technology loaders in volume manufacturing capability, financial performance, and sustained delivery

Through joint quality improvement planning sessions, we agree on stretch goals that reflect leadership strategies for both our companies. To achieve these goals, we transfer technology to suppliers to improve their quality, cost, and process capability. We supplement this technology transfer with education to ensure that suppliers become self-sufficient as soon as possible. Essential areas of supplier improvement are:

- Application of SPC to critical processes
- Electronic Data Interchange (EDI) to simplify purchasing transactions
- Application of leading-edge process equipment
- Adapting our product development tools to enhance their development capability
- Training in Continuous Flow Manufacturing (CFM) cycle time reduction principles
- Incorporation of Computer Integrated Manufacturing (CIM) technologies

Similarly, these suppliers have technology and process expertise that we apply to our products and services. We achieve these benefits through their early and continuous involvement in our development and manufacturing process.

We agree on measurement methodology and consistency, have periodic reviews of the results and focus on improvement initiatives. Our suppliers are actively involved with us in initiatives to achieve our 10x, 100x quality improvement goals and our 50% cycle time reduction goal.

3.3.d. Anticipated Changes in Competitive Quality Position: By integrating our organization and our customers and suppliers into planning and product development, our prevention based process has enabled us to more than double the reliability of our products in two years (fig. 6-9), reduce our maintenance costs by over 50% (fig. 6-5), extend our warranty duration from 3 to 12 months, and reduce total cycle time by over 80%. Our break even time (time for accumulated revenue to equal product development and introduction investment) has been reduced 62% since 1983. Our S/3X and AS/400 system install base of over 400,000 systems has grown by 50% in the last three years, our market share has grown in each of the last two years, and our worldwide revenue growth was 24% last year compared to 9% growth in the industry.

To improve our competitive quality position in the 1990's, we have set the following quality goals.

- To improve our key quality measures 10x by 1991, and 100x by 1993, through the application of new tools and technology, and prevention based design processes
- To reduce our total cycle times an additional 50% by 1995 through closer customer and supplier partnerships, enhancing productivity tools, cross-functional integration, and increasing support service productivity
- To increase the productivity of our people 30% by 1993 through deployment of quality ownership, on the job training, and new tools to simplify and reduce process steps

Achieving these goals will enable us to fully implement our market-driven quality strategy (fig. 3-2). Our customers' success will guide us in setting new goals that will improve satisfaction (fig. 3-8), and ensure the business results (fig. 3-9) that come from quality improvement.

	Average Competition	IBM	Composite BOB	IBM Goals 1990	1991	1993
Customer Sat Index	XX	XX	XX	XX	XX	XX

Source: 1989 M&S Survey (fig. 7-12)

Figure 3-8. Customer Satisfaction Index. The index is comprised of 7 indicators such as hardware, service, and sales. The composite best of breed is the best company in each indicator.

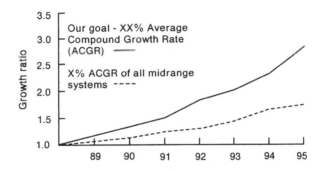

Figure 3-9. Business Results of Quality Improvement and Customer Satisfaction.

4. Human Resource Utilization

In 1988, IBM received the first annual Secretary's Opportunity 2000 award from the U.S. Department of Labor. This award recognizes outstanding achievement by an employer in human resource and social responsibility programs. In her presentation speech, Secretary McLaughlin praised IBM's human resource and community involvement practices as being worthy of emulation by American companies if they are to be competitive in the year 2000.

4.1. Human Resource Management

4.1.a. Integrating Human Resource Plans: Human resource plans and business plans are inseparable in IBM (fig. 3-1). This relationship was reinforced in January 1989, when John Akers defined our market-driven strategy (fig. 3-2). This strategy reshaped our company's fundamental approach toward our customers, requiring new commitments from employees to the quality of their work and the quality of IBM products and services.

Our business plans and human resource efforts come together in our human resources strategy. Through analysis and systematic planning, we develop human resource plans to support our business needs and to further improve our quality culture. To prepare our human resource plans, a team of representatives from all areas work together to study the quality requirements in our functional strategy and our operating plan (item 3.1.d.). They assess the availability and skills of people necessary to meet those requirements and determine any additional training and facilities that must be provided. Using the results of this work, the personnel planning team develops a strategy and a series of plans to meet our needs for staffing, recruiting, educating, promoting, compensating, and rewarding.

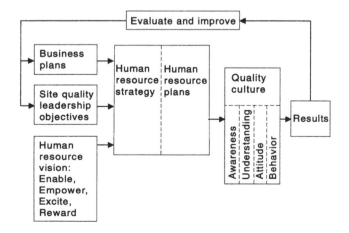

Figure 4-1.   Integrating Human Resource Plans into Quality and Business Plans.

246

This process (fig. 4-1) also reinforces our quality culture in which employees move from an awareness and understanding of quality to a personalized attitude and behavior that produces improved results.

4.1.b. Key Strategies: Our human resource vision is: to enable, empower, excite, and reward all employees to achieve our business and quality goals. Our strategies to achieve this vision are:

- Communication and teamwork
- Education and training
- Management development
- Job flexibility
- Decision-making participation
- Recognition and compensation

Communication and Teamwork: A strong communication strategy is the cornerstone of our employee-manager partnership, our quality initiatives, and the effectiveness of our employees. Our business plans are communicated through area meetings, team meetings, and one-on-one discussions. Managers provide leadership, coaching, and feedback. Employees consult with each other to ensure that requirements are understood and plans are synchronized. Understanding and commitment are reinforced through informal as well as regularly scheduled meetings among cross-functional teams.

Education and Training: We provide extensive education and training to ensure that all employees have the skills they need to meet our quality objectives. One hundred percent of our employees receive on-the-job training. Last year, each person received an average of 51 hours of formal education. Most of our 770 separate classes were offered on site and on company time. To achieve our education goals, we have many partnerships with educational institutions to develop programs for our needs, and we provide them with teachers and equipment.

We work with suppliers to improve their processes, from administrative to manufacturing. We work directly at supplier locations, providing training and assistance in areas such as Continuous Flow Manufacturing (CFM, a continuous flow of parts on an assembly line with minimal inventory) and Statistical Process Control (SPC) to ensure the quality of their products and services.

Management Development: To keep up-to-date on their people-management, business, and quality skills, all of our managers receive a minimum of 40 hours of management development training each year. All Rochester managers attend two 2-day Management Colleges that focus on meeting employees' needs (item 1.3.a.).

Job Flexibility: IBM's full-employment practice ensures that employees receive new job opportunities when they initiate improvements that simplify, eliminate, or change their current role. We maintain full employment by offering temporary assignments, transfer opportunities, and retraining. Employees have flexibility to define their job assignments through performance planning sessions with their managers, and they have flexibility to move to other jobs.

Decision-Making Participation: Each employee participates in decision making through day-to-day contact with their team members and manager. Through this interaction, employees build confidence and assume ownership of their jobs. Managers are available to spend more time managing processes and building strategies for the future.

Recognition and Compensation: The primary means for recognition and compensation is our merit pay plan, which provides salary increases based on level of performance. Managers also use a wide variety of reward mechanisms, ranging from a simple thank you to monetary awards, reinforcing commitment to quality and recognizing accomplishments. For examples of those reward mechanisms see item 4.4.a.

4.1.c. Priorities: Our principal human resource priorities support our quality priorities described in item 3.3.a. Our short-term human resource priorities are:

- Educating employees in quality concepts and methods
- Empowering employees and enhancing teamwork
- Achieving quality results through employee evaluations, compensation, and awards

Human resource priorities provide the tools, training, and reinforcement for employees to implement the quality priorities.

Our long-term human resource priorities are intended to:

- Reinforce a culture that turns quality values into personal values
- Ensure an integrated approach to prevent defects across all organizations
- Provide online productivity tools, databases, and communication links
- Establish clear leadership in ergonomic standards for workplace comfort and safety

Implementing these human resource priorities creates a paradigm shift in the way employees work. Their increased commitment and ownership will achieve our leadership objectives (fig. 3-6), fulfill customers' expectations of ever-increasing quality, and reduce the cycle time of our processes.

4.1.d. Evaluating and Improving: Our human resource strategy drives aggressive plans for employee morale, attendance, overtime, performance evaluations, staffing, workload, and awards. We measure progress against goals set in those plans by collecting appropriate data (much of it updated weekly), analyzing it to identify trends, and determining root causes. Based on the results of our analysis, we take action to improve our processes and our business and human resource plans.

We evaluate data from other companies and industry associations and assess our leadership in human relations. We use the Mayflower Survey (fig. 3-5), an annual opinion survey of a random sample of employees in 34 leading companies, to obtain company-specific data and set benchmarks. As a result of analyzing the data, we made significant changes to assist employees in balancing their work and home lives. In 1988, we expanded our flex-time system, allowing employees to adjust their schedules up to one hour, and instituted an unpaid leave of absence of up to three years for child or family care. In addition, we introduced a work-at-home pilot program.

4.2. Employee Involvement

4.2.a. Approaches to Group Participation: IBM Rochester is an exciting place to work! There is a family feeling of joint responsibility, a comradery born of shared challenges and successes. The work ethic and commitment to excellence in Rochester contribute strongly to our success. This environment is nurtured by the peer-to-peer relationships among all our people and is reinforced by managers who lead by example. People want to learn and contribute, and we give them the opportunity and tools to do so.

We are organized into departments and larger units to provide a formal structure, but our real organization exists in teams. Often, they are self-initiated and operate without management participation. We work to make boundaries between departments invisible, to approach each task on a team basis, and to create organizations without walls. The synergism that takes place in these teams often reveals unexpected opportunities and promotes the cross-exchange of ideas when members participate in other teams.

Our employees work in teams within a function, across functions, and in joint teams with suppliers and customers. Teams in production areas improve the processes and quality of our manufacturing line. Our Site Services and Support area hosts internal customer advisory councils (item 5.6.c.) to evaluate customers' perceptions and improve customer satisfaction. Teams of customers, marketing representatives, engineers, and programmers participate in planning discussions, design reviews, and early tests.

4.2.b. Opportunities for Contribution

Individual Opportunities: On-going, one-on-one contact with managers and team members provides an opportunity for discussion, questions, and suggestions on any topic. We also provide opportunities for contribution through the more than 11,000 online terminals that provide employees access to extensive communication capabilities, databases and forums, and design and analysis tools. The result is that employees ask questions, share information, and contribute in many ways. Employees with new ideas submit invention disclosures online. These ideas do not have to be related to the employee's job. Any employee can send a proposal to Larry Osterwise or any other person on site. Later this year, all employees will be able to submit suggestions online. These and other online applications give individual employees fast access and feedback every day.

Opinion Survey: Our annual employee opinion survey provides another opportunity to contribute to improvement. Employees are asked approximately 100 questions about such issues as quality, work environment, and communications. While participation is voluntary, typically 94% of our employees respond: an excellent rate. In addition to requesting answers to multiple-choice questions, the survey asks for write-in comments. The 1989 survey responses contained 33,533 comments, including 2417 about operating effectiveness and quality. We analyze all comments, identify key concerns, and develop site action plans to improve the quality of our processes.

Within a month after the survey is completed, managers review survey results with their departments. In these sessions, employees and their managers identify trends, determine causes, and create action plans to improve satisfaction. We track the results in action and status reviews. One example concerned the satisfaction, availability, and response time of online computer support. We investigated and installed three additional IBM 3090 systems in 1989 and plan to install four more in 1990 to improve performance and upgrade capacity. We will review the response to the same question in 1990 to determine the effectiveness of these actions.

Other Opportunities: Other opportunities to contribute include the suggestion plan, skip-level interviews, roundtables, the Open Door process, and Speak Ups. Our suggestion plan encourages employees to contribute ideas for quality improvement and formally recognizes the value of their ideas. Cash awards are based on the amount of savings to the company and range up to $150,000. Skip-level interviews (one-on-one meetings with an upper-level manager) and roundtables (discussions among several employees and an upper-level manager) allow employees to express their views on quality to upper management. Employees who are not satisfied with their manager's response are free to pursue their concern with any level of management (including the Chairman of the Board) through the Open Door process without fear of retribution. Strict measures are enforced to protect the employee's privacy and right to be heard. Employees receive direct feedback within two weeks. Speak Ups allow employees to anonymously present ideas or concerns in writing. All issues are investigated and action is taken within two weeks.

4.2.c. Approaches to Empowerment: Our full-employment practice supports an environment in which employees are willing to accept full ownership and take risks to improve the quality of our products and processes. We understand that mistakes are part of that risk and must be balanced against the opportunity for improvement. At our Corporate Technical Recognition Event last May, Terry Lautenbach said, "If you haven't been told by your immediate manager once or twice, and recently, that you have exceeded the limits of your authority, you have no idea what those limits are."

We focus on understanding the issue, sharing all available information, and deciding what resolution will produce the best quality for our customer, internal or external. This approach promotes win-win solutions.

Employees are expected to take action to prevent defects. Our prevention-based software development process empowers everyone in our programming lab to contribute to the software quality before it is shipped. Through peer reviews and Problem Tracking Reports (PTR), manufacturing, development, and assurance employees can raise concerns, and the product cannot be approved for shipment until the issue is resolved. Production employees can even stop the manufacturing line.

The highest performance rating an employee can earn, "far exceeded the requirements of the job," is defined in part as follows: "The employee's judgement, resourcefulness, and depth of knowledge are superior. The employee not only anticipates and adapts to changes in the job environment but often creates new ways of doing things that change the nature of the job. In short, the employee breaks the bounds of the job." Employees who measure up to this standard and take responsibility for acting are rewarded through our merit pay system.

Encouraging Innovation: We want careers in IBM to be fulfilling and rewarding. For many people, the opportunity for innovation is the most satisfying and rewarding stimulus they could receive. To provide those opportunities, we use a dual-ladder concept that affords technical professionals and managers equal opportunity for promotion and compensation.

Our goal is to be the leader in technology and innovation. Employees create aggressive plans for our products and aggressive goals for themselves. We support them with:

- Advanced design and problem-solving tools
- Comprehensive information about technology and other products
- Access to customers and our marketing and service people
- Freedom to solve problems their own way
- Authority to act

We encourage employees to participate in activities such as publishing in professional journals; joining technical societies; attending technical vitality seminars, conferences and Interdivisional Technical Liaison meetings; participating in the mentor process; and teaching. This environment stimulates the free exchange of ideas, which results in innovative product and service quality improvements.

Means of Increasing Responsibility: Employees assume additional workload when someone is absent, take temporary assignments in other areas, and work as team leaders. Employee initiatives, new processes, and new products produce new jobs and redefine existing ones. Last year 2200 employees took on new assignments, and over 13% of our employees were promoted. Employees are encouraged to go beyond their basic responsibilities and assume additional ones in order to participate in these opportunities. To recognize what an employee is doing, these expectations are built into individual performance plans jointly developed by the employee and manager. The results produced by the employee are the basis for the performance evaluation, and this evaluation is directly tied to our merit pay system.

We prepare employees to be successful in new jobs with increased responsibilities by providing education and personal development (item 4.3.). These classes include Leadership Workshop, Team Leader Workshop, Project Management, Management Preparation Seminars, and technical education.

The team leader approach is used across our product and service organizations. The nonmanager team leader takes ownership of a project and works with other team members to follow the project through to completion. The team sets priorities, defines quality measures, establishes timetables, holds reviews, and continually improves the process.

To give production employees and teams knowledge, experience, and increased responsibility, we are implementing Manufacturing Skills Integration (item 4.3.b., MSI).

4.2.d. Involvement, Empowerment, and Innovation: We are continually working to improve processes through employee teams. The number of processes that have been defined has grown from 105 in 1987 to over 300 in 1990. Each employee is involved in one or more process and has individual responsibility to continually improve it.

Personal involvement is a normal and on-going part of the Rochester culture. One way to evaluate employee involvement is by their voluntary participation in the suggestion program, opinion surveys, and Speak Ups. Figure 4-2 shows these trends.

	1987	1988	1989
Suggestions submitted	XXXX	XXXX	XXXX
Suggestion awards (× $1000)	XXX	XXX	XXX
Speak Ups	XXX	XXX	XXX
Opinion survey participation (%)	93	94	94

Figure 4-2. Trends in Employee Involvement.

During the past three years, we offered employees the opportunity to volunteer to work in branch offices with our marketing organization and make calls on customers. One hundred and fifteen people participated in these six-week assignments and gained a whole new dimension of customer and marketing needs. An additional 108 people volunteered to call customers shortly after their AS/400 system was installed to determine their satisfaction. Others have made calls to prospective customers to determine their interest in an AS/400 system. Through our Everyone Sells program, Rochester employees furnished over 4300 sales leads to our marketing team.

Voluntary participation in teams is widespread, and teams often operate without management participation. We estimate that more than three-quarters of our 653 departments have one or more teams operating within them. They focus on quality topics such as hardware and software products, publications, supplier quality, education, recruiting, financial procedures, emergency procedures, and library services. All production areas have team activity. We estimate that 50% of our production employees are involved in teams today and this will grow to 75% by year-end 1990.

We empower employees in a variety of ways. Production employees inspect and evaluate their own work and audit their own processes. They shut down the line immediately if parts or processes need correction. Manufacturing engineers resolve problems and notify suppliers directly about defective parts. Programmers and engineers initiate reviews of products under development. Employees enroll themselves in education classes and initiate actions to have courses developed. MSI empowers production employees with increased self-sufficiency, involvement, and ownership of their work. Through the Customer Partnership Call process, employees are also empowered to take action in the important area of customer contact and support (item 7.2.d.).

The technical vitality of our employees contributes to innovation. We emphasized this vitality during the past several years and as a result have produced a very positive trend in some important innovation indicators (fig. 4-3).

4.2.e. Evaluating Involvement: The effectiveness of all Rochester employees is reflected in our quality results (category 6.) and customer satisfaction (category 7.). Individual employees receive effectiveness ratings in their performance evaluation. At the team level, effectiveness is demonstrated in the quality results and process rates for the department. For example, through weekly team meetings the Circuit Packaging and Production Center has reduced cycle time by 87% and reduced in-process defects by 38%. We have increased production capacity by 85% from 1987 to 1989.

Type of Innovation and Involvement	1987	1988	1989
Technical memos	13	31	93
Technical reports	35	58	78
Trade press articles	6	15	18
Published internal presentations	53	70	77
Published external presentations	25	25	54
Author recognition awards	0	7	15
Disclosures submitted	459	358	652
Patents filed	33	33	47
Technical vitality seminars	NA	32	70
Tech. vitality seminar attendance	NA	4000	9500

Figure 4-3.   Trends in Employee Innovation and Involvement.

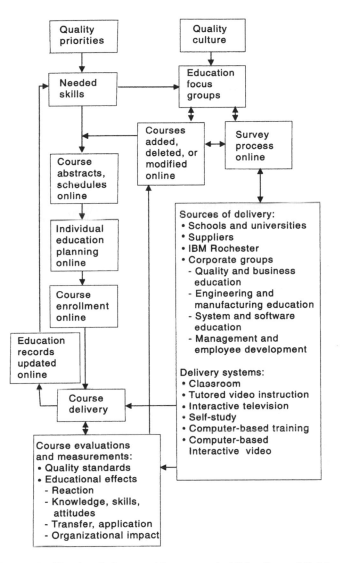

Figure 4-4. Planning, Delivery, and Improvement of Education and Training.

Managers analyze their own management characteristics for effectiveness in delegation, communication, recognition, and motivation. Employees and their manager voluntarily complete Management Activities Profile forms. Employees' responses are compared with those of the manager. The manager feeds back aggregate data to the department and develops action plans in areas for self-improvement.

We also focus on the effectiveness of organizations, processes, education, and plans. We measure the effectiveness of our training, instructors, and certification process by the output of our employees.

4.3. Quality Education and Training

4.3.a. Approach to Education and Training: Quality priorities drive our education process to deliver the right education to the right people at the right time (fig. 4-4). Education in quality concepts, methodologies, and tools support our business plans. Market-driven quality education is being implemented for all levels of management and employees. Our approach to quality education is to move people from awareness and understanding to personal commitment and behavior. Quality education for our employees combines formal classroom instruction with on-the-job training in new responsibilities. This education enables our employees to improve the effectiveness of their work and the quality of our products and processes.

The quality education that is required is determined by comparing existing skills of employees with our estimated future skill requirements. Managers are responsible for understanding how the functional strategies and quality priorities relate to their area of responsibility and for defining new skills required. Employees develop an education plan jointly with their managers. All courses have learning objectives to ensure that students know what skills they will obtain from the course. An employee's course selection is influenced by: business plans, department needs, new skill requirements, anticipated business environment changes, and personal career goals.

Annually, the site conducts an education survey to help define our quality education needs for the coming year. As business plans change, quality education plans are reviewed and adjusted to provide necessary education. Education focus groups of representatives from across the site help support this process. Employees have instant access to course abstracts and schedules, and enroll themselves online. Employees initiate action to get new classes defined when new needs are recognized.

We review our suppliers and business partners' capabilities to meet our quality priorities. We view our suppliers and business partners as extensions of IBM. To ensure that they understand our goals, we share information, work with them to establish their goals, help them become self-sufficient, and provide some of the education they need. In some cases, our suppliers' employees attend the same courses as IBM employees. In other situations, we customize our courses for our suppliers and deliver them at IBM or at their location. Some of the courses we have delivered to our suppliers and business partners are AS/400 Operation, Continuous Flow Manufacturing (CFM), Electronic Data Interchange (EDI), and Statistical Process Control (SPC).

Each employee has an education record as part of a personnel database. It contains a listing of courses taken, the dates they were taken, and the length of each course. As courses are completed, the education records are updated electronically. Summary reports are compared with the skills needed to support our business plans. We use the results to modify the education courses offered. On request, we also create reports for managers who want to know who in their area has taken a particular course.

To improve the education planning process, we are implementing a Management System for Education (MSE). In addition to our existing process, MSE offers skill planning, needs assessment, individual education plans, and education road maps online. It also offers the ability to incorporate individual education plans into department, function, and site education plans, thus eliminating the need for an annual education survey.

4.3.b. On-the-Job Reinforcement: After employees receive quality education, they reinforce their new skills by using them on the job. Managers acknowledge employees' new skills by creating opportunities for them to share their learning through peer-to-peer interaction and by modifying their responsibilities. Obtaining and applying education affect an employee's performance rating, promotion, or transfer to another job.

In 1986, we determined that additional programming skills were required. At the same time, we had a surplus of nonexempt employees. Since that time, 213 people have completed programmer training that included computer architecture, structured design, and program validation. This training was provided at a local university and college credits were awarded. Those successfully completing the education were placed in programming assignments where their knowledge and skills are reinforced by their new department objectives and individual performance plans. They will take additional college courses to continue their skill building. Many have now been promoted to professional programmer status.

In recent opinion surveys and from other feedback, production employees said they want greater variety and flexibility in their jobs, more decision-making opportunities, and increased promotional opportunities. Manufacturing Skills Integration (MSI) is the solution. Production employees are taking on additional job responsibilities previously handled by production control, maintenance, and manufacturing engineering. Education is being expanded to include CFM, equipment maintenance, and process engineering. After employees return from classes, managers reinforce skills on the job by adding responsibility for statistical process control and for maintenance and repair of their machine.

Other successful quality processes begin with peer-to-peer training. CFM was introduced by Larry Osterwise in 1983. Multiple CFM projects were introduced in 1984, and classes, presentations, and videotapes were used to spread CFM techniques. Those principles are reinforced by changes in job responsibilities. By 1987, CFM became a regular part of the Rochester way of doing business, and our procurement team helped our suppliers and customers implement CFM (item 5.7.b.). Today, professional organizations, such as the American Production and Inventory Control Society, and universities, such as Winona State University, are benefiting from the training we provide in CFM principles and techniques.

To promote on-the-job reinforcement, employee experts act as consultants and teachers to other employees and suppliers. They present subjects such as statistics, CFM, design of experiments, quality functional deployment, and project management. Company-wide focus groups, such as Interdivisional Technical Liaisons and centers of competence, meet to discuss advances in technology.

4.3.c. Summary and Trends by Category

New Employee Orientation: During their orientation, new employees are introduced to our quality values by a site executive. They also learn of our commitment to quality through frequent meetings with their managers and departments and through their performance plans. Classes tailored specifically for new employees include information on our business cycle, quality process, and statistical process control, in addition to specific job training. Figure 4-5 depicts the number of hours of classroom education provided for new employees and the percent of employees participating. In 1987 education hours were higher because certain skills were required to support the initial development of the

AS/400 system. In 1988, much of that education was communicated among employees on the job, so less classroom education was needed.

	1987	1988	1989
Education per new employee (hours)	160	133	140
Participation of new employees (%)	99	100	98

Figure 4-5. New-Hire Formal Orientation Received during First 12 Months.

Management development courses include elective courses and those defined by corporate management development. This year all Rochester managers will receive education in key quality initiatives. In turn, they will provide that same education to their employees by the end of this year.

Employee Categories	% of Site	Sample of Quality Education Courses	Hours/Employee		
			1987	1988	1989
Engineer	XX	Engineering verification Statistical methods Failure prevention	38	37	48
Programmer	XX	System performance planning Problem determination Defect prevention	57	62	76
Manager	XX	Market-driven quality Participative management Sys leadership by design	34	38	72
Other exempt	XX	Decision analysis Measurement and testing Quality func deployment	28	29	40
Production	XX	Statistical process control Continuous flow mfg Automated applications	XX	28	27
Other nonexempt	XX	Failure prevention Problem solving Software testing	30	19	41

Figure 4-6. Education and Training Received per Person by Job Category.

Costs per Employee: The average annual cost to provide education and training for the past three years is $1878 per employee and has increased steadily over that period, from $1740 in 1987 to $2103 in 1989. The amount we spend for education is equivalent to about 5% of our payroll. This percentage is five times the national average.

Hours per Employee: Figure 4-6 shows the number of classroom education hours per employee by job category.

Percent Receiving Education: The percentage of employees who receive formal education each year is significantly higher than the amount received by other employees of

U.S. industry, as shown in figure 4-7. The percent of participation will continue to increase in 1990 as a result of the delivery of our new market-driven quality education.

Employee Categories	Rochester			U.S.
	1987	1988	1989	1988
Engineer	84	82	84	57-59
Programmer	76	83	87	61-65
Manager	92	85	98	47
Other Exempt	76	77	81	58-64
Production	72	89	87	22-36
Other Nonexempt	83	82	84	32-52

Figure 4-7. Percent of Employees Receiving Education vs. United States Average.

4.3.d. Indicators of Effectiveness: Certain education evaluation topics are qualitatively different from others (fig. 4-8). For example, evaluating some topics requires simply measuring student reactions subjectively, whereas evaluating others requires measuring changes in employee performance on the job. Pretests and post-tests, on-the-job results, and the opinion survey (which includes the question "How satisfied are you with the education or training you have received from IBM to do your job effectively?") provide this feedback. Input is gathered from design reviews, pilot classes, instructor observations, and student reactions. In 100% of formal courses delivered, students are asked seven questions. Two are "What is your overall evaluation of this course?" and "Rate the quality of the course delivery." The average response to each of these questions, where one is lowest and five is highest, is over four. This input is analyzed and used to determine what quality education should be added, deleted, or modified and which instructors should be coached to meet quality expectations. As a result of indicators, we reduced the length of some courses, introduced videos, and changed lectures to workshops.

Evaluation Topics	Indicators
Course quality	Learning objectives Design reviews Course evaluations
Employee reactions	Course evaluations Opinion survey Feedback to manager
Knowledge, skills, and attitudes	Tests Instructor observations Follow-up with students
Transfer, application	Job responsibilities Performance evaluation Promotion, transfer
Organizational impact	Improved quality Lower costs Reduced cycle time

Figure 4-8. Indicators of Effectiveness of Education.

Quality education and training contributed to the results shown in category 6. Courses such as computer-aided mechanical design and simulation increased output per employee. Courses in failure avoidance and decision analysis helped increase revenue per employee. CFM and SPC courses improved supplier quality. Courses in defect prevention and system performance analysis improved system software quality. Courses in failure prevention and design of experiments reduced manufacturing and development cycle time.

4.4. Employee Recognition and Performance Measurement

4.4.a. Key Strategies for Ensuring Contributions: Our key strategy for encouraging contributions to quality is to integrate performance plans and evaluations with merit pay, recognition, and additional rewards. Performance plans are developed to stimulate individual achievements and contributions to team success. A quality focus is required in all performance plans. With input from peers, team leaders, and other employees, managers determine the extent and level of an individual's contributions. Our merit-pay plan provides compensation based on those achievements and contributions.

Managers select from a wide variety of monetary and nonmonetary rewards, ranging from a simple thank you to individual monetary awards, team recognition, and sitewide recognition for significant quality milestones. When Rochester won the IBM U.S. Quality Award last year, all employees were invited to a celebration event. In addition to other individual and group awards, managers recognize their department members through department lunches or other events of their choice.

To encourage individuals to work as team members, we also reward team efforts. Based on team accomplishments and recommendations from managers and other employees, our senior managers determine team awards. Balance and equity between team and individual awards is achieved through this review process. For example, at our May 1989 Corporate Technical Recognition Event, we recognized individuals and team winners from Rochester for innovations and unique technical efforts. A team of five employees shared $175,000, two employees as a team shared $90,000, and one employee was awarded $35,000.

4.4.b. Reinforcing Quality: Overall quality results determine an employee's performance and appropriate recognition for the individual and team. We reinforce quality in a variety of ways through our recognition and compensation strategy. Employees develop measures of quality through performance plans developed jointly with their managers. In addition, we reinforce quality through bulletin board notices, employee newspaper articles, department meetings, and publicity on individual and team quality achievements.

With our merit-pay system, quality performance is recognized through higher salary increases. Our four levels of acceptable performance range from "far exceeds requirements" to "consistently meets requirements." Currently, 55% of Rochester employees are evaluated as far exceeding or consistently exceeding requirements, while 45% are evaluated as exceeding at times or consistently meeting requirements. IBM traditionally promotes employees from within the company on the basis of merit, a practice our employees regard very favorably. In 1989, our promotion rate was 13% of the site population; in 1990, it is projected to be 14%.

4.4.c. Trends in Recognition: Sitewide events, such as cafeteria receptions with refreshments, recognize the collective quality accomplishments of the Rochester team. One event was held in 1988 to recognize the AS/400 announcement. In 1989, three events were held. One celebrated the first anniversary of the AS/400 announcement. The second recognized shipping 1.5 million hard disks from Rochester. The third, hosted by Terry Lautenbach, celebrated winning the IBM U.S. Market-Driven Quality Award as best site.

Another indicator of nonmonetary recognition is attendance at technical vitality luncheons, which continue to increase from 300 in 1987 to 390 in 1988 and to over 500 in 1989. Also, attendance at inventor breakfasts has risen from 402 in 1987 to 479 in 1988 and 525 in 1989.

Managers set objectives to ensure that monetary awards are equitably distributed. A variety of formal recognition programs are in place to award outstanding contributions to quality and excellence. Monetary awards range from $50 to $150,000. Quality accomplishments, leadership, process improvements, and outstanding problem solving are recognized by the ABS Excellence Awards ($1500 to $25,000) and the Management Excellence Awards ($5000). In 1989, 107 employees received ABS Excellence Awards and 27 managers received Management Excellence Awards. In 1989, 40% of our employees received monetary awards to recognize their contributions. Forty-five percent of the awards given in 1989 recognized individual contributions to a team effort, such as programming teams developing new applications.

Figure 4-9 shows the distribution and trend of monetary awards for recent years.

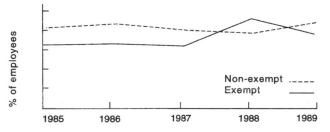

Figure 4-9. Percentage of Employees Receiving Monetary Awards.

The 1988 results rose significantly for exempt employees because of recognition associated with the development phase of the AS/400 system, while results for nonexempt employees declined slightly because production of the AS/400 system had not begun. In 1989, as AS/400 system volumes increased, nonexempt employees were recognized for outstanding quality contributions and process improvements.

4.4.d. Evaluating Effectiveness of Recognition: To evaluate and improve the effectiveness of our recognition and performance measurement system, we use the following process. First, we identify the key indicators of effectiveness, such as employee morale and business results. Then we set goals and gather appropriate data. For example, to evaluate the effectiveness of our merit pay plan, we gather monthly data about salary increases. To measure progress toward our goals, we identify trends in the data. We analyze negative trends and assign owners to develop action plans. Next we implement the action plans and regularly review feedback from sources, such as the opinion survey, manager (skip-level) interviews, roundtables, peer reviews, Speak Ups, and Open Doors to ensure that we are continually improving our process.

4.5. Employee Well-Being and Morale

4.5.a. Health, Safety, Satisfaction, and Ergonomics: For quality improvement activities in health, safety, and satisfaction, we use the process management approach explained in item 5.6. Individual process owners, such as our Medical, Facilities Engineering, and Personnel departments:

- Set standards to meet internal customers' needs
- Gather data to determine trends
- Determine causes of trends
- Develop and implement plans to prevent problems
- Monitor results of their actions to ensure continual improvement

For example, one standard for our Medical department's process is to have a safe, comfortable work environment. The results of their assessment of work-related injuries revealed an opportunity to improve the workplace design. In 1989, we created an Ergonomics department to review all manufacturing processes and implement improvements to prevent injuries.

4.5.b. Analysis of Causes: Our Medical department strives to have no job-related accidents or illnesses. They check medical data for certain high-risk job categories to determine medical trends. When an accident occurs, teams of Medical, Safety, and management personnel immediately begin an investigation of root causes and complete it within 10 days. They develop an action plan to correct the condition and prevent the problem from reoccurring. After a medical-related absence, the Medical department works with the employee's physician to assess the need for any temporary or permanent change in job activities. They also work with Mayo Clinic physicians, who serve as our site physicians, to integrate community medical information into our review of employee health trends. For example, to help prevent repetitive motion trauma illness, we changed our production process by using job rotation.

4.5.c. Flexibility and Retraining: Our full-employment practice reinforces our supportive work environment, instills employee loyalty, and makes us a more desirable employer. We hire the best available people to give us the flexibility to respond to industry changes. When technology shifts and new skills are required, we retrain our employees. The steps taken from 1986 to 1989 to ensure job security were:

- Voluntary retraining for new positions
- Voluntary temporary production assignments
- Voluntary transfers to other IBM locations
- Voluntary retirements

Last year alone, we provided retraining and new job opportunities for one-third of the site population.

4.5.d. Special Services: Our employee benefits plan provides employees and their families with a broad foundation of protection and security at no cost to employees. This plan is recognized as an industry leader. *Working Mother* magazine named IBM as one of the top 10 companies for working mothers.

Our medical staff provides a wide array of services to help maintain a healthy work environment, including voluntary health screening physical exams at five-year intervals. The IBM Club provides extensive recreational facilities and intramural activities. The Employee Assistance Plan provides confidential, professional assistance to employees and their families experiencing problems such as mental distress, substance abuse, and marital and family difficulties. A Plan for Life is an industry-first plan providing health education companywide. We also accommodate disabled employees, by providing telephone amplifiers and voice-enabled computer systems.

We invest in our community by matching, two for one, employees' donations to nonprofit cultural and educational organizations. Our Fund for Community Service grants money and equipment to nonprofit organizations. Our Voluntary Education program provides opportunities to increase employees' knowledge in areas both directly and indirectly related to their jobs.

4.5.e. Determining Employee Satisfaction: Employee satisfaction is determined through the annual opinion survey (item 4.2.b.), one-on-one discussions, executive roundtables, skip-level interviews, frequent department meetings, and the Speak Up process. We measure the results of these processes, identify trends, determine causes, and develop action plans to improve satisfaction. Examples of recent actions we took as part of this process include constructing a new building and parking lot, purchasing additional ergonomic furniture, and restricting smoking.

4.5.f. Trends in Key Indicators: As measured by the percent of favorable responses to six key opinion survey questions in 1989, morale for nonmanagers in Rochester rose again and remained the highest of all 17 IBM manufacturing and development locations. Management morale also rose and was the third highest. The external survey comparisons indicate that IBM's morale versus other companies surveyed was 6% higher for managers and 8% higher for nonmanagers. When responding to the opinion survey questions asking employees to rate their satisfaction with working for IBM, Rochester employees consistently respond more favorably than the corporate average for IBM manufacturing and development sites (fig. 4-10).

Safety: In each of the past 10 years, we received the Minnesota Safety Council's Award of Honor. Over the past five years, our OSHA incident rate has been approximately 40% of the electronics industry average (fig. 6-19).

Attendance and Turnover: In 1989, our employees had an absence rate of 2.4%. Normalized to the Bureau of National Affairs (BNA) criteria, our absence rate for the past three years has not exceeded 1.3%, compared with the 2.5% median absence rate for companies with more than 2500 employees. Our employee turnover rate has not exceeded 1.1% for the past three years, compared with the BNA median of 9.6%.

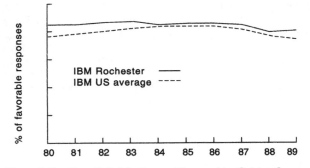

Figure 4-10. Overall Satisfaction as Measured by Opinion Survey.

5. Quality Assurance of Products and Services

Our market-driven process is designed to exceed customer expectations by delivering high-quality products in a dramatically reduced cycle time.

5.1. Design and Introduction of Quality Products and Services

Quality assurance spans our entire process illustrated in figure 5-1 (see p. 264). We accomplish this by:

- Integrating planning, marketing, service, development, and manufacturing functions into the process
- Involving customers and suppliers continuously in planning for, validating, and introducing products
- Preventing defects in all parts of our business
- Improving processes continually

5.1.a. Converting Needs and Expectations to Requirements: **1** To confirm our understanding of our customers' expectations, we analyze information from several sources including customer councils, visits, surveys, business partners, and from our marketing groups. For details about our customer requirements process, see item 7.1.a.

2 As a first step in defining product and service specifications, we translate customer expectations into requirements using critical success factor matrices.

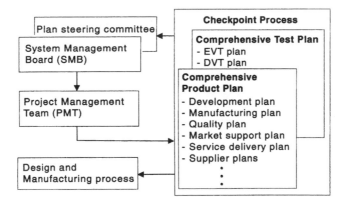

Figure 5-2.   Project Management Process.

Next, we use input from conjoint analysis studies, Analytic Hierarchical Processes (item 3.1.a., AHP), and financial business models to determine requirement priorities. Through Quality Function Deployment (QFD) techniques, we identify key requirements and match these requirements to the best available technologies. **3** We use the results of this

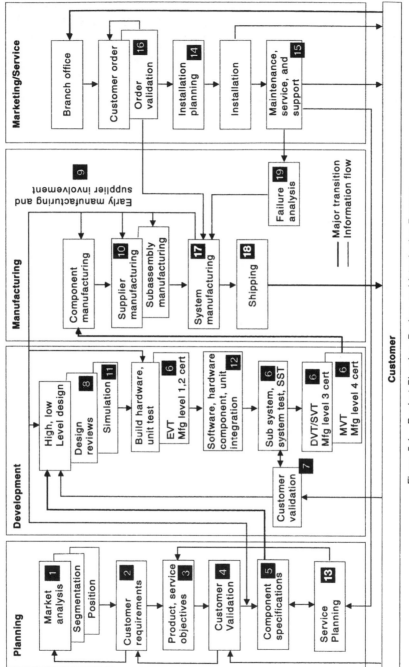

Figure 5-1. Product Planning, Design, and Introduction Process.

analysis to develop detailed product, process, and service objectives. Customers review, provide feedback and recommendations, and validate that the objectives meet their needs **4** .

5 Using matrix chart techniques, we systematically set system-level performance, reliability, cost, and service objectives. We use our knowledge of how each component affects the system to break down the product, process, and service objectives into component-level objectives. Design teams, comprised of cross-functional representatives, use proven design tools and languages to convert the component objectives into specifications.

5.1.b. Quality Assurance in the Design, Development, and Validation Process:
Figure 5 2 illustrates our process for quality assurance in design, development, and validation. Based on specifications, teams of experienced planners write detailed plans for designing, validating, developing, testing, marketing, and servicing a product. We combine over 20 detailed plans into the Comprehensive Product Plan (CPP). We use that plan, along with the Comprehensive Test Plan (CTP), and the checkpoint process to manage the product development cycle. The CTP includes the following design and manufacturing assessments: **6**

- Engineering Verification Test (EVT)—Verifies the hardware design; manufacturing process certification levels 1 and 2
- Software System Test (SST)—Verifies the software design
- Design Verification Test (DVT)—Verifies that the product as designed can be manufactured; manufacturing process certification level 3
- Manufacturing Verification Test (MVT)—Verifies that the production processes can produce the product at the necessary quality and volume levels; manufacturing process certification level 4
- Serviceability Verification Test (SVT)—Verifies that the product will meet its serviceability specifications

At each checkpoint, our manufacturing quality engineering team ensures that the certification criteria are met and our Rochester Systems Product Assurance (RSPA) team assesses design and schedule risks.

The plan steering committee controls the CPP, and any change requires System Management Board (SMB) approval. The Project Management Team (PMT) uses the CPP to manage product introduction and ensure schedules and specifications are met.

7 Throughout the planning and product development process, we review our progress with customers to ensure that our plans meet their requirements. At customer councils, held 10 times per year, we present our plans and solicit feedback. We modify our process and plans based on this feedback. During the planning and development of the AS/400 system, customers and business partners representing over 4500 establishments worldwide participated in these councils.

8 Before we begin to code or build a component, cross-functional teams conduct formal design reviews. These teams examine the design to ensure it meets all quality, function, performance, reliability, service, health, safety, and environmental objectives. They also look for potential problems that could lead to customer dissatisfaction, process upsets, or inaccurate measurements. The review team formally documents all problems and identifies the responsible owner. Each problem is tracked until it is resolved.

265

Validation: **6** We evaluate design quality and the progress of manufacturing process certification at a series of key internal validation checkpoints (EVT, DVT, SST, SVT, MVT). At each checkpoint, the design is verified and the manufacturing process is certified at a level that reflects the maturity of the product.

As we validate our products, our customers validate the conversion of their requirements into our products. We enlist our business partners (value added retailers and industry remarketers) to assist in the development and validation of key software functions. For example, through our Early Support Program (item 7.6.a., ESP), the MARCAM company received a prototype AS/400 system six months after we started development.

Feasibility Assessments: **9** Our Early Manufacturing Involvement (EMI) teams of cross-functional experts assess the feasibility of producing our products at the beginning of the design process. Through EMI we ensure that production and supplier process improvements are integrated into the design of a product. We also ensure that preparation for production stays on schedule. Manufacturing and development teams work together to identify opportunities for simplifying their processes. We reduced the complexity of the part logistics management process for the AS/400 system by 50% compared to the previous process. We identify critical process steps and insert SPC points. In our latest 3.5-inch hard disk product, 18 test operations, 21 parts, and 11 processes have been identified for SPC by using fishbone diagraming. We continuously assess the feasibility of producing our design through common verification and assessment checkpoints.

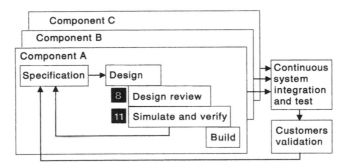

Figure 5-3.   Continuous Integration of Component Quality.

5.1.c.(1) Selecting and Controlling Key Process Characteristics: Based on our quality priorities (item 3.3.a.) we select key process characteristics that improve requirements planning, defect prevention, product reliability, and supplier performance. Based on knowledge of our customers' requirements, our current processes, and our tools, we select and set those key process characteristics to be controlled that minimize sources of variability.

We establish two levels of process characteristics, operational and intrinsic. An operational characteristic is indirectly controllable and an intrinsic characteristic is directly controllable through statistical measures and techniques.

- An example of an operational process characteristic is early and continuous customer and supplier involvement
- An example of an intrinsic process characteristic is defect prevention

We have a control plan and proactive management system with a clear set of decision priorities: quality, schedule, function, and cost.

Customer Involvement: 2,4,7 We invite customers to review our designs and evaluate our products throughout the development cycle. During development of the AS/400 system, over 250 customers participated in these reviews. Through early customer involvement, we stabilize our requirements and minimize variability.

Supplier Involvement: 18 We involve key suppliers as partners early in the development cycle to participate in our quality improvement initiatives, and contribute to reduced cycle times.

Defect Prevention: We systematically build defect prevention into our process by:

- Empowering People—Employees participate in setting our goals, objectives, and priorities (item 4.2.). They have authority to make decisions about their jobs. Management's role is to manage the process.
- Investing in Tools 11 —We invest substantially in developing tools to support our processes and are now working on the next generation of tools that will support more quality improvements (item 3.3.b.).
- Getting Involved Early—We integrate all functions into the development process, and ensure that decisions account for the requirements of all groups. Our processes require early involvement with development by the following organizations:
    - Worldwide manufacturing operations
    - Marketing/Service
    - Industry application developers
    - Site support services
- Designing Robust Products—Our products meet worldwide, total product life requirements.

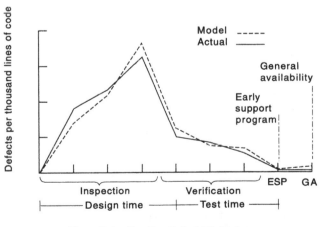

Figure 5-4.   Tracking Defect Elimination.

12 By validating the quality and performance of each component before integrating it into the system, we shorten system test and debug time and ensure a higher quality product. Figure 5-3 shows the component quality process.

Control Plan and Proactive Management System: Our process has four levels of quality assurance control:

- Operational-level control by component developers, team leaders, and first-line managers
- System design control
- Management control by the PMT, and the SMB
- Independent audits/peer reviews

Operational-Level Control: To ensure component quality, all of our organizations exercise continuous, day-to-day control. As a result, the higher level control tasks are much easier. Figure 5-4 is an AS/400 control chart typical of those used by developers and managers to track removal of software defects against models.

System Design Control: Detailed implementation plans aimed at bringing together all of the various elements of the product and service design are the responsibility of the product managers. They focus on solving problems that occur during integration of multiple engineering and programming components. They are responsible for ensuring the system meets the entry requirements of various test phases ⬛6 , and that the product and service features satisfy the product plans.

Management Control: The PMT represents all functions. It ensures that the checkpoint process requirements in the comprehensive IBM Development Guide are met. This process identifies a series of key checkpoints, which have review and evaluation requirements, as well as strict entry and exit criteria. The SMB meets biweekly to review progress, resolve major issues, and approve any plan changes.

Independent Audits and Peer Reviews: In addition to our process controls, we reinforce quality assurance by using audits and peer reviews (item 5.4.).

5.1.c.(2) Service Process Control: Our service objectives are to provide 100% on-time product delivery and industry leading system reliability to our customers. To meet these objectives, we automate our order and delivery process, design our products for easy field upgrades, choose highly reliable components, and design problem analysis, isolation, and resolution capability into our products. We use the same process and validation checkpoints for controlling service and delivery design as we do for products.

Service Characteristics as an Integral Part of Product Design: ⬛13,14 We integrate service and delivery characteristics into our products during the development process using the same control systems associated with hardware and software. Requirements for service simplicity have produced hardware designs that are rugged, easy to install and keyed to prevent incorrect assembly. We design self-diagnostic features into our products to reduce repair time. We verify the order process at key checkpoints ⬛6 with a set of tests and measurements that ensure we meet our objectives. To simplify the order and delivery processes we offer a Total System Package (TSP) which consolidates all hardware, software, and documentation into a single package.

Measures of Service Parameters: Our objective is to prevent disruptions to our customers' business. We establish measures of service performance (fig. 6-7) to compare to our objective and take action to improve.

Service Planning: Service and delivery planning starts at the beginning of the development process with plans for training customer support personnel. We estimate the people and equipment required (the Service Cost Estimate [SCE]) to meet service performance goals by projecting service measures such as repair actions, maintenance parts costs, and repair time. This forms the Service Cost Estimate (fig. 2-2, SCE). Monthly tracking of service performance against our plans ensures timely process control. `15`

5.1.d. Minimizing Introduction Time: The major process improvements that we have made to minimize introduction time are described below.

Simplifying our Process: We eliminated process steps that previously required manual conversion of information. New development tools, such as VHDL (item 1.4.b.), logic synthesis, object oriented programming, and programmer workbenches have eliminated routine translation between conceptual and detailed design.

Introducing New Tools for Defect Prevention in Design: By preventing defects in design, we reduced our software development cycles by 35%. We have implemented sophisticated development tools, such as the Engineering Verification Engine (EVE), to simulate and evaluate the design of hardware components and subsystems *before* building them. On the AS/400 project, initial prototype systems were operational in one-sixth the time of previous systems. Our manufacturing team built 40 systems for our programming team's use 10 months earlier than had been previously possible.

Integrating Customers and Suppliers into the Development Process: `2,4,7` Through customers participating in product planning (item 7.1.), we stabilize requirements, thereby preventing major design modifications, and achieve shorter development cycles. We engage suppliers at the beginning of our development processes and work with them to implement our joint quality initiatives.

Automating Transfer of Design Data Worldwide: In order to achieve our business objective of simultaneous worldwide product availability, we use common worldwide databases and logistic systems to eliminate the time required to convert data and reduce the possibility of errors. These systems and databases enable critical product and process control data to be automatically distributed to manufacturing locations and suppliers worldwide. See figure 2-2 for descriptions of Engineering Design Systems (EDS), Enterprise Materials Logistics System (EMLS), Development Production Records System (DPRS), CADAM and CATIA (engineering design and analysis tools), and other data systems.

5.2. Process and Quality Control

5.2.a. Process Control: We systematically *design* control into our production processes. Our EMI teams develop manufacturing process requirements during the initial stages of product design and development. These requirements are translated into specifications and measures by our manufacturing process design teams. We use an online system to convert design data into manufacturing process control limits and to collect data at critical stages in our process. We use this data and statistical process control techniques to control performance within preset limits, and take action if we observe any process irregularities. Our techniques for controlling processes are described below.

Translation of Design and Customer Data: We use the automated data translation features of our online Manufacturing Control System (MCS) to prevent defects. This eliminates the misinterpretation of specifications and the miscoding of manually entered data. Product consistency across the world is assured since every location uses the same data source. **16** Customers' orders from branch offices are validated using an AI order configurator (item 2.1.c.), transmitted to the appropriate manufacturing location, and used by the MCS to control and verify the system assembly process and load the software. This has saved thousands of hours of manual effort, and has improved cycle times.

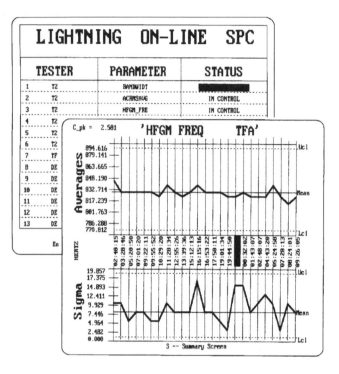

Figure 5-5. Online SPC Screens. Our operators view key control parameters and detailed history.

Computer Integrated Manufacturing: **17** We integrate our component production lines, subassembly production lines, and final assembly and ship areas using the MCS. The production process and test equipment calibration and specification is monitored and controlled, and each assembly is tracked by serial number.

Statistical Process Control (SPC): We use SPC to identify and prevent potential process upsets. Operators monitor which parameters need attention (fig. 5-5), select the parameter, observe its history, and take action.

5.2.b. Assurance: We assure our products and services through comprehensive specifications for developing test processes, service plans, and performance goals. Hourly tests and measurements in production, and regular service performance measurements are compared to projections. We review our product and service assurance processes through regular audits and manage improvements with our change control process.

Test processes: EMI teams establish test plans that specify limits for product and service performance. To assure consistency, we use unique test software that rigorously tests system interfaces and devices much more thoroughly than using a standard operating system. We test successive levels of assemblies, throughout the production process, starting with parts and partial assemblies. We bring all of the hardware and software elements of the customer's system together before shipment, load all programs, and test every system against its specifications. We then ship the complete, preloaded package to customers ▮18▮ to improve their ease of installation (item 6.1.a., Trends in Delivery Time, TSP).

Audits: We use audits to supplement our product assurance and service measurement processes. Each week, an audit of five system assemblies is completed, testing them for 100 hours and looking for any sign of early product life problems. Radio frequency emissions of our products are audited to ensure they conform to national standards. We audit service measurements such as repair time and compare them to goals, correcting any adverse trends. Results are fed back to improve processes, specifications, or plans.

Change Control: We use our automated change control process to review and validate the impact of any change on other processes. Changes are implemented after approval from our quality, service, development, manufacturing, and finance teams.

5.2.c. Measurement Quality: To ensure quality, we establish and document measurement requirements for products and services, certify equipment against national standards, and control accuracy through regularly scheduled calibrations.

Requirements Established and Documented: We establish and internally publish requirements for the accuracy and frequency of service data collected, which is used to monitor our performance. We define and document requirements for precision, limits, and acceptable bias parameters of key measurements. We qualify measurement systems as part of the MVT level 4 certification and then cross-correlate related measurements to validate our equipment. Owners are informed online of any calibration required to control the accuracy of our equipment.

Equipment Certification: Our calibration lab, tool and test equipment lab, systems assurance lab, material lab, and Statistical Competency Center calibrate tools and test equipment and measurements for accuracy. National Institute of Science and Technology (NIST), UL, CSA and other standards are used for calibration. We calibrate and test over 800 frequency-based instruments by using the HP5061A Cesium Beam Frequency National Standard. Output data is compared, using a receiver-comparator system, to WWVB. Where test instruments are used for critical measurements of key processes, stability is established during an annual calibration. As other instruments are installed, stability is verified and reviewed on request thereafter.

Process Measurements: Control measurements, such as solder temperature and humidity, and statistical measurements, such as the number tested versus failed, are two types of process measurements tracked. As process elements approach control limits, statistical measurements are validated through audits, before taking other actions.

5.2.d. Root Cause Determination: To ensure that the precise source of the problem or upset is found so that preventative action can be taken, we use root cause analysis that consists of part traceability, process analysis, and failure analysis.

Traceability: We design traceability into all processes that produce our products. We track production date, process steps, the tools used for assembly, and the origination of the part for key parts of an assembly. Service, production process, and SPC measurement data is analyzed, using Pareto techniques, to identify trends in types and frequency of failures.

Process Analysis: Data is collected on parts conformance and tools performance for critical production processes. SPC data trends in one process step are compared to those in another step. This comparison identifies the effect of change in one step that may influence follow-on operations. Statistical techniques, such as design of experiments, are used to isolate the root cause of a process upset. In software development we monitor defect rates and compare them to models. When we observe a deviation, we use Pareto methods to determine major categories of problems and take corrective action.

Failure Analysis: **19** Material analysis labs, Auger analysis equipment, and scanning electron microscopes are used to analyze returned parts to identify the source of the problem. Our analysis continues until the cause of an upset is identified and the action required to prevent it is identified and taken.

5.2.e. Approaches for Correcting Process Upsets: When we encounter process upsets, we take immediate action to protect our customers from interruptions to their businesses. We determine the source and cause of a process upset or problem and take corrective action to prevent it from reoccurring. If analysis calls for lengthy corrective action, short-term measures are designed to contain the upset.

Preventive Based Action: To prevent process upsets, we take actions to redesign our products, change component sources, or utilize new tools. We team up with our suppliers to correct problems by developing a better process or by redesigning the part. Additional tools are used if capacity is a problem, or replacement tools are installed to handle reliability upsets. If failure analysis indicates usage or environmental design deficiencies, we redesign the product to meet the new requirements. New measures verify that actions are having their intended result. Process recertification and product change regression tests confirm product and process quality improvements.

Containment Actions: The production process is stopped, and inspections are introduced to detect problems in the product until corrective design, tool, or process improvement can be implemented. Tool owners are immediately notified of the need to increase calibration frequency. Documentation is updated and employees responsible for improving the process step are taught new equipment operation procedures. We assign employees with the correct skills to improve process operations.

Locations worldwide that design or produce similar products are immediately informed of an upset in a process. Root cause analyses and corrective plans are communicated to the appropriate locations and organizations. To prevent upsets, alternate component usage, equipment requirements, and assumptions about process operation are reviewed. We disseminate analysis data and improvements through technical reports and Interdivisional Technical Liaison (ITL) conferences.

5.2.f. Using Information for Improvement: We compare information (fig. 2-2) obtained from process control to models, projections, and our goals to identify any action required for quality improvement.

Continuous Focus on Improvement: Information from IDSS (item 2.1.c.), the primary data source for software analysis, is reviewed with developers at regular meetings to compare quality goals and current performance. We use these results to project future quality performance of our products. Opportunities to improve are initiated early enough in our development cycle to have significant impact before our product reaches our customer. EMI teams maintain and analyze process upset databases to improve future product designs and processes.

Throughout the production process, equipment and part parameters are fed back to the MCS and are continuously monitored against preset upper and lower limit specifications, usually more stringent than the product specifications. If we determine that the process or equipment parameters are shifting toward an out of conformance condition, operators are notified and take preventative action.

Lessons Learned: At the completion of major checkpoints, we review our processes, their results, and goals to prepare our teams for the next process cycle. We identify successful techniques and areas for improvement. We prioritize and assess the feasibility of these improvements and modify plans for the next product cycle accordingly.

Root-cause analysis, based on long-term data collected and correlated across critical processes, leads to significant improvements and dramatically reduced cycle times. Correlation between different phases of our process is used to optimize each individual phase and the process as a whole. Using these techniques, our circuit card assembly process was streamlined: 25% more volume capability was achieved, 11 inspection stations were eliminated, 60% of defects were prevented from moving downstream, first pass card yields were improved from 75% to 89%, and cycle time through the card process was reduced from 25 days to two days.

5.3. Continuous Improvement of Processes, Products and Services

5.3.a. Continuous Improvement Opportunities: Benchmarking is key in defining new quality improvement opportunities. Comparing our current performance to benchmarks, we constantly raise our goals, and identify opportunities to improve our products, services, and processes.

Benchmarking: New product announcements and superior process performance by any company are opportunities to learn new improvement techniques. We use these opportunities to expand our benchmark base. New technology leaders emerge regularly and we study their characteristics too, such as level of technology integration, the extent of product redesign from one generation to the next, or their disclosure of breakthrough techniques through technical papers or conferences.

Soliciting Customer Input: Customer recommendations are evaluated and become improvement initiatives throughout our processes. Customers who are either new users of our products and services or who are expanding the use of our products into new areas provide feedback on additional environments that set new expectations and require us to improve our products and services.

Assessment of Our Current Processes: Each process has a management owner who is responsible for and committed to improving the process. The owner establishes measures that quantify the process' capability and focuses on continually finding new measures, raising goals, reducing cycle time, and improving customer satisfaction. Product cycles are followed by extensive analysis that assess areas of improvement identified in the previous cycle. We concentrate on improving those steps of the process that currently require human interaction or interpretation and seek new tools or methods that simplify the process and eliminate the possibility of errors.

Evaluating Technology Capabilities: We look for the best technology available to improve our products, processes, and services. We compare IBM technology, benchmark competitive products, and fund research at universities. These activities identify alternatives offering improvements in cycle time, cost, reliability or service delivery which are evaluated against our quality objectives and, if feasible, integrated into products, processes, or services. The AS/400 processor design team assessed and implemented new chip technology and reduced the amount of electronics by two thirds when compared to the System 38.

5.3.b. Optimizing Process Characteristics: To ensure continual process optimization, we:

- Use advanced information systems to provide us with current data about our processes
- Focus on using the most advanced manufacturing technologies
- Empower individual employees by giving them total responsibility
- Use recognized statistical techniques

MCS: We optimize our processes by using the MCS as the central control point for our production facility. It monitors inventory, cycle time, and quality levels, provides tracking information, avoids duplicate data collection, and is used by process owners for instantaneous analysis of their data.

Technology Selection: Our process controllers are designed with state-of-the-art technology to obtain optimal reliability and availability from our manufacturing process. Our production line is designed with redundant cells so that it rarely stops because of a single cell failure. We use a pull system in manufacturing as part of our continuous flow manufacturing implementation to simplify process management.

Individual Assignments: Process owners take total responsibility for specific measurements and key process parameters. They ensure constant attention to process performance, and continually look for ways to optimize the process.

Use of Statistical Techniques: We use exploratory data analysis, design of experiments techniques, and response surface analysis, to identify and optimize parameters that affect the production of our products and services. We are currently using design of experiments to optimize the design of critical mechanical assemblies. Our analysis has identified variables (such as the velocity and force that an alignment assembly uses to position hard disk platters) that effect hard disk edge scratching and marking due to tool contact.

5.3.c. Verifying Improvements: After opportunities for improvement are identified, we evaluate their feasibility, set goals, and develop plans to implement them. We use measurements, analysis, and our checkpoint process to confirm the results of the improvements. We assess potential process upsets and verify that improvements will not adversely affect any current processes. We confirm that our expectations are met through ongoing monitoring of processes, recertification of improved processes, and engineering change regression tests on products.

Once a change is implemented, we confirm our expected results using SPC measurements and other process tracking indicators. We recertify key production processes that are changed including processes modified by our suppliers. Design changes are verified through extensive regression tests which confirm original objectives or validate new ones. Major product changes introduced during or after one of the checkpoint tests, EVT, DVT, MVT, or SVT, 6 may require that we repeat key parts of the test.

We use process measurements such as cycle time to indicate when improvements reach their expected results. On the AS/400 system, software updates are distributed through our Electronic Customer Support (item 2.2.c., ECS) product and are installed by our customers. We used benchmarking and assessment of our current upgrade process to identify a number of ways to reduce the installation time of software updates. By optimizing our process, we cut the installation time in half and reduced the amount of verification data by 97%. We have since established new installation time goals of a 20% reduction in 1990, and a 50% reduction in 1991. This initiative minimizes customer disruptions and improves satisfaction.

5.3.d. Integrating Continuous Improvement: We integrate continuous improvement by adjusting targets in our processes, improving process design to handle change and reduce cycle time, and transferring knowledge throughout the company.

Adjusting Targets: After we achieve stability and sustained performance in a process, we reestablish new, more aggressive process limits. In hard disk production, we improve our key quality indicator limit by 10% after three months of on-target performance.

Designing Flexible Processes: Our processes, in addition to being well defined and repeatable, are flexible and adaptable. No process is considered permanent or unchangeable. Our announcement process has been continuously improved by involving our marketing and service teams earlier in the preparation of announcement material, and by using a tool called a customer value matrix, which optimizes our announcement documentation by making it easier for the customer to find key product changes.

Transferring Knowledge: We use information from process improvements to standardize and implement changes worldwide. New process techniques are communicated among our implementation teams, assuring effective integration. Manufacturing quality action teams hold daily meetings, share performance results of the previous day's production, and act on improvement suggestions. International assignees in Rochester communicate process or technology improvements to their home locations, assuring consistent worldwide implementation. By participating in the development process, service interns use their acquired knowledge to educate teams at their branch locations. Quality action teams in development review process measurements, formulate plans to improve their quality measures by implementing new tools or techniques, and assign responsibility for learning what other teams across the company are doing for quality improvement. Worldwide quality reviews share process initiatives implemented in the previous quarter.

5.4. Quality Assessment

5.4.a. Assessing Quality: Our approaches to assess quality, quality systems, and quality practices are internal and external audits. Using audits, we ensure that our products, processes, and services are properly controlled, meet expected results, and are continuously improved. Audits are performed, with teams evaluating audit results against government, product, legal, and ethical standards. Recommendations and actions from key audits are tracked and reported quarterly to the Rochester Management Committee (item 1.3.c.).

We compare our audit tools and services with other IBM locations and outside agencies. Before a peer review, teams evaluate their checklists for accuracy and pertinence to the review. As new audit tools are deployed, the audience, application, and results expected from the use of the tool are reviewed with the audit tool developer to ensure that it is suitable and effective for our intended application.

5.4.b. Types of Assessments: RSPA, Business Controls, and Corporate Internal Audit are our primary internal product and service auditing groups. RSPA is involved from design to customer operation, providing independent quality assessments in all major product and process areas. RSPA also provides a customer's view of the product and its delivery. Figure 5-6 illustrates additional system, product and service quality audits.

System Audits: System and procedure audits assess the efficiency and effectiveness of our quality assurance processes, product service mechanisms, and quality and business controls by having internal and external experts review our operations in detail.

Our business process is audited by external firms such as Price Waterhouse, and A. T. Hudson. The Stanford Research Institute International audit compared our software development processes with those used by 17 others in our industry and concluded that we had the most advanced programming process.

Product Audits: Product audits assess the quality of our hardware and software products. We submit our product to independent labs and national agencies to receive certification before general availability. Customers help us review our products by providing regular input at user group meetings or by returning comment forms on specific aspects of our business such as documentation quality.

Service Audits: RSPA assesses service plans and the service design at development checkpoints. Regular service process audits are performed by business controls and Corporate Internal Audit. We compare monthly service performance measurements against our goals, correlate the comparisons to external customer satisfaction surveys, and take action.

5.4.c. Translating to Action: Our process for translating the findings of audits into improvements consists of the following steps.

Documenting the Findings: We document all audit findings and include a summary of the control status, any major positive points, issues, or recommended improvements. Each issue or improvement item contains a description of the facts to support the findings, and the severity (only with issues). We then present these findings to the audited areas.

Auditor (Frequency)	Type of Review
Internal	
Rochester employees (continuous)	Functional process self-audits
RSPA (continuous)	Hardware, software, service, manufacturing support and customer view assurance
System test team	Final test on the system using customer-like configurations
Procurement team (at least annually)	Suppliers' quality
Business Controls (continuous)	Process controls, procedures, and effectiveness
IBM (corporation)	
Peer reviews (qrtly)	Functional support systems
Readiness reviews (as required)	Conformance to Comprehensive Product Plan
IBM early internal users (each upgrade)	System and service
Corporate audits (yrly.)	Functional systems & procedures
External (non-IBM)	
Price Waterhouse (annual)	Finance, accounting practices
U.S. Government (annual or as needed)	EEO, OSHA (safety/health), Security
State Government (annual)	Hazardous waste Safety
Stanford Research Institute (one time)	Software development processes
A.T. Hudson (as needed)	Administrative services
Customers (ongoing)	Order processing, billing, service
UL, VDE, CSA National Test Labs (each upgrade)	Product safety
Customer (each upgrade)	Early Support and pilot programs audit of products and service
Contracted test groups (each upgrade)	Comprehensive Test Plan

Figure 5-6. Examples of System, Product, and Service Audits.

Assigning Responsibility for Action: We establish and agree upon new goals, a plan, and a review schedule with the audit team and process owner. Using facts from the audit, the owner assigns detailed process analyses to be done to determine the root cause of the problem. Owners evaluate recommendations to improve processes and deploy education plans to ensure proper awareness and interpretation of the changes.

Implementing the Improvement: We review and agree upon the action plan, including any new measures, with our suppliers and customers. We agree upon final approval to close an audit issue with the review team. When suggested improvements are made to a small area, we communicate and teach on-the-job. When larger process improvements are made, we communicate them through department or area meetings.

Reassess Corrective Actions: We review key audit findings and follow-up to ensure that corrective actions are completed. After we implement a change, we maintain close measurements and surveillance. Audit reviews remain open until we demonstrate improvement.

5.4.d. Improvement Verification: Our improvement plans guide us in setting goals to assess our success in addressing audit results. We continually compare process or product parameters to these goals to verify our improvement objectives. Our subsequent reviews, audits, or certification plans ensure that we achieve predicted results by concentrating on issues from prior audits. We publish audit results and action plans to ensure consistent implementation.

5.5. Documentation

5.5.a. Documentation System: To ensure consistency of our product and process quality worldwide, we use a comprehensive and consolidated documentation system to preserve and transfer information instantaneously. An integral part of every process, our documentation system uses consistent formats and offers instantaneous access. We are continuously adding more of our documentation to online libraries to improve access to information and ensure that the latest versions are always available. This enables quality assessments from any audit or review to be updated immediately and shared worldwide. Since specifications, plans, and standardized processes are developed and maintained in an online documentation control library (item 2.1.c., IDSS), a design document can be updated in Rochester and, within minutes, be available to a component developer in our Hursley, England, laboratory.

Our documentation system also provides a complete, comprehensive base for educating and training new employees, ranging from online course schedules, abstracts, and enrollment to online process documentation about how to record their timecards. Figure 5-7 lists some of the major types of quality assurance documentation we use to define products, procedures, measurements, and standards.

5.5.b. Timely Updates and Documentation Disposal: Our online documentation system is interactive and dynamic. Updates are made quickly and easily and users are electronically notified as soon as a new level of the document is available. Our Corporate Information System and Administration (CISA) tool gives every employee access to a growing online database of national standards, corporate directives, and guidelines. In addition to the technical vitality seminars (item 4.2.c.), technical reports and memorandums on the latest technological advances and trends are available in our worldwide documentation database. Our corporate retention guidelines clearly specify data retention and disposal periods for all documentation. Vital information (for example, the latest technology specifications, designs, personnel data, and process documentation) that need to be recovered in case of a disaster is stored in vaulted salt mines in Kansas.

Employee   ***
  Personnel systems* for   Education courses*,
    salary and performance   schedules*, abstracts*
Planning
  Comprehensive product plan*   Customer requirements
  Business planning   Quality plans*
Development
  Development guide*   Reliability & engineering
  Quality plan*   specifications*
  Design & process info   Assurance test & problem
    on IDSS*   log*
Manufacturing & Purchasing
  Test & process specs*   Mfg & supplier procedures
  Bill of materials & routing*   Component quality
  Certification/quality plans*   assurance system
Marketing & Service
  Authorized program   Sales procedures
    analysis report* (APAR)   Diagnostic manuals
  Technical bulletins   Newsletters
Customer
  User guides & references   Question & answer (Q & A
  System-delivered educ*   database)*
  Installation video   COMMON presentations
Corporate Standards
  Corporate Standards index*   CIs and directives*
Industry & Gov't Req'ts
  NIST   Canadian Standards Assn
  U/L   OSHA procedures
Site Operations
  Operating procedures*   Chemical control system*
  Management memos*   Quality control video
Note: Asterisks indicate online documents.

Figure 5-7.   Examples of Documentation Types.

5.5.c. Accessibility: We assess the responsiveness of our documentation system to both internal and external customers and continuously improve and expand the content and capabilities of the system. Our information is updated and verified instantaneously through worldwide networks of data systems that assure the best response and access possible. We use advanced computer communication networks and provide systems support 24 hours a day, seven days a week, to enable electronic conversations (fig. 2-2, conferencing disks) between employees worldwide. Our office system (PROFS) uses the latest technology to provide electronic messages and documents, calendars, and access to databases. From their computer workstations, our customers use AS/400 online education, search product documentation, access IBM question and answer databases, and share information with other customers through our ECS network. This improved access and new modes of sharing documentation are effective ways to closely monitor customer needs and environments throughout the world.

5.6. Quality Assurance, Quality Assessment, and Quality Improvement of Support Services and Business Processes

5.6.a. Principal Means for Quality Assurance: Figure 5-8 lists functions that directly support our products and that provide services to all site organizations.

Product Support Functions	Internal Support Functions
System Evaluation, RSPA	Facilities Mgmt and Security
Performance Evaluation	Education
Usability Evaluation	Legal services
Translation	Finance and Accounting
Marketing	Communication Services
Integration/Build	Personnel
Service	Administrative Support
Distribution	Tools & Test Equipment
Plant Management	Information Services

Figure 5-8.   Rochester Product Support and Internal Support Functions.

Our method to assure the quality of our support services and business processes is to assign an owner to manage each process. Owners gather customer requirements, set standards, design our processes, and continually review their performance against our standards. They are responsible for assessing, controlling, and improving their processes. They translate employee (our internal customers') requirements into objectives, improvement plans, and quality measures. Process documentation, measurements, and analyses are used to ensure that our product and internal services support our quality priorities. The process owner manages (keeping standards in mind) by using the method illustrated in figure 5-9.

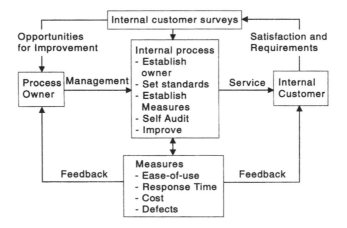

Figure 5-9.   Process Management to Improve Quality.

Gathering Requirements: Our employee opinion survey (item 4.2.b.) questions, internal customer advisory councils, and process specific surveys are used to analyze supplier service-level satisfaction and collect process improvement requirements. Employees analyze survey results, review process improvement action plans, and feedback comments.

Process Design: In process design, we use our internal customer performance expectations to set standards and measures of service. Each process is assessed by comparing the service-level performance to our standards.

Functional Self-Audits: Self-audits are used to supplement our internal measures. Internal customer and process owner teams analyze our processes and identify quality improvement opportunities. Owners modify their processes and update process documentation. Figure 5-10 summarizes examples of nonproduct process assessment results.

Process	Frequency	Type	Results
Chemical control	Continuous	Site/gov't	60% warehouse space reduction
Information processing capacity and performance	Daily	Self-mgmt	Tripled programmer productivity Compile time improvement from 4 hours to 5 minutes
Fixed asset control	50% annually	Site	26% improvement in accuracy
Education functional reviews	Annual	Site	More accurate education plan
Reproduction services	Bi-Weekly	Site	62% output increase/$126K saved
Furniture repair requests	Annual	Self	Saved 730 hours per year
Corporate Education Network	Annual	Site	Saved $240,000 per year in travel expenses

Figure 5-10. Examples of Nonproduct Process Assessment and Improvement.

5.6.b. Continuous Improvement: Process owners continually identify differences in service performance between their current levels and levels expected by their customers. We use the following methods to improve our service levels.

Identifying Opportunity and Setting Goals: We compare our support services to leading companies and establish benchmarks. Process measurements are compared to these benchmarks and opportunities for improvements are identified. Owners of support service processes meet regularly with their internal customers to understand new requirements. The process owner sets goals to raise standards based on:

- Customer requirements
- Benchmarks set from similar support services at all IBM locations and other companies
- Applicable laws and governmental requirements and standards
- Acceptable professional and ethical practices
- Corporate guidelines

Implementation: We improve service levels to meet our customers' requirements, adjust processes to correct upsets, and add measures to accurately reflect our customers' satisfaction. Our customer order processing team used the results of a survey of competitive processes to modify their product introduction process for new announcements and improved their cycle time by 20%.

Verifying Improvement: We continually measure our performance and compare our data to benchmarks to meet increased customer requirements. We periodically review our benchmark sources for accuracy. Goals are reviewed as requested by the customer or at least annually.

5.6.c. Improving Participation: In order to achieve our cycle time quality priorities, all aspects of our business focus on process management. Our strategy is to broaden the base of our quality assurance and improvement comparisons in our support services and business processes. As stated in item 3.2.c., we are benchmarking industry-leading quality systems and are implementing new techniques and initiatives aimed at total quality improvement across our business. Current efforts and plans to enhance participation include:

Expanding Benchmarking: We are expanding nonproduct benchmarking in our support and business process areas. Exchanges with leading companies that have similar support organizations help us to compare our service levels, and establish new industry leading improvement goals. We are currently assessing total quality systems of leading companies and implementing new goals and methods based on our findings.

Internal Customer Councils: Our support organizations have initiated advisory councils comprised of internal customers. These councils provide feedback and suggestions to our administrative and service functions much as our external customers do in their advisory councils. The result is a more customer driven view of the needs of our internal organizations.

5.7. Quality Assurance, Quality Assessment and Quality Improvement of Suppliers

5.7.a. Supplier Assurance Process: Our goal is to develop full-service suppliers who demonstrate that they have the capability to insure defect free purchases from their suppliers. Our procurement strategy has progressed toward acquiring advanced electronic subassemblies. Our suppliers are responsible for total component planning and purchases, as well as assembling complex units. Our approach for assuring supplier quality has four steps, selection and approval, establishing statistical controls, process certification, and regular audits.

Supplier Selection and Approval: All potential suppliers' quality, financial, and business control processes are surveyed to verify their ability to perform to our requirements. Our quality surveys consist of a series of questions relating to the key aspects of a potential supplier's total quality system. Quantitative analysis of the survey findings is compared against benchmarks. Each approved supplier is audited annually for compliance. We select suppliers based on sustained high quality performance and competitive bidding.

Establishing Statistical Controls: We require the use of SPC methods and process capability indices (CPK). Our goals are to achieve 10x improvement in parts per million performance by 1991, and 100x improvement by 1993. We will achieve these quality levels by working with our suppliers on education, early involvement, and through emphasis on the total quality management discipline reflected in the Malcolm Baldrige criteria.

Certifying Processes Producing IBM Units: Our commodity specialists and electronic engineers work closely with suppliers to verify that their key processes are capable of producing required results. Once certified, changes may be incorporated into the process only with our approval.

Audits, Inspections, and Testing: We use the same rigorous set of process reviews with our suppliers that we use internally. We require detailed quality plans from each supplier, defining their processes and assuring that our requirements are met. For complex subassemblies, we hold design reviews and perform the same verification tests (DVT and MVT) that we use internally. We do not *inspect* quality into products. Since our results give us confidence in our supplier selection, approval, certification, and control process, we inspect until five consecutive lots are verified as 100% defect-free. We then reduce inspections to periodic audits.

We regularly audit our suppliers' processes, conduct reliability sampling, and perform aggressive failure analysis. We procure and manage selected major acquired subassemblies, such as flexible disks, tape, hard disks, and their supplies, for the IBM corporation worldwide. In addition to extensive pretesting and test data analysis, we require that our suppliers disassemble tested units and look for any indication of unexpected product wear.

We track quality data for our suppliers in an online database, maintaining a *rolling* 12-month record for every part. Suppliers who do not conform to our standards are identified. We work with them to help recover their performance, or if that fails, we no longer approve them. Figure 5-11 shows an example of a supplier who, after working with us and implementing specific recommendations, demonstrated significant improvement. These recommendations included technology changes and process sequence improvements.

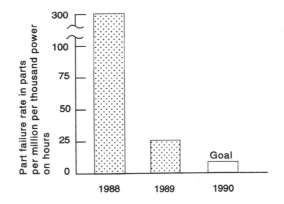

Figure 5-11.   *Example of Supplier Success, 10x Improvement in One Year.*

5.7.b. Improvement Strategy: Our strategy for improving supplier quality is to integrate joint development processes and make suppliers partners with us in our business. Our improvement initiatives are:

- Establishing long-term relationships
- Recognizing exceptional performance
- Offering education on CFM, SPC, and EDI

Selecting Suppliers and Establishing Long-Term Relationships: Using continuous improvement as a theme, we establish long-term relationships with suppliers who continue to demonstrate excellence in service and technology. Figure 5-12 shows our long-term supplier trend.

	Number of Years as IBM Supplier			
	<2	2-5	6-10	>10
% of Suppliers	11%	21%	20%	48%

Figure 5-12.   Years of Partnership with Suppliers.

We select exceptional suppliers to ensure quality and technological leadership in our products. Twenty-seven of our key suppliers have received a total of 88 quality awards from major companies other than IBM. Twenty-four of these suppliers received awards from IBM.

Supplier Recognition and Training: Excellence in supplier performance is recognized through our corporate and local supplier awards programs. Each year, suppliers meeting our defect free objectives are recognized via a corporate award or a local letter of commendation. In 1986, we started a local awards program that complemented our corporate program. In 1988, we gave 36 local awards and 23 corporate awards.

We hold formal meetings twice a year to provide training on SPC techniques and applications, CFM (item 4.3.b.), part profiling techniques, EDI, or other topics as requested. See item 6.4.b. for our supplier education program and results.

We have recently updated our primary supplier control process, corporate specification 216, to help suppliers focus on quality improvements. We require that our key suppliers perform self assessments using the MBNQA guidelines and take action to correct any deficiencies.

Summary: Early and continuous involvement by customers, suppliers, business partners, and all of our internal teams, results in products that exceed our customers' expectations. Our employees' commitment to continuous quality improvement and our emphasis on defect prevention, have improved the quality of our products while dramatically reducing our total cycle time.

6. Quality Results

This category compares our current product family to our previous product family, as well as to other industry and world leaders. Figure 0-3 and figure 0-4 in the Overview show our products that are used in the following discussion.

6.1. Quality of Products and Services

Figure 6-1 identifies the key internal product and service quality measures derived from our customers' view of IBM quality (items 7.7, 7.8). The trends shown in the following pages demonstrate the continuous improvement resulting from our quality priorities (item 3.3.a.). These figures clearly illustrate the results of continually assessing and improving our internal targets.

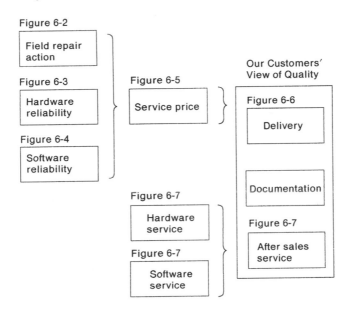

Figure 6-2

> Field repair action

Figure 6-3

> Hardware reliability

Figure 6-4

> Software reliability

Figure 6-5

> Service price

Figure 6-7

> Hardware service

Figure 6-7

> Software service

Our Customers' View of Quality

Figure 6-6

> Delivery

> Documentation

Figure 6-7

> After sales service

Figure 6-1. Key Product and Service Quality Measures.

6.1.a,b. Trends in Field Repair Actions and Preventative Measures: Figure 6-2 shows the dramatic improvement in actual field performance, resulting from our continuous analysis of repair actions and subsequent improvements to hardware and software reliability. This improvement was made across a population of installed machines which is growing at a rate of 20% a year.

In 1988, our field Repair Actions (RAs), although still meeting target, increased slightly. Through timely, extensive root cause analysis (item 5.2.d.,e.) and feedback, we corrected the problem and took steps to prevent these problems in the future. Our analysis identified that the increase in RAs was caused by insufficient installation planning associated

285

with the AS/400 introduction, not hardware failures. Immediate corrective action was taken to enhance the effectiveness of our field support team, including improving installation planning guidelines and training. To prevent recurring RAs on future products, we simplified the installation process and improved the system environment. For example, we reduced the number of steps in our software installation process by 74%, and the time to install software by 50%. In addition, we enhanced the AS/400 system to increase its immunity to external electrical disruptions. In 1989, RAs continued on a positive trend.

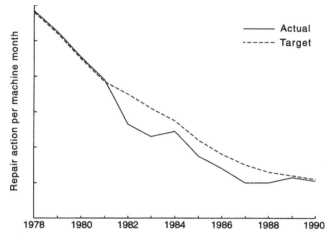

Figure 6-2. Trends in Repair Actions. System 3X and AS/400 System Hardware and Software.

6.1.a. Trends in Hardware Reliability: We achieve superior reliability by selecting the latest advanced technology, preventing defects early in design and manufacturing, and performing dynamic stress tests of our systems and hard disk products. We design for manufacturability and reliability. As a result, our 1989 hard disk products have 60% fewer parts than their predecessors—contributing to dramatic improvement in the Mean Time to Failure (MTTF).

Figure 6-3 depicts improved reliability trends for large systems and small midrange hard disk subsystems.

6.1.a. Trends in Software Reliability: Total system reliability is a combination of software and hardware. Software reliability is internally measured as the number of defects per Million Lines Of Code (MLOC). Improved processes, tools (such as IDSS, item 2.1.c.), and software quality modelling (fig. 5-4) have steadily improved the quality of our output. Defects per MLOC have decreased at a compound rate of 15% from 1981 to 1989. Our target for 1990 is a 37% reduction over 1989 levels.

In 1988, we added a measurement process to focus on a customer view of software quality. We now measure the average number of times a user requests IBM assistance per month of operation. Improvements in this measure are illustrated in figure 6-4. Software installation improvements implemented throughout 1989 drastically decreased the number of problems users experienced (fig. 6-7).

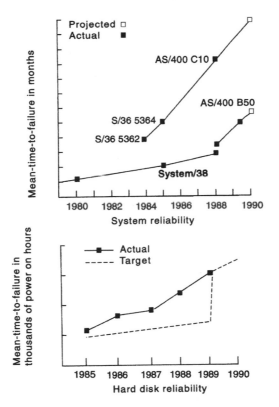

Figure 6-3.   Improved Hardware Reliability from Product to Product.

6.1.a. *Trends in Service Price:* Warranty and service objectives are integrated into our development quality process (item 5.1.c.(2)). Higher reliability in hardware and software means reduced maintenance prices for our customers.

Figure 6-5 clearly demonstrates our product-to-product improvement in service price.

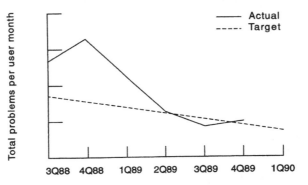

Figure 6-4.   AS/400 System Software Quality. Customer requests for assistance.

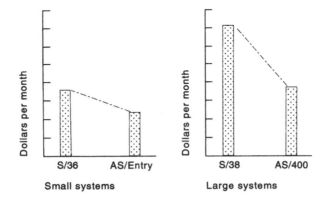

Figure 6-5. Average Service Price for Small and Large Midrange Systems.

6.1.a. Trends in System and Hard Disk Performance: System performance is a quality indicator. We design superior performance into our systems by selecting advanced electrical component technology and pioneering new techniques in system software architecture. Our key performance measure is response time, the time from a user-initiated input to a response from the system. Studies have identified that customers improve their productivity significantly when using systems with subsecond (less than one second) response time. Our performance evaluation tool correlates response time, transaction rate, and number of active users to a standard interactive workload. We exceeded system response time targets and achieved subsecond performance for our customers.

The hard disk subsystem is critical to overall system performance. Through our many advancements in hard disk technology, we are able to compress higher data storage capacity into a smaller physical package, thus enabling improvements in performance. The industry measure for disk performance is the time it takes to read a 10,000 byte block of data (access time).

6.1.a. Trends in Price/Performance: Our customers want increasing levels of performance, function, and reliability at a competitive price.

6.1.a. Trends in Cost of Ownership: Cost of ownership is defined as the price customers pay for software, hardware, documentation, and maintenance. Our quality initiatives focus on improvements in service price and price for performance, so that our customers benefit from a reduced cost of ownership.

6.1.a. Trends in Delivery Time: As a result of our initiative to improve our responsiveness to customers, we have reduced the time from customer order to system installation by 12 weeks, from 3.5 months to two weeks (fig. 6-6). Two key process improvements are:

- Using the capabilities of our Manufacturing Control System (item 5.2.a., MCS), we have achieved, for the past three years, over 99% on-time delivery to our customers.
- The Total System Package (TSP) program consolidates all hardware, integrates documentation, and preloads software into a single package at the factory. TSP

greatly improves the ease of installation at the customer's site and accounts for 15 days of our 12 week reduction in delivery time.

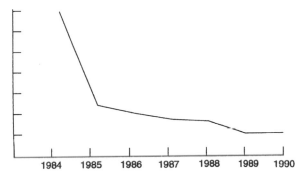

Figure 6-6.   Delivery Time.

6.1.a. Trends in User Documentation: The quality factors in documentation are ease of use, retrievability, readability, and technical accuracy. These factors are indicators of our customers' satisfaction with our system. We assure the quality of our documentation through a four step internal review process. Documentation accuracy, as measured by readers' comments, has improved 100% since the time the AS/400 system was introduced to 1989. During the same time, the total output, documenting new system functions, has increased by 38%.

6.1.a. Trends in After-Sale Service: We added new customer-oriented service standards in January 1988 that are key indicators of service quality and performance (item 7.3.a.). Improving trends in hardware and software calls are demonstrated in figure 6-7. Service calls are sometimes deferred by a customer's request or by mutual agreement. Service calls that have not been deferred are currently achieving a *Same-Day Fix* standard more than 86% of the time. The percentage of AS/400 hardware service requests meeting this standard improves steadily and has achieved or surpassed the levels of the S/3X family within a year of its availability.

A key strategy for improving AS/400 software service responsiveness is the implementation of our Electronic Customer Support (ECS) technology (item 2.2.c.). ECS is a service tool that is invaluable in reducing the time that a customer's system is down. As of March 1990, approximately 57% of AS/400 software service requests were made through ECS, and over 85% of those were resolved by ECS. Before we introduced ECS, the average time for a S/3X customer to get a corrective software fix was 24 hours. With ECS, this time has been reduced to 30 minutes.

We measure AS/400 service quality by the percentage of our customers who choose our maintenance agreement over competitors'. This has improved by 50% since the introduction of the AS/400 system (1988). Currently, we provide 90% of all maintenance contracts for the AS/400 system.

6.1.b. Overall Trends and Preventative Action: Key product and service measurements demonstrate no long-term adverse trends. This confirms that our quality management system is effective. Processes are continuously improving, and we are able to react quickly to correct short-term deviations as described in the discussion of field repair actions. The results of root cause analysis (items 5.2.d.,e.) of problems are fed back and process changes are made to prevent recurrence.

	3Q88	4Q88	2Q89	4Q89
Hardware				
Return Call to				
Customer Within 1 Hr				
S/3X	XX	XX	XX	XX
AS/400	XX	XX	XX	XX
Response Time to				
Site Within 2 Hrs				
S/3X	XX	XX	XX	XX
AS/400	XX	XX	XX	XX
Same-Day Fix				
S/3X	XX	XX	XX	XX
AS/400	XX	XX	XX	XX
Software				
First Contact Fix				
S/3X	XX	XX	XX	XX
AS/400	XX	XX	XX	XX

Figure 6-7.   *After-Sales Service Performance.* Percent meeting standard.

6.2. Comparison of Quality Results

6.2.a. Basis for Comparison: We analyze over 200 domestic, European, and Japanese competitors' products in detail. We estimate product development and manufacturing cycles and processes, failure rates, and performance. The composite best of breed is used to establish benchmarks (fig. 3-4) that set design, manufacturing, and procurement specifications at a level that ensures our products will achieve a global leadership position.

Our major independent sources of competitive information are DataPro consulting services, Info Corp consulting service, the Sierra Group, and approximately 40 industry publications that are routinely scanned and consolidated into a bimonthly newsletter. Competitive hardware disassembly and analysis (50 over the last five years) is a major source of information.

Our quality leadership vision is to be better than the best competitor and to continuously strive to exceed the composite Best-Of-Breed (best of breed) in every category that is critical to total customer satisfaction with our products and services.

The figures in this category reflect comparisons with worldwide and industry-leading competitors in our markets.

6.2.b.,c. Component Failure Rate Comparisons with World Leaders and Leadership Objectives: Our competitive analysis groups and the Component Quality Reliability Lab (CQRL) determine the failure rate trends of competitors based on analyses of the technology they use. Our 100,000-times logic circuit reliability improvement (fig. 6-8) is dramatic and places us in a world-leading position (our best-of-breed objective).

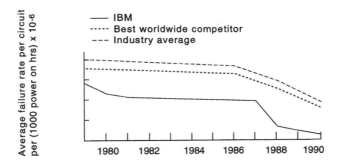

Figure 6-8. Component Reliability Trends.

6.2.b.,c. Hardware Reliability (MTTF) Comparisons with World Leaders and Leadership Objectives: Component reliability translates to product hardware reliability measured in MTTF. We have quadrupled the MTTF of our large systems, and more than doubled the MTTF of our small systems, keeping us well ahead of the best competitor in any year, as shown in figure 6-9.

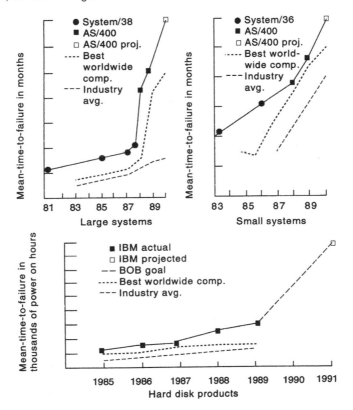

Figure 6-9. Reliability Trends.

Although the MTTF of our hard disk products was exceeding the industry average and the best competitor, the rapid rate of improvement by our competitors convinced us that additional action needed to be taken. We re-examined every key element of our business and defined critical success factors for a breakthrough product. Through integrating development and manufacturing teams, using advanced simulation techniques and simultaneous product and manufacturing process design, we introduced a new product in 1989 that surpassed current levels and set a new best-of-breed benchmark. Our design goals for our 1991 products ensure that we will continue this leadership (fig. 6-9).

6.2.b. Software Comparisons with Industry Leaders: As shown in figure 6-10, data from an independent survey of midrange system owners shows Rochester software quality leads the competition. We are the only major software developer that does not charge for maintenance.

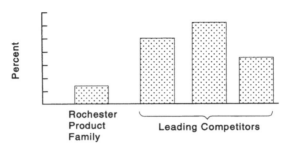

Figure 6-10. Percent of System Failures Caused by Software.

6.2.b. System Performance Comparisons with Industry Leaders: Using our performance evaluation tools, we set design goals to ensure that our systems consistently perform at a higher level than those of our competitors. AS/400 systems provide superior response times in a commercial environment (our target market) at equivalent transaction rate capacities versus competitive systems.

6.2.b.,c. Hard Disk Performance Comparisons with World Leaders and Leadership Objectives: In 1985, we lagged both the industry average and the best-of-breed goal. In 1989, our previously described breakthrough product (fig. 6-9) overtook the average access time in the industry and now sets the best-of-breed benchmark. Future products are being designed to maintain this status.

6.2.b.,c. Service Price Comparisons with Industry Leaders and Leadership Objectives: As a direct result of focusing early in the design process on making our AS/400 system easy to service (item 5.1.c.[2]), service price is another area where the AS/400 system sets the competitive best-of-breed benchmark. As shown in figure 6-11, the average monthly price of service is almost half of the industry average and is lower than all other leading competitors.

6.2.b.,c. Cost of Ownership Comparisons with Industry Leaders and Leadership Objectives: The Sierra Group, a highly respected industry consultant, publishes an annual survey that compares cost of ownership of competing systems. As shown in figure 6-12, our current product family is better than the industry average and all but one competitor. Since this survey was published, we have responded to this challenge in the

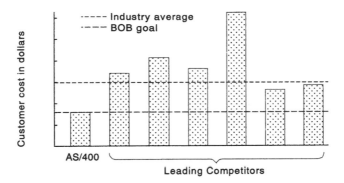

Figure 6-11. Average Monthly Service Price. Sierra Group compares AS/400 to leading competitors.

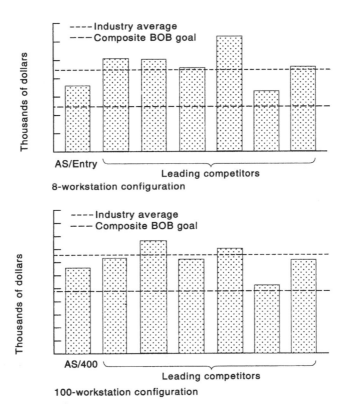

Figure 6-12. 5-Year Customer Cost of Ownership.

marketplace by introducing a new model with a 20% increase in performance at the same price, thus enhancing the system's value to our customers.

6.2.b. Documentation Comparisons with Industry Leaders: Independent consultant surveys are used to compare our documentation (item 5.5.) to that of competitors. The results of a 1990 study, which focused on online information, indicated that the AS/400 online information, in particular the index search help facility, ". . . has no equal." Ninety percent of the customers surveyed indicated that they would recommend the AS/400 online information system and they had ". . . outstanding praise for AS/400 online information."

6.2.b. After Sales Service Comparisons with Industry Leaders: We perform quarterly competitive assessments against both direct product competitors and third party service providers to ensure that our service standards (fig. 6-7) continue to meet our customers' needs and expectations. These assessments are conducted by an independent consultant and contain a yearly sample of over 2500 customers. The results of these assessments demonstrate that the AS/400 service quality (as measured by response time to the customer's site and first-time repair) exceed the average of our leading competition and is equal to our best competitor.

6.3. Business Process, Operational, and Support Service Quality Improvement

By continually assessing (fig. 5-9) our progress toward our leadership objectives, we improve all of our operational, business, and support service processes. We have over 300 processes, each with an identified owner who employs quality improvement techniques. Results are demonstrated by the examples in figure 5-10. Figure 6-13 identifies processes that are key to supplying superior products and services to our customers and driving our employee and business productivity.

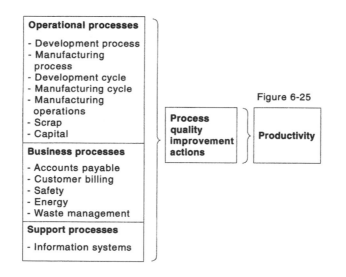

Figure 6-13.   Continuous Process Quality Improvement Drives Increased Productivity.

6.3.a.,b.,c. Trends in Key Operating Measures, Preventative Measures, and Industry Comparisons

6.3.a. *Manufacturing and Development Process:* As a part of our cycle time reduction initiative, we improved our process for designing and introducing new products (item 5.1.b.). The improvements have prevented defects from occurring and significantly shortened the time to achieve a fully operational system (fig. 6-14).

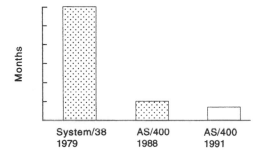

Figure 6-14.   *Results of Focus on Early Defect Prevention.* Time from initial build to full operation.

Controls are in place for all of our manufacturing processes (item 5.2.a.) ensuring they remain within the limits we set for them. First-time yields are tracked at each process step, and defect distribution charts for each element within the process are used for continued improvement.

Figure 6-15 illustrates two of our key process measures showing continued improvement over time (item 5.3.). Our goals are to reduce defect levels by 10x in 1991 and 100x in 1993 (over 1989 levels). By using high-quality processes for circuit cards and subassemblies, we prevent problems from occurring in system manufacturing. Fewer problems requiring card removal occur at system test, resulting in a dramatic 50% reduction in rework.

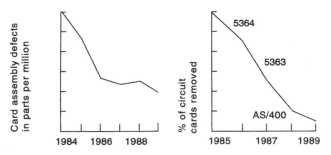

Figure 6-15.   *Defect Prevention.* Card assembly defects and system level card removals.

6.3.a.,c. *Development Cycle:* As a result of our development cycle analysis the cycle times for our full range product line are better than for our full range competitors. Competitors with *niche* (limited range) product lines generally have shorter development cycles. However, the XX-month development time for the AS/400 B10 and B20 systems (of comparable complexity to the systems in the niche market) equals or betters these competitors (fig. 6-16).

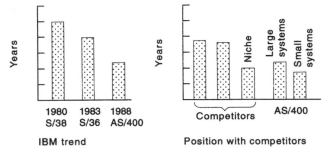

Figure 6-16. System Development Cycle Times. Comparisons to our previous products and our current competitors.

6.3.a. Manufacturing Cycle Time: We analyze each stage in our process to determine how to create a flow that minimizes bottlenecks and eliminates unnecessary steps. The total cycle time from supplier part order to customer installation has been reduced by 67% from 1984 to 1989. Figure 6-17 shows trends in system build times for Rochester products, a 78% improvement since 1986.

6.3.a.,b. Manufacturing Operations: Early involvement in design, a customer-driven *pull* system, and just-in-time delivery techniques with our suppliers have resulted in improved quality and efficiency of our processes (fig. 6-17). As an example, the number of square feet required to produce a system has decreased by 88% from 1986 to 1990.

System Year	S/38 1986	S/36 1986	AS/400 1989	1990 Proj
Inventory turnover	X.X	X.X	X.X	X.X
Card build, test (days)	XX.X	XX.X	X.X	X.X
System build, test, pack & ship (days)	X.X	X.X	X.X	X.X
Assemble time (hrs.)	XX.X	X.X	X.X	X.X
Systems per day (capacity)	XX.X	XX.X	XXX.X	XXX.X
Sq ft per system	XXXX.X	XXX.X	XXX.X	XXX.X

Figure 6-17. Manufacturing Operation Measures. Trends from S/3X to AS/400.

During 1989, we intentionally held high levels of component inventory throughout the year to ensure immediate product availability for projected increases in customer demand. In 1990, we reassessed our methodology for demand forecasting and implemented a more balanced supply-vs-demand process. Year to date, 1990, the inventory turnover rate is eight times.

6.3.a. Cost of Scrap: Our high quality manufacturing processes (fig. 6-15) not only reduce rework but result in lower scrap costs. Total cost of scrap as a percentage of output decreased by 20% from 1986 to 1989, during the introduction of the AS/400 system in 1988 and its new releases in 1989.

6.3.a. Capital Expenditures: We focus on investment to support our leading-edge technologies, and future product plans, and improving the efficiency and quality of our manufacturing processes. We concentrate on eliminating capital expenditures that no longer support this investment strategy. Over a five-year period, these actions reduced the site Net Book Value (NBV) by $XX million while production output grew XXX%. Furthermore, capital assets were reused wherever possible, saving $13 million in the past two years alone.

6.3.a. Trends in Support Services

6.3.a. Information Systems: Rochester employees use the Information Processing (IP) computing systems for a multitude of tasks (fig. 2-2). The availability of those systems (up and ready for sign-on and activity) during normal working hours is a key factor in increasing the productivity and the quality of our work. In 1983, system availability was at 97.3%.

Since 1985, we have maintained an availability rate of 99.6%, or better, while continuing to add systems, function, and work stations. We are the best in IBM.

Item 6.1.a. states that response times under one second increase customer productivity. Our internal measurement shows that response times have averaged 0.7 seconds or less from 1986 to 1989.

6.3.a.,b.,c. Trends in Business Processes, Preventive Action, and Industry and World Comparisons

6.3.a.,b. Accounts Payable: We continuously self-assessed and improved our accounts payable process. Figure 6-18 demonstrates that the percentage of early payment discounts lost and late referrals has declined substantially. We achieved our goal of zero defects in late referrals in 1989. The percentage of late payments has followed these trends with the exception of 1988 and 1989. During this time, the number of invoices we processed increased greatly due to a consolidation of missions from other sites and the resultant personnel changes, which required additional training. February 1990 late payments have beaten their target.

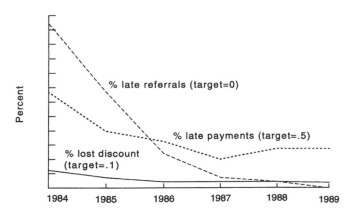

Figure 6-18. Accounts Payable Efficiencies.

6.3.a. Customer Billing: Our quality self assessment extends to the administration of our customer billing process. The quality indicators for this process are the accuracy of our bills (percent without repeat billing), time to collect, and the overall efficiency of the process. Since 1984, the time to collect our bills has decreased by 26%, while the overall cost of the process has been reduced by $XX.X million. During this time, we have maintained a monthly billing accuracy level greater than 90%.

6.3.a.,b.,c. Safety: Rochester consistently maintains an OSHA incident rate (fig. 6-19) that is a fraction of the industry average. We have received the Minnesota Safety Council's Award of Honor for the past 10 years.

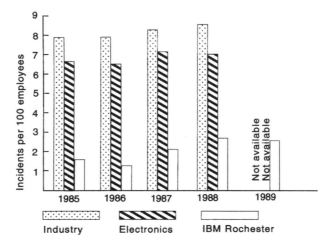

Figure 6-19.   OSHA Recordable Incident Rate.

During 1987, Rochester instituted an industry-leading process for classifying and recording all incidents, particularly focusing on ergonomics. In 1989, we established an Ergonomics Project Office that conducted manufacturing process reviews and employee training throughout the site. This resulted in an improvement in the 1989 results over 1988.

6.3.a. Energy: We deploy quality improvement measures to conserve our total energy usage. These efforts culminated in winning the 1989 Energy Saver's Award of Excellence from the Minnesota Department of Public Service. We were first in the industrial category and the overall statewide competition. Total energy use as a percentage of output has decreased dramatically over a period of time when energy unit costs have been rising (fig. 6-20).

6.3.a.,c. Waste Management: IBM Rochester will eliminate Chlorofluorocarbon (CFC) emission by year end 1993. These actions far exceed the requirements of the Montreal Protocol, an international agreement on CFCs (fig. 6-20). The Rochester site has twice received the Governor's Award for Excellence in Hazardous Waste Management and has a solid waste recycling rate of 60%, two times IBM corporate average and five times local industries. Savings from these recycling processes have increased by 15% since 1988 and were over $1.2 million in 1989.

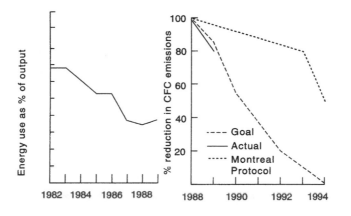

Figure 6-20.   Key Conservation Programs and Worldwide Environmental Program Comparisons.

6.3.a.,b.,c. Overall Productivity: The results of quality improvements in all our business, operational, and support service processes are measured by trends in the productivity of our employees (revenue per employee). Figure 6-21 shows revenue per employee compared to the best competitor each year and the industry average.

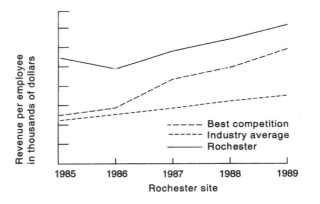

Figure 6-21.   Improvement in Key Productivity Measure—Revenue Per Employee.

6.4. Supplier Quality Improvement

6.4.a. Trends in Key Quality Indicators: As a result of our strategic supplier partnership initiative targeting defect prevention (item 3.3.c.), the defect rate of all incoming production parts has improved by 52% from 1987 to 1989 (fig. 6-22). We project another 40% improvement year-to-year in 1990. Our ultimate goal is to have zero defects. We have achieved these improvements by increasing our use of suppliers who provide us with defect-free parts and services. Almost 85% of our production dollars in 1990 will go to suppliers producing zero-defect output, up from 35% in 1987.

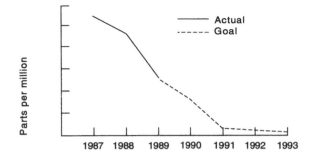

Figure 6-22.   Improvement in Defect Rate of Incoming Parts.

Our strategic partnership initiative includes extending the application of Continuous Flow Manufacturing (item 4.3.b., CFM) operating procedures to our suppliers' processes. In 1989, 37% of our production purchases were delivered via a CFM *pull* signal. This has increased to 50% and is projected to be 62% by year end 1990. This partnership initiative has reduced the average purchase part lead time by 50% since 1988.

Quality improvement is not limited to our production purchases, it extends to all suppliers of products and services. The quality of our nonproduction services is measured via internal user surveys. These surveys are performed on a wide variety of procured services, ranging from the travel agency to cafeteria to cleaning services. We achieved improvements in space utilization, inventory level and turnover by implementing CFM with our nonproduction suppliers of packaging materials as shown in figure 6-23.

Working with our software vendors, we have achieved significant improvements in the quality of their software. The actual defect rate for a key vendor has decreased by a factor of 50% over the past three years (fig. 6-23). Throughout the fourth quarter of 1989, this vendor achieved zero defects on software provided.

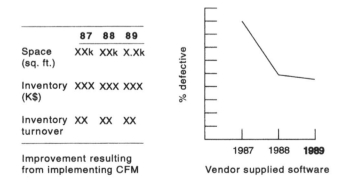

Figure 6-23.   Results of Quality Improvements with Nonproduction Suppliers.

6.4.b. *Trends in Improving Supplier Quality:* To improve our quality to our customers, we continue to *raise the bar* on the quality level of incoming parts. This bar has been set at 10x improvement by 1991 and 100x by 1993 from 1989 base (fig. 6-22).

Our strategy to improve supplier quality starts by establishing long-term relationships with fewer suppliers (fig. 5-12). We have reduced the number of production suppliers by 35% over the past five years. We involve our suppliers early in the design cycle to assist in defining efficient, high quality processes. This partnership produces designs that are correct the first time, thus preventing problems from surfacing late in the manufacturing cycle.

To help our suppliers meet our high quality standards, we provide training programs for their specific applications. From 1985 to 1989, we trained over 1000 supplier employees in CFM techniques, 300 suppliers in statistical process control, and 150 suppliers on Electronic Data Interchange. This training covers 100% of our key (critical parts) suppliers.

The results of these actions not only have improved the quality of our processes, but our suppliers' quality as well. The following table demonstrates the improvements realized from the implementation of a CFM process with one of our key AS/400 suppliers.

	Before	After	% Improvement
Supplier			
Workload	XX	XX	46%
Space (K sq ft)	XXX	XXX	43%
Inventory	$XXXXK	$XXXK	50%
IBM Rochester			
Inventory	$XXXK	$XXXK	66%
Lead time	X wks	X wk	80%

Figure 6-24.   Results of CFM Implementation.

Rochester experts work directly in our suppliers' locations, integrating experimental methods into our suppliers' capabilities raising them to the state of the art. One of our many examples is the following experience with a supplier of thin film media.

A durability problem occurred with a supplier's disk during qualification testing. Contaminants were appearing on the surface of the disk. Root cause analysis revealed that microscopic fractures caused particle alignment differences from our internally produced product. At a technical meeting with the supplier, we discovered that the process introduced too much heat. Testing was done at reduced temperatures, and the new disk exhibited no signs of fractures.

6.4.c. Trends in Rewarding Quality Suppliers: The IBM company has an annual supplier award that is presented to qualified suppliers. The criteria for receiving an award is three consecutive years of corporate-wide defect-free delivery. Awards are presented at the supplier's facility by our procurement team, so that supplier employees participate in the award ceremony. The benefits of, and incentives for, the award are that winners can display the certificate and gain publicity and be assured of continued consideration for new IBM business.

Between 1985 and 1989, 310 IBM awards were presented to a production supplier base that averaged XXX companies. In addition, 27 of our key suppliers have received a total of 88 quality awards from other companies over the past five years. These awards have been received from companies such as Ford Motor, Xerox, Digital Equipment, John Deere, Motorola, and Hughes Aircraft.

7. Customer Satisfaction

"How do you know if you have quality? How do you know if you have excellence? There is only one measure, and that is delighted customers."
—John Akers, IBM Chairman of the Board

7.1. Knowledge of Customer Requirements and Expectations

7.1.a. Defining the Marketplace: Our products are sold worldwide. Figure 7-1 illustrates the two major customer and potential customer groups we evaluate when segmenting our markets.

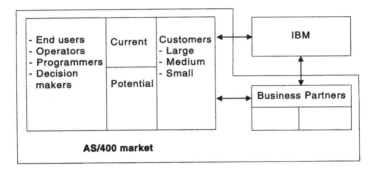

Figure 7-1. AS/400 Customer and Potential Customer Groups.

The first group consists of small, intermediate, and large business customers who have, or will purchase, products and services directly from us. The second group consists of current and potential business partners. These independent companies assist us in selling, installing, and maintaining our products. Business partners compliment our products with their own functions and services, having a major effect on customers' satisfaction with our product and services. Forty percent of our products are sold through them.

We begin our systematic segmentation process at a global level by identifying the criteria needed to achieve leadership in every major geographic area. The customer requirements, market opportunity, competition, and methods we use to sell and support our products vary by geographic region. To understand details of these differences, information from each successive segmentation step is analyzed to develop the criteria for the next level of segmentation until sufficient information is available to assess a market opportunity and identify requirements for success.

Figure 7-2 depicts our process for segmenting global markets and understanding customer and potential customer opportunity groups. From industry segmentation, we select our target markets. The requirements of the targeted groups are identified, evaluated, prioritized, and translated into product and service quality features. These prioritized features are validated by customers and then incorporated into the operating plan (item 3.1.a.).

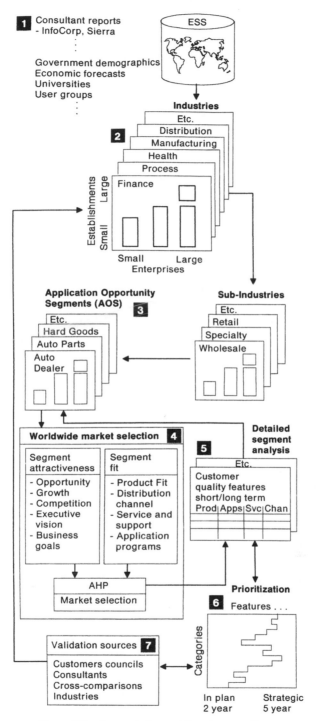

1 Consultant reports
- InfoCorp, Sierra
⋮

Government demographics
Economic forecasts
Universities
User groups
⋮

ESS

Industries
Etc.
Distribution
Manufacturing
Health
Process
2 Finance

Establishments
Small — Large

Small   Large
Enterprises

**Application Opportunity
Segments (AOS)** **3**
Etc.
Hard Goods
Auto Parts
Auto
Dealer

Sub-Industries
Etc.
Retail
Specialty
Wholesale

Worldwide market selection **4**

Segment attractiveness	Segment fit
- Opportunity - Growth - Competition - Executive vision - Business goals	- Product Fit - Distribution channel - Service and support - Application programs

AHP
Market selection

5   **Detailed segment analysis**
Etc.
Customer
quality features
short/long term
Prod|Apps|Svc|Chan

Prioritization
6 Features . . .

Validation sources **7**

Customers councils
Consultants
Cross-comparisons
Industries

Categories

In plan   Strategic
2 year   5 year

Figure 7-2.   Segmentation and Requirements Process.

In step **1** , our market segmentation team segments worldwide geographies. The criteria for this segmentation are economic stability, growth, political environment of nations, cultural similarities, population demographics, and our current product support structure. The team groups continents and countries together by cultural and political similarities. Using government demographic information, economic forecasts, and information from our worldwide operations, we assess the feasibility of success in specific geographic areas. From this geographic segmentation, we select markets for industry segmentation. Our Executive Support System (item 2.2.d., ESS) contains monthly IBM and independent industry data and provides information for segmentation and decision support.

In steps **2** and **3** , our market research team further segments selected geographic markets into industry, sub-industry, and Application Opportunity Segments (AOSs). These steps identify the industry segment opportunity for data processing solutions and identify our customers' and potential customers' requirements.

We base our industry segmentation steps on the employee size of companies; industry growth projections; local, regional, national, and multinational makeup; major industrial classifications, such as manufacturing; and our current position versus our competitors. Analyzing industry and government information, we identify the number of industries and the number and growth rate of small, intermediate, and large businesses within them. Applying Pareto techniques to this data, the 180 AOSs are prioritized by revenue opportunity, market share, and profit potential. With industry consultants, academic experts, and our own market planners, we conduct in-depth studies of selected high-opportunity, high-growth industry segments to assess our strengths and weaknesses in meeting specific customer requirements.

Through surveys, interviews, literature searches, and attendance at industry-specific conferences, we collect requirements needed to achieve success in an industry segment. In 14 studies done in the last five months of 1989, in-depth interviews were conducted with 3054 customers and competitors' customers, 327 business partners, and 54 business partners of our competitors. We evaluate our product placements, gains and losses, and competitive product placements to assess the market penetration and requirements to achieve new opportunities. Each year, we use the results of over 40 similar studies to identify customer and potential customer requirements at the industry AOS level.

Our business partners and those of competitors are experts in industry AOSs. We evaluate their requirements closely as they are a major influence to success in these segmentations.

The purpose of step **4** is to prioritize industry AOSs for customer product and service feature segmentation. We weigh the relative importance of each segment's attractiveness against how well our product and service plans fit customer requirements. Using a decision support tool called Analytical Hierarchical Process (AHP), we mathematically assess the strength of one option over the others.

7.1.b. Identifying Product and Service Quality Features: Having selected the customer segments that represent the most viable, achievable business opportunities, our approach **5** is to analyze and identify specific product and service quality features in detail. The criteria used for this level of segmentation are the type of user (end user, operator, programmer), new business, competitive business, industry leaders, emerging technology, and competitive offerings. To collect information, we conduct surveys, workshops, and interviews and host customer councils. We train our technical people in market planning and analysis techniques. Consultants, academic experts, and our own integrated teams develop specific objectives, study tools, and methodologies for understanding customer needs and benefits. We group the needs into four categories that we call our critical success factors: products, software applications, service and support, and marketing channels. We studied 10 specific customer segments in the last 18 months to collect product and service quality feature needs. We interviewed 737 end users and 281 business partners—ours and competitors. We also place special focus on the needs of industry leaders. They are innovative, push current offerings to their limits, and most accurately project strategic product and service quality features.

In step **6** , the product and service quality features, expressed in customer terms, are translated into more product-specific items. For example, a customer definition of a product or service quality feature might be "better communications," which would be translated into categories such as Communications and Connectivity with functions such as Ethernet, Local Area Network, etc. Teams who understand both the customer environment and product-specific technology perform the translation and build a matrix of categories and features.

We rank features by their relative importance through applying Pareto techniques to survey and interview feedback data that specifically probe customer group preferences. We estimate resources required to produce key features. The prioritized matrix is weighed against the affordable investment required to achieve our quality and business goals. This results in a plan that identifies current (In Plan) and strategic product and service quality features.

*7.1.c. **Cross-Comparisons with Other Key Data and Information:*** The purposes of our cross-comparisons are to:

- Validate the accuracy of our prioritization process
- Gain additional detail on key quality features
- Keep aware of current customer satisfaction, as well as market and competitive dynamics that are relevant to current or new product and service quality features

Our approach **7** is to continuously collect data from customer satisfaction surveys, consultant reports, complaints, gain and loss reports, and feedback from customer councils. Quality features, needs, issues, or opportunities are grouped and prioritized by the number of times the feature was identified, the level of dissatisfaction, or survey preference indicators. Based on this prioritized data, product planners develop justifications to change the current plan. A cross-functional plan steering committee approves or rejects this input. If approved, the plan is changed immediately. If rejected, the quality feature is given future consideration in the next plan prioritization cycle.

As a result of cross-comparisons, within 160 categories and functions in our 1989 plan, we lowered the priority of 16 items and added 19 new product and service quality features.

Internal Dissatisfaction Indicators: Data on product and service feature requirements from the complaint management process and Customer Partnership Calls is analyzed monthly by product planners. This data is compared to the current plan to determine adjustments to the plan (item 7.7.b.).

Surveys: We survey hundreds of customers quarterly. Key satisfaction indicators are translated into product and service features and input is given to the prioritization process two times each year.

Independent Reports: Consultants, such as the Sierra Group, report satisfaction and rank feature needs by major competitor. Using this data, we are able to objectively evaluate customer expectations for new features and see how our competitors' customers evaluate their product needs and shortcomings. The Computer Intelligence Corporation publishes gain/loss comparisons (fig. 7-31). We use this data to cross-compare our performance in specific industry segments.

7.1.d. *Process Evaluation and Improvements:* To continually improve our ability to satisfy our customers' requirements, we analyze our overall process (fig. 7-2) for effectiveness, efficiency, and adaptability. Measures of customer satisfaction, business results, amount of change, amount of resources required, and ease of making improvements are used to evaluate our process. Our approach to evaluating and improving the segmentation and requirements process is to:

- Evaluate other companies' segmentation methods and consultants' studies
- Set benchmarks
- Identify areas for improvement
- Set goals
- Establish improvement plans
- Implement improvements
- Measure results
- Document the process improvements

We set benchmarks by comparing our process with other IBM sites, our competitors, and other businesses. This establishes an objective reference to judge the overall effectiveness and efficiency of our process. Comparisons to the benchmarks highlight areas for improvement such as new data sources, segmentation methods, etc. The process owner sets improvement goals such as use of new data sources, better tools and methods, education, etc.

To establish improvement plans to achieve the goals, we work with university experts in market planning to evaluate the latest academic concepts. New planning tools, segmentation techniques, and cross-comparison sources of data are implemented as a result of this industry and academic partnership. Education and training, both on-the-job and academic, is provided to all product and market planners. When improvements are implemented, all changes are communicated to the areas involved and are documented by the process owner.

Changes are tracked to ensure successful implementation. IBM Corporate audits are done on a periodic basis to assess the control and effectiveness of the process.

Recent improvements to the process include:

- Resegmenting across industry segments with what we call "end-user compute scenarios." A newly formed team called The Solution Managers analyzes how computers are being applied by customer groups across industry AOSs.
- Using new global information sources, such as Computer Intelligence Corp., and

adding new computerized tools, such as System User Analysis (SUA), to improve requirements gathering

- Customer councils organized for feature-specific improvements. Councils held in the first quarter of 1990 focused on product and service quality requirements.

To share our segmentation and requirements process across the corporation, we televised a week-long workshop to all IBM locations. At the request of Wharton School of Business, IBM Rochester presented our process at the XVI International Research Seminar in Marketing sponsored by the American Marketing Association and the Foundation Nationale Pour L'Enseignement de la Gestation Des Enterprises (France) where we received accolades from the academic community for our practical implementation of a leading-edge process.

7.2. Customer Relationship Management

One of IBM's basic beliefs is "Provide the best possible customer service." Our customer focus studies have determined that our customers' key service and support requirements are responsiveness, ease of doing business, technical ability, and knowledge of their business.

7.2.a. Process for Understanding and Responding to Customer Service Requirements: Excellent service is the foundation of our customer relationship. Detailed surveys, on-site interviews with customers, and recommendations of lab consultants (experienced Systems Engineers [SEs] dealing with customer support requests) identify key customer service needs. We correlate these needs with the segmentation results in the planning process (item 7.1.) to establish accurate requirements for product and service improvements. Our Comprehensive Product Plan (fig. 5-2, CPP) ensures that the service requirements are understood and responded to throughout the company. The CPP contains a development plan, in which we describe and commit to the development and verification of new service features. The CPP also contains the market and service support plan, which describes how Marketing and Service will support the product in the field using the new service features. To ensure the market and service support team understands the customer relationship requirements, we disseminate support requirements through our Field Television Network (FTN) to all customer contact employees. We verify the service characteristics of our products internally through our service verification test and externally through our Early Support Program (ESP) with customer and service personnel (item 7.6.a.).

Every marketing and service representative is appraised and paid based on account satisfaction. Our customer satisfaction management process (item 7.6.) measures the final outcome of our service relationship through customer satisfaction survey feedback.

7.2.b. Ensuring Easy Access for Customers: Through our Customer Partnership Call Process (fig. 7-3), we take a proactive role in ensuring customer access to IBM. This provides easy access for customers to comment, seek assistance, and identify complaints. We are also continuing to expand our traditional survey methods of providing customer access.

Another enhancement that ensures easy access for customers seeking assistance is the question and answer databases available through our Electronic Customer Support (item 2.2.c. ECS). Through ECS, customers can access the Hands On Networking Environment (HONE) for the IBM Sales Manual and marketing information, and the Electronic Quick Answer Library (EQUAL) for quick and accurate responses to questions related to IBM, the AS/400 system, and selected products.

We assign a marketing representative, systems engineer, and customer engineer to each customer and are establishing programming support representatives. We support our field personnel with responsive administrators in each local branch office. The account manager is the customer advocate and is personally responsible for the satisfaction of all customers within a sales territory. This team represents IBM to the customer and is specifically trained and motivated to represent the customer to IBM. Customers anywhere in the world can get IBM hardware or software service anytime (24 hours a day, 365 days a year) by calling a toll-free number.

7.2.c. Following Up with Customers on Products and Services: Our feedback sources (fig. 7-9) include customer partnership calls. We call every AS/400 customer 90 days after installation and ask if they are satisfied. Partnership calls identify any customer concerns early and measure the effects of improvements. Timely information is key to continually improving our high level of customer satisfaction and maintains our leadership in the industry.

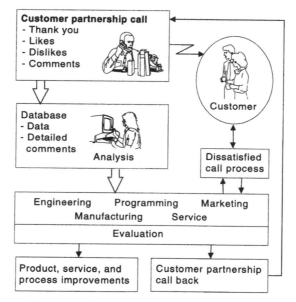

Figure 7-3. Process for Customer Partnership Calls.

If, during a call, our customer expresses any dissatisfaction with their IBM relationship, a series of follow-up actions are invoked to resolve their concerns and restore complete satisfaction (fig. 7-4). Thirty days after resolving a customer's concern, we call the customer again to confirm that they are satisfied. This additional follow-up ensures the customer has the final say.

7.2.d. Employee Empowerment: IBM Chairman John Akers stated that we want every product and service, every contact with our company, to be perfect in the eyes of our customers. Market-driven quality starts by making total customer satisfaction an obsession and empowering our people to use their creative energy to satisfy and delight their customers. We provide our employees the freedom of action to do everything necessary to satisfy our customers.

Key to employee empowerment is disseminating our quality vision (item 1.1.a.) and education program (item 4.3.). We train employees in technical, interpersonal, and problem-solving skills. We empower them by fostering a partnership with them using a participative management style. We work with our employees, solicit their views, coach them, and include them in the decision-making process. Total employee involvement has been an IBM tradition: one of IBM's demonstrated basic beliefs is respect for the individual.

Taking Extraordinary Measures: Our project office provides a critical situation management process that is devoted to resolving difficult technical problems in customer accounts. We deploy a team with the technical knowledge to support our marketing team in problem resolution. The Project Office has authorized replacement systems or *loaner* systems and even chartered air transportation to expedite system delivery in emergency situations.

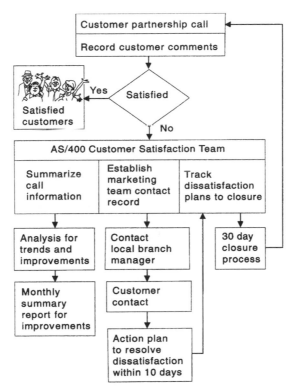

Figure 7-4. Process for Dissatisfied Customer Partnership Calls.

Dedicated IBM employees have stepped in after tornados, floods, fires, or other natural disasters affected our customers. The IBM employees not only helped our customers restore their businesses (item 7.4.b.), but also contributed to the community recovery effort.

7.2.e. Hiring, Training, and Recognizing Employees: Improving customer relationships and maintaining customer satisfaction are deeply ingrained in the training programs for our sales, service, and support personnel.

Hiring and Qualification: Interpersonal skills and behavioral characteristics are important factors evaluated in the hiring decision for all employees, but they are essential for our customer contact employees. After hiring, intensive qualification training programs ensure the employee has a complete understanding of how to work with customers. In addition to technical education, qualification training includes IBM basic beliefs and values, business practices and ethics, customer relationship management, market-driven principles, and communications skills.

Ongoing Training: Customer contact employees participate in a balanced ongoing training program that includes technical education and professional development. IBM Customer Engineers (CEs) average XX hours of technical and professional education each year. SEs and marketing representatives spend about XXX hours each year in education. Our Advanced Business Institute classes, taught by respected business school professors, instruct field personnel in the challenges facing customer executives, notably CEOs, CFOs, and MIS executives, in today's business environment.

Recognition: IBM Means Service awards are earned by CEs who have demonstrated leadership and achieved outstanding customer satisfaction ratings. Systems Engineers are selected to attend an SE symposium based on several criteria, including their customers' satisfaction. Customer solution bonuses are an incentive for marketing representatives to successfully solve specific business problems for customers. Branch managers have funds, which they can use to recognize customer satisfaction achievements.

Employee Morale: All IBM employees are encouraged to participate in the annual IBM employee opinion survey (item 4.2.b.). Executive interviews, Speak Up programs, and executive roundtables are also frequently used to solicit employee ideas and monitor morale. Special attention is paid to questions intended to measure employee opinions on our company, our practices, and our environment compared to other firms. Maintaining high morale of our field personnel is an important management responsibility. Team building, group functions, and other events are frequently used for this purpose.

7.2.f. Technology and Support: We have a comprehensive support system to provide service to our customers. Our support structure (fig. 7-5) provides an increasingly specialized hierarchy of technical experts to resolve problems.

Effective and Timely Customer Service: We maintain effective and timely customer service through our use of a worldwide information network and advanced technology.

Information Network: Our worldwide information network links all service personnel to development and manufacturing locations and to a central IBM database called Remote Technical Assistance Information Network (RETAIN). Service, support, marketing, and development personnel use RETAIN.

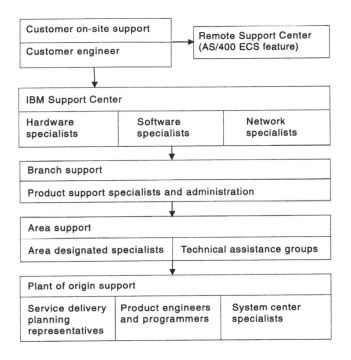

Figure 7-5. Service Support Structure.

Advanced Technology: Our service personnel are backed by the Advanced Technology Service Dispatch System. When a customer makes a hardware service call to 1-800-IBM-SERV, the call is automatically switched to one of twelve round-the-clock area communication centers. The CE receives all customer and call information on a portable service terminal, ensuring quick customer response.

An artificial intelligence tool is being tested in the Rochester and Chicago support centers to assist in software problem diagnosis and support. The tool will guide support representatives through a series of logical paths to a known solution or direct them to the software defect discovery process. Through the automatic diagnostic capability of ECS (item 2.2.c.), a problem can be detected, analyzed, and reported, and a CE dispatched for warranty service before the customer becomes aware of the problem.

7.2.g. Information Analysis: We collect and analyze data on all customer service characteristics. The reasons for customer dissatisfaction are as important to us as our knowledge of customer satisfaction. We collect and analyze information on gains and losses, and order and cancel volumes in addition to complaint data. If negative trends are discovered, we find the root cause and prevent its reoccurrence.

The analysis is reported to our Rochester Management Committee (RMC), Critical Success Factors Council, and LOB general manager (fig. 7-11) for consideration when evaluating the need for policy changes. Our Customer Satisfaction Management (CSM) team is responsible for measuring, evaluating, and communicating the results of a change in any customer relationship policy. Adjustments to policy implementation are made, evaluated, and reported as the new policy solidifies.

In the second quarter of 1989, our evaluation of business partner sales indicated that our business results targets were jeopardized in three areas:

- New business sales
- Business partner sales
- Business partner customer satisfaction

We then fully reviewed our business partner marketing channels and determined that additional education was needed. We put in place an education program to equip our business partners to better support the AS/400 system. In three months, we educated 1300 business-partner employees. Additionally, our general manager of market operations directed that a technical support plan be developed and reviewed for each business partner.

As a result we implemented the following policy and organizational changes:

- An assistant general manager position was created to increase focus on marketing to new and small businesses. All business partner sales operations were consolidated under this individual.
- A marketing executive was named in each of our 11 marketing areas to focus on new and small business.
- We increased from 17 to 40 the number of branch offices focusing specifically on new and small businesses.

In the second half of 1989, new business sales set records and business partner satisfaction improved.

7.2.h. Evaluating and Improving the Process: Our customer satisfaction management process (fig. 7-11) is established to measure and improve our services to customers. We use data from our feedback sources (fig. 7-9) to evaluate service characteristics. Our Customer Satisfaction Management Team is responsible for identifying areas for service improvement to both product and service management. Priorities for improvements are established during the product planning process based on customer satisfaction input. Improved services are checked via internal testing, if they are product related; or by the service delivery organization, if they are service related. Once implemented, products and services are tracked to ensure they are meeting customer expectations, closing the loop from customer input to customer satisfaction.

7.3. Customer Service Standards

7.3.a. Setting Customer Service Standards: Our high standards for customer contact employees are based on our strong ethical and professional guidelines. All employees receive training in these guidelines. Customer contact employees receive additional training in interpersonal relationships and professionalism.

Our customers' service requirements are the basis for our customer service standards. We develop our customer service standards by using information from:

- IBM and independent surveys
- Customer requirements and ongoing feedback
- Competitive benchmark comparisons
- Service councils involving IBM and our customers

Our products are critical to the successful operations of our customers' business and when problems occur, our response is governed by the following standards:

- Professionalism (courtesy, interpersonal skills)
- Responsiveness (time from call to on-site service)
- Ease of doing business
- Technical ability and coverage
- Knowledge of our customers' business

We measure these standards through surveys and other feedback sources.

7.3.b. Employee Involvement in Setting Standards: We use the experience of our customer contact personnel to improve our customer service standards. During our development cycle, experienced service personnel participate on teams (item 5.1.a.) that establish the required service standards relating to technical skills, coverage, and responsiveness. Employees also participate on the Service Delivery Council, which provides customer feedback on improving our service delivery. Service and development teams work together during the design, build, and test stages of product development to define and establish improvements to the service and quality features of our product offerings. These teams also participate in the Serviceability Verification Test (item 5.1.b., SVT) that verifies the effectiveness of our service procedures against the service standards.

Our customer contact personnel participate in improving our order delivery process (i.e., order configurator (item 2.1.c.)) and in improving our diagnostic capabilities (item 2.2.c., ECS). To ensure that required technical ability and coverage is provided to our customers, the market support plan and Service Cost Estimates (item 5.1.c.(2), SCE) for our products are developed using early service involvement input from our customer contact personnel.

7.3.c. Deployment of Standards: Effective deployment of our service standards is accomplished through two processes: product education and manager-employee performance planning and measurements (item 4.4.a.).

Education: Customer contact employees receive specific product training on the support standards, procedures, structures, and tools available to service our products. Customer satisfaction training is given to customer support employees, which helps provide effective support for our customer contact personnel. Our senior managers, through the Executive Assistance Program, have been trained to support customer contact personnel in customer questions, problems, and briefings.

Performance Planning and Measurements: At sessions held at least semiannually, the manager and support staff employees discuss and agree on the appropriate customer support standards. There is freedom to modify the standards based on new product requirements, responsiveness issues (i.e., travel time), improved tools, etc. The final criteria is formally documented in a performance plan and the employee is measured against that plan.

7.3.d. Tracking: Customer support standards are tracked and objectively measured by our marketing, service, and administration teams (fig. 7-6) to ensure these standards are maintained.

7.3.e. How Standards Are Evaluated and Improved: Our customer service standards are evaluated using key measurement data (fig. 7-6), customer feedback, surveys, customer contact employees, and consultants for trends and changes in customer requirements. The service standards are reviewed for effectiveness and *value* to customer satisfaction. The Service Delivery Council reviews our service leadership position derived from our customer service standards relative to benchmarks and our customers' expectations. Rochester management reviews field service activity and performance against established criteria generated in the SCE to identify and correct service problems.

Product improvements, technology advancements, and education are used to improve our customer service standards. Product enhancements improve the serviceability of our products. All product changes are analyzed, validated, and measured against established benchmarks to ensure service improvements. Responsiveness and ease of doing business is improved by using new technologies, such as cellular phones and the digital communications network. Enhanced education provides customer support personnel information required for timely and accurate service that aids in our responsiveness.

	Responsiveness	Ease of doing business	Technical ability	Knowledge of customer business	Professionalism
Service					
ORIGINS online information system	D		D		
Time analysis report	M		M		
Service delivery management system	M		M		
Service delivery monitor	D		D		
Quality account reviews				O	O
Customer appreciation program		O			
Administration					
Purchase billing quality		M			
Days sales outstanding	M				
Account visits				O	O
Sales					
Customer Executive opinion survey	Y	Y	Y	Y	Y
Quota attainment	M	M	M	M	
Mktg mgr contact	O	O	O	O	O

D = Daily   Y = Yearly   M = Monthly   On-going

Figure 7-6. Methods for Tracking Service Standards.

7.4. Commitment to Customers

7.4.a. Guarantees and Warranties: We stand behind our commitment to customer satisfaction.

Comprehensiveness: We provide warranty coverage on all our products "24 hours a day, 7 days a week." The hardware warranty for our machines is 12 months and covers installation, parts, and labor. Software maintenance is included in the basic license fee. Customers who buy licensed software are entitled to updated releases of the software for the life of that product at no additional charge. Our software license provides the most comprehensive support available and is rare in an industry where most competitors charge for software support and updates. Our hardware warranty periods and software support practices are shown in figure 7-7.

Comparative Warranty and Software Support Practices
Warranty in Months

Vendor	Pro-cessor	Magnetic Disk Storage	Software Defect Support	Software Release Updates
AS/400	12	12	Life of product*	Life of product*
DEC	12	12	12	Add'l charge
HP	3	3	Add'l charge	Add'l charge

*Within basic software license fee.
Source: Vendor-Published Information

Figure 7-7. Standard Warranty Period and Software Support in Months.

Conditions: To ensure consistent high-quality service, IBM conditions its warranty applicability upon certain reasonable and clearly defined customer responsibilities. The customer, for example, must maintain a suitable operating environment for the machine during the warranty period. The IBM software warranty is conditional on the customer's proper use of programs on designated machines and operating environments. IBM will, however, continue to service a customer's altered or improperly operated machine for a reasonable charge.

Understandability: To ensure a clear understanding of our product warranties and associated conditions, we write our warranties in crisp, concise, easy-to-read language. Software programs are used to validate that our language is understandable and simple. Teams review our contracts, including our warranties, for proper language. We use competitive benchmarks to ensure clarity and brevity.

Credibility: All problems that arise during the warranty period are corrected by skilled IBM CEs, who use the same standards that they would use for a customer with a maintenance agreement. Approximately XX% of our AS/400 customers maintain IBM as their hardware service provider after the warranty period expires. They expect and receive highly skilled, responsive service.

7.4.b. Other Commitments: We go above and beyond our guarantees and warranty commitments to support and satisfy our customers by:

- Preserving customer investments
- Providing timely, worldwide support
- Providing extraordinary response in disasters

Preserving Customer Investments: We make a significant effort to preserve customers' investments in current products. Our customers can use their existing terminals and some printers and hard disks on their new AS/400 system. To help preserve our customers' investments in software, we provide products that help System/36 and System/38 customers convert their software to the AS/400 system. Our Software Partner Lab helps customers and business partners in this software conversion.

Timely Worldwide Support: We support 27 national language versions on the AS/400 system. Development cycle process improvements have given us the ability to ship products in all translated languages simultaneously worldwide. This means that customers do not have to wait for translated versions of the product. We provide 24-hour worldwide support (item 7.2.b.).

Disaster Response: IBM has a long history of helping our customers when natural disaster strikes. When Hurricane Hugo destroyed a System/36 in South Carolina, the Rochester Project Office and the local marketing team shipped a reconditioned replacement system to the customer within a week even though that model was no longer in production.

7.4.c. Recent Improvements: Because of improved product and service quality, we extended our warranty period from 3 to 12 months. We reduced maintenance prices to our customers (fig. 6-5) through new service tools such as the portable terminal. Using ECS, we handle customer calls electronically. We enhanced the Total System Package by preloading software to make system delivery and installation faster, thus reducing CE and customer time (item 6.1.a., Trends in Delivery Time). Even though we added significant software function across our product line, we do not charge for software release upgrades and fixes. With enhanced terms and conditions, IBM is an easier company to do business with. Examples include total system lease, extended maintenance offering, and service offering improvements.

7.5. Complaint Resolution for Quality Improvement

We define a customer complaint to be any expression of dissatisfaction by a customer.

7.5.a. Aggregation and Use of Complaint Data: There are three avenues through which customer complaints arrive at IBM (fig. 7-8). They are:

- Direct to our area or branch offices **1**
- Formally to IBM headquarters and/or key line-of-business executives **2**
- Through customer feedback programs described in figure 7-9 **3**

We have established a Customer Satisfaction Management (CSM) team **4** to be the primary focal point for complaint activity. This team ensures that the aggregate information from all feedback programs and executive complaints **5** is put into the planning process and used to improve products and service quality features. Complaints are regarded as opportunities for quality improvement that fall into three categories:

- Business practices
- Service and support provided by customer contact employees
- Product capabilities

Data in each of these categories is presented to the appropriate management team along with the recommendations for improvement. 6

7.5.b. Ensuring Quick Response: We have empowered the branch office manager to do everything necessary to resolve a complaint to the satisfaction of the customer. Decisions on financial assistance, equipment replacement, or loans, etc. can be made by the branch manager. The branch office is in closest contact with the customer and has the complete backing of the service support structure (fig. 7-5). Through the branch office employees, complaints are handled expediently and all levels of management give complaint resolution top priority.

Complaints reported to the branch office 1 enter the resolution process directly. Complaints received through other avenues 2,3 are communicated to the branch office for prompt attention 5 .

Branch Office Complaint Management: 1 All complaints that come directly to our branch office are logged and tracked. The branch manager is responsible for resolving complaints and immediately assigns an investigator to contact the customer, analyze the problem, and take corrective action.

Corporate or LOB Executive Complaint Management: 2 Our Customer Relations department has processes in place for handling complaint letters to corporate executives and telephone calls to a toll-free number. Complaints are logged and assigned to a marketing manager for action. The Customer Relations department monitors and retains control over the investigation until it is resolved and then completes a close-out package on each complaint. Complaints are categorized by type, product, and geographic location. Resolutions are reviewed by the area complaint coordinator and the division president and reported back to the chairman's office. The CSM team reviews all of these complaints.

Feedback Program Complaint Management: 4 Our CSM team collects, analyzes, and acts on all adverse indicators from customer feedback programs. These proactive initiatives, such as Customer Partnership Calls and Customer Councils, provide easy access for customers to express their opinions openly on our product and service quality. Because of the broad scope and coverage of these programs, they are an invaluable source of information for product and service process improvements. 7 Direct communication access to the local account team and manager ensures fast and effective resolution for the customer. 5

Indication of Improved Response: The most important indicator of improved response is a customer's satisfaction with our response to a complaint. We call customers back 30 days after resolution of complaints received through the Customer Partnership Call process. The percent of dissatisfied customers has continually declined (fig. 7-16).

7.5.c. Analyzing Complaints: 6 Our process for analyzing and resolving complaints is also our customer satisfaction process (item 7.6.e.). The process has four phases de-

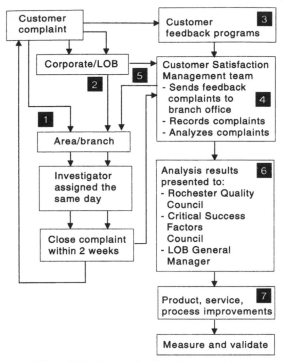

Figure 7-8.   Process for Handling Complaints.

signed to resolve dissatisfaction. In the first phase we aggregate complaint data with feedback from sources like the COMMON user group and Customer Advisor Councils. We analyze the data for trends and problem similarities and establish improvement actions based on the quantity of similar complaints. The analysis of this data identifies problems to the development, manufacturing, marketing, and service organizations.

In the next phase the problem owner clarifies the problem definition and root cause. This is followed by the corrective action and validation phases. The problem is resolved only after the CSM team confirms that the customer considers the problem corrected and all action to prevent further problems is completed.

7.5.d. *Improving the Complaint Handling Process:* The CSM team is responsible for identifying areas of process improvement in conjunction with our Corporate Customer Relations, Marketing, and Service Teams. Our internal benchmarks indicated IBM Japan and IBM Canada excelled in complaint and inquiry management. Their processes provided a prototype for creating and improving the process we use. Two pilot programs are being implemented in three marketing areas to improve our process for deployment across the country.

We have initiated a pilot program for an improved complaint management process. After successful pilot testing of the program in our Philadelphia marketing area (four states), we will deploy it to all marketing areas by year-end 1990. Complaints are electronically transmitted for collection and further analysis at the area level. The consolidated information and analysis is reviewed for action within the area and forwarded to other lines of business for action.

A complementary pilot program in our Chicago and New York City marketing areas will improve handling of customer inquiries. Customer relations centers will receive customer inquiries and immediately engage the appropriate expert, ensuring that customers get the information they need as quickly as possible. The centers will also be a resource for customer contact employees who cannot handle a customer's inquiry directly. Complaint calls will be entered in the complaint management process.

7.6. Customer Satisfaction Determination

7.6.a. Methods—Ensuring Their Objectivity and Validity: We measure customer satisfaction through:

- Early Support Programs (ESP)
- Customer Partnership Call Process
- Surveys: IBM, independent
- Feedback sources

Figure 7-9 summarizes the major types and frequency of customer satisfaction data.

Type	Frequency	Coverage
IBM surveys		
M&S cust sat	Annual	IBM & competition
Cust exec opinion	Qtrly	IBM product line
AS/400 cust sat	Qtrly	USA midrange
AS/400 mkt tracking	Qtrly	Last qtr AS/400 installs
Foreign marketplace	Annual	IBM product line
Independent surveys		
DataPro	Annual	USA midrange
Sierra Group	Spot/update	USA midrange
Yankee group	One time	USA midrange
Feedback Programs		
AS/400 customer partnership calls	90 days after install	USA AS/400
SE network	Ongoing	USA midrange
Complaints	Midrange	USA AS/400
Project Office	Ongoing	World midrange
Advisory Councils	Ongoing	World AS/400
Field measures	Monthly	World midrange
User groups (COMMON)	Biannual	World midrange
ECS	New prod.	World AS/400

Figure 7-9.   AS/400 Surveys and Feedback Programs.

Early Support Programs: This program enlists the aid of our customers prior to general availability and tests our process of delivering a system from manufacturing to installation to full use at our customer's site. ESP checks order entry, manufacturing, delivery, and installation as well as post-installation service and support. It does this by using all the procedures customers will use after products are made generally available. We collect data at each step in ESP.

Customer Partnership Call Process: We call customers 90 days after the system is installed to determine if they are satisfied with all aspects of our total business relationship (item 7.2.c.).

Surveys: We sponsor several ongoing surveys and monitor independent vendor and consultant surveys. These complementary surveys provide an objective perspective of how our customers feel about our products and services, as well as how satisfied they are compared to our competitors' customers.

The AS/400 Customer Satisfaction Survey addresses specific attributes such as quality, reliability, documentation, ease of use, service, and support. We analyze results to identify factors that contribute most to overall satisfaction and address areas for improvement.

To ensure the objectivity of our results, some of our surveys are blind surveys—the customer is unaware of who commissioned the survey. For all other surveys, we hire professional survey firms to remove potential process or question bias. We compare our internal results with those of industry-accepted surveys.

For statistical validity, a broad marketplace sample with a large population size is surveyed. Survey questionnaires have a design review and are pre-tested. The research firm then assists us with the survey design and tabulates the results. Our Statistical Competency Center provides consultation services to assist with CSM team analysis.

Feedback Sources: All our feedback sources are designed to reach out to our worldwide customers and actively solicit their opinions of our performance. Our product, business, and market planners and our executives are required to call on our customers to maintain an awareness of customer satisfaction levels.

One of our most important feedback sources is COMMON, an independent users' group. This group contains over 4000 worldwide members and meets twice a year. The fall 1989 meeting defined 788 resolutions (requests for product and service improvements) for the AS/400 system. Ninety percent of them are currently being evaluated for future development. Ninety-two resolutions are already being implemented and 103 have been accepted as future requirements.

7.6.b. Segmenting Satisfaction Data

Segmentation: We segment customer satisfaction data into the following categories:

- Geographic area
- Industry segments
- Application type
- Customer size
- Previous computer experience
- Channels (IBM and Business Partners)
- Competitive comparisons
- System (model and configuration)
- Operating environment

These categories are available instantly using the query capability of our customer satisfaction database files and ESS (item 2.2.d.).

We segment survey and customer partnership calls by industry or previous computer experience to determine if products or services targeted for specific industries or backgrounds are meeting our expectations. We also segment complaint data by system, reason, and geographic area to identify trends developing in a specific area of our products or services.

Competitors: With data from our Marketing and Service (M&S) customer satisfaction survey, we compare our customer satisfaction with our competitors' using the same indicators. We avoid analytical bias by applying the same analytical techniques against competitive data as we apply against our own. We also use independent surveys and ratings to compare our products to our competition and to validate our research.

7.6.c. Correlation of Satisfaction Results with Other Satisfaction Indicators: We correlate product satisfaction with the results of our ESP and pre-release testing. We survey early customers and test subjects using questions, topics, and response categories common to our post-release surveys and obtain any early view of the final satisfaction levels. By correlating test results with the final satisfaction levels, we establish the validity of our testing and use the test data to make decisions about the effectiveness of customer satisfaction enhancements.

We also correlate trends in complaint data to problem resolutions. For example, we provided our customers with performance and migration and conversion improvements during the second quarter of 1989. Figure 7-10 shows the resulting dramatic drop in complaints.

Complaint Issue	1Q89	2Q89	3Q89	4Q89	1Q90
Performance	X	X	X	X	X
Migration/conversion	XX	X	X	X	X

Figure 7-10. Complaints Concerning Performance, Migration, and Conversion Problems.

We also use correlations to validate complaints. We analyze data from several other sources, such as Customer Partnership Calls and surveys, to find other indicators of the same problem. Cross-correlation studies are used to correlate system performance to overall customer satisfaction. Our latest survey data shows that our recent performance improvement had a significant impact on customer satisfaction.

7.6.d. Extracting Customer Preference Satisfaction Data: We extract information from customer satisfaction data in the following ways:

Structuring Survey and Customer Partnership Call Questions: Initial results from customer satisfaction surveys and Customer Partnership Calls are gathered using consistent questions and tabulation techniques. We generate reports for product planning purposes and present these results to executive, product, and service managers and their staffs.

Cross-Correlating Survey Questions: We obtain more detailed information by running statistical cross-correlations between survey questions to determine if there are indicators of developing problems or trends. If so, we analyze them further and in more detail.

Analyzing Segments: We analyze the responses from each category (item 7.6.b.) to determine trends. Declining trends indicate rising customer preference for needed features. Our analysis helps us determine in what areas focus groups should be used.

7.6.e. Using Customer Satisfaction Information to Improve Quality: Our overall process for using customer satisfaction data to improve quality is shown in figure 7-11 and consists of four phases:

- Problem Identification **1**
  - Analyze feedback to identify problems, missing requirements, or opportunities
  - Substantiate with multiple source data
  - Understand the problem and customer impact
  - Initiate special studies
- Problem Ownership **2**
  - Clarify definition to ensure correct root cause analysis
  - Confirm ownership
  - Confirm action plan
  - Obtain short-term improvement or circumvention if required by customer
- Action Plan **3**
  - Ensure solution is *in plan*
  - Ship improvement to the field
- Validation **4**
  - Measure results with customers

Our CSM team is the focal point for customer satisfaction information feedback. It collects and analyzes data and substantiates issues. **5**

The team reviews these issues with the providers of information **6** and support organizations to verify and validate them. This is done to help prioritize issues presented to management and to our Quality and Critical Success Factors Councils for resolution.

Our Quality Council **7** is made up of senior functional managers who direct problem analysis and drive corrective actions.

Our Critical Success Factors Council **8** provides senior executive direction for process improvement, focusing on product, marketing, and service to ensure customer satisfaction leadership.

Quality indicators and results are reviewed monthly with our Line of Business General Manager (LOB GM) and the Rochester Management Committee (RMC). **9**

10 Worldwide requirements and customer feedback are translated into quality and product improvement activities through the process described in item 7.1.b.

7.6.f. Processes Used to Improve Customer Satisfaction Methods: Our process evaluation encompasses two basic paths: an external validity check of customer feedback accuracy and an internal analysis based on statistical techniques.

322

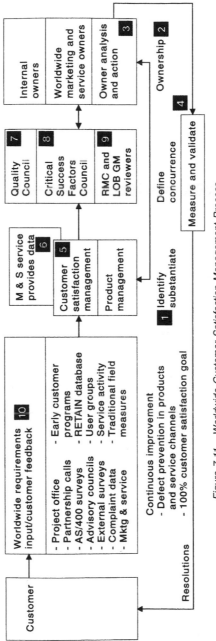

Figure 7-11. *Worldwide Customer Satisfaction Management Process.*

Evaluating by Checking External Validity: We evaluate our process by taking the results of our indirect customer feedback (surveys, etc.) and comparing them to the results of our direct customer feedback (complaints, advisory councils, etc.). A close comparison indicates that the satisfaction determination process accurately reflects the field satisfaction level. A lack of a comparison indicates the need for improving the customer satisfaction process.

Evaluating by Checking Internal Validity: We perform internal checks and reviews on our satisfaction process in the form of technical data analyses. We determine the relevancy of our survey questions by statistically correlating specific questions to our satisfaction index questions. The results of these correlations identify questions that do not contribute to our assessment of customer satisfaction.

Improving by Correlating Questions: The results of such analyses are used to eliminate less meaningful questions from our surveys. These questions are replaced with more direct questions regarding higher correlation satisfaction issues. Ongoing checks also provide input to our improvement process. The CSM team identifies problems and implements corrective measures. This ongoing analytical process allows us to address specific questions to potential issues, enabling us to proactively address dissatisfaction items.

The process reviews have enabled us to identify several areas within our process that have been improved. We enhanced our Customer Partnership Call process through such a review—branch offices may now more easily relay reasons customers expressed dissatisfaction during a call.

7.7. Customer Satisfaction Results

7.7.a. Customer Satisfaction Trends

Transition to the AS/400: System/3X products have consistently ranked at or near the top of internal and external customer satisfaction surveys. We are committed to build upon the standards established by our System/3X products. The immediate acceptance and success of the AS/400 system indicates that we were correct in our assessment of customer requirements. Early demands over-stressed our support structure, resulting in a dip in customer satisfaction. Recent internal surveys demonstrate that our customers' satisfaction has improved significantly, indicating that we solved our earlier problems (fig. 7-12). Recent independent surveys show that the AS/400 system already leads the competition. The AS/400 system is extending its customer satisfaction leadership tradition of the S/3X products and will continue to improve.

% Satisfied	S/3X				AS/400
	1986	1987	1988	1989	1989
Hardware	XX	XX	XX	XX	XX
Hardware service	XX	XX	XX	XX	XX
Software	XX	XX	XX	XX	XX
Partnership	XX	XX	XX	XX	XX
Technical support	XX	XX	XX	XX	XX
Sales representative	XX	XX	XX	XX	XX
Satisfaction Index	XX	XX	XX	XX	XX
Source: M&S Customer Satisfaction Survey					

Figure 7-12.   Customer Satisfaction Indicators.

Customer satisfaction indices and indicators are measured by our yearly M&S survey. Using this blind survey, we also survey customers of our competitors. It provides an impartial comparison of their customer satisfaction to ours.

Figure 7-13 demonstrates significant improvement in AS/400 customer satisfaction since publication of M&S survey results (fig. 7-12). The AS/400 Customer Satisfaction Survey provides us with timely trend data. The survey is designed and scheduled to measure the results of important product and service improvements. The most recent survey reflects the effects of system improvements in our October 1989 announcement.

The AS/400 Customer Satisfaction Survey is an IBM-identified survey and, as such, we often see a more critical response than in the M&S survey. The combination of the early AS/400 surveys and our other customer feedback programs led to product and service improvements that resulted in the increases shown.

AS/400 Customer Satisfaction Surveys (% satisfied)				Trend
	4/89	8/89	3/90	
Overall satisfaction	N/A	87	91	↑
Recommend system	90	91	95	↑
Sales	74	75	77	↑
Systems engineer	78	85	89	↑
Hardware quality	86	86	92	↑
Hardware service	93	88	93	−
Software quality	79	83	89	↑
Software service	68	62	79	−

Figure 7-13.   AS/400 Satisfaction Indicators.

Segmented results by previous computer experience and industry are shown in figures 7-14 and 7-15. We analyze user satisfaction by industry segment to refine our product to meet our customers' needs in target industries (item 7.1.b.). Segmenting by customer's previous computer experience identifies requirements to ease the migration of System/3X customers and to appeal to new customers and customers of our competitors. Feedback from the AS/400 Customer Satisfaction Survey and other sources revealed that former System/36 users were less satisfied than new customers or System/38 users. As a result, several product and service improvements were made to the AS/400 system and satisfaction of former System/36 users is improving.

Previous Computer Experience	Percent satisfied	
	8/89	3/90
S/34 S/36 Replace	XX	XX
S/38 Replace	XX	XX
Other IBM Replace	XX	XX
Competitive Replace	XX	XX
Additional	XX	XX
New	XX	XX
Source: AS/400 Customer Satisfaction Survey		

Figure 7-14.   AS/400 Customer Satisfaction by Computer Experience.

Industry Segment	4/89	8/89	3/90
Distribution	XX	XX	XX
Manufacturing	XX	XX	XX
Process	XX	XX	XX
State and Local Government	XX	XX	XX
Health	XX	XX	XXX
Finance	XX	XXX	XX

Source: AS/400 Customer Satisfaction Survey

Figure 7-15. Customer Recommendation Ratings by Industry Segment. When asked if they would recommend the AS/400 to peers, most users say yes!

Our customer partnership call process (item 7.2.c.) is a powerful tool to aggressively seek and improve our customer satisfaction. Figure 7-16 shows the trend of dissatisfied responses. Our dissatisfied customers receive follow-up attention from branch offices and they also receive a call back. We measure the effectiveness of this process to continue our quest for 100 percent customer satisfaction. The percentage of customers dissatisfied when we call back has significantly decreased (fig. 7-17).

As part of the customer partnership call process, we identify, categorize, analyze, and report indicators of dissatisfaction to product and service teams monthly for action. Major or frequently mentioned items receive immediate attention. Minor items are recorded by our product planning team and are used in the plan prioritization process (item 7.1.c.). Figure 7-16 shows the breakout of concerns identified through this process.

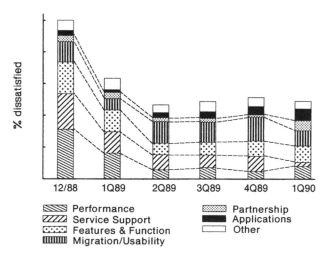

Figure 7-16. Customer Partnership Call Dissatisfaction. Reasons for dissatisfaction are categorized and Pareto analysis is used to identify improvement.

Examples of actions we have taken to correct problems include:

- Performance: Improved system performance planning tools and customer training sessions (performance invitationals) held in the first half of 1989
- Service & Support: Improved training and use of Electronic Customer Support during the first half of 1989

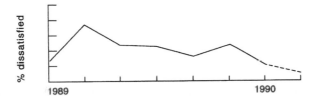

Figure 7-17.   Customer Partnership–Call Back Satisfaction. We improved the resolution process through closer linkages and follow-up with the account team.

Our service team also surveys to measure our customers' views of service. Recent survey results are shown in figure 7-18.

	2H88	**1H89**	**2H89**
Dispatch & arrival	X.X	X.X	X.X
Actual repair	X.X	X.X	X.X
Quality & value	X.X	X.X	X.X
Service relationships	X.X	X.X	X.X
Administration	X.X	X.X	X.X
Knowledge of Rep	X.X	X.X	X.X

Scale: 1=Very dissatisfied; 4=Very satisfied
Source: NSD Competitive Assessment

Figure 7-18.   Service Survey. Customers are consistently satisfied with S/3X and AS/400 service.

We focus on customer satisfaction worldwide—60 percent of our customers are outside the U.S. International project offices for each of the major geographic units, working with the Rochester Project Office, monitor customer satisfaction. Surveys and other information are provided to our CSM team.

7.7.b. Trends in Adverse Indicators: We track complaints, critical situations, and warranty costs.

Customer Complaints: Figure 7-19 shows our complaint trends. A favorable decline is shown over the last two years even though we added a new AS/400 product and discontinued the previous products. This indicates the positive acceptance of our current product and service quality features.

Critical Situation Management: Our project office is the focal point for resolving and tracking critical situations. The project office reviews all unresolved situations weekly. Critical situations that are open more than four weeks are reviewed by the ABS General Manager. New critical situations have been reduced (fig. 7-20) by our product and service im-

	Install	Number of Complaints					Complaints
	Base	S/32	S/34	S/36	S/38	AS/400	per Thousand
1987	XXX,XXX	X	XX	XXX	XX		X.XX
1988	XXX,XXX	X	X	XXX	XX	XX	.XX
1989	XXX,XXX	X	X	XXX	X	XXX	.XX
Source:	S/3X and AS/400 Complaint History						

Figure 7-19.   *S/3X and AS/400 Complaints.* We received very few complaints from our customers.

provements. The increased skills of our field personnel have given them the ability to provide improved customer assistance. Satisfying our customers' needs results in customer referrals and increased product sales.

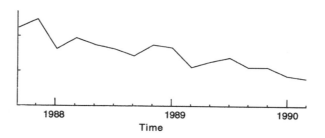

Figure 7-20.   *S/3X and AS/400 Critical Situations.*

Warranty Costs: Warranty costs as a percent of output (fig. 7-21) have stayed below 0.3% even though the warranty period was increased from 3 months to 12 months. This warranty improvement increased the attractiveness of our products and demonstrated to our customers our commitment to quality.

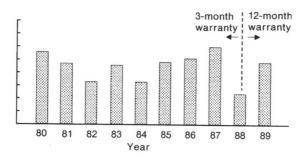

Figure 7-21.   *Warranty Costs as a Percent of Output.*

Replacement Systems: In 1989, we replaced XX of our more than XX,XXX AS/400 systems shipped. To date (1990), we have replaced three. System replacements exemplify our commitment to ensure customer satisfaction.

Sanctions: While Rochester's portion was less than X%, on December 29, 1989, IBM paid U.S. Customs $18.5 million to resolve underpaid *assists* on imports for 1983–1987. IBM fully cooperated in both the inquiry and determination of duties. We conducted a search and found no other sanctions under regulation or contract over the past three years.

Compliance with Regulations: Rochester products have an unblemished record of compliance with health, safety, and environmental regulations. All IBM Rochester products comply with FCC standards for Class A computing products as well as with UL, CSA, and IEC safety requirements. We measure our products to the most rigorous standards to ensure worldwide product compliance. For example, in anticipation of more restrictive compatibility requirements in some European countries, we shielded new circuit cards to ensure future compliance. Our ongoing audit programs ensure continued compliance with safety and environmental regulations. There have been no issues with the health, safety, or environmental effects of Rochester products. There has never been a group action by or on behalf of customers regarding our products.

7.8. Customer Satisfaction Comparison

7.8.a. Comparison to Competitors: We provide world-class products and services and compare ourselves to the *best-of-breed* competitors around the world by using internal and independent surveys.

The Marketing and Service Customer Satisfaction Survey measures satisfaction levels in the United States. Figure 7-22 shows the results of the 1989 survey.

S/3X customer satisfaction has been outstanding. AS/400 customer satisfaction is very good and has improved continuously in our AS/400 Customer Satisfaction Survey (fig. 7-29).

In fact, the most recent Sierra 5000 research (2/90) puts the AS/400 ahead of the competition in hardware service, software support, and system performance (fig. 7-23).

European Competitive Assessment: In Europe, our competitive assessments compare our customers' satisfaction to leading European competitors. Our product line, on average, has the highest customer satisfaction ratings (fig. 7-24).

Nikkei Computer Customer Satisfaction: In the competitive and quality-conscious Japanese market, AS/400 small systems occupy the first position and the AS/400 large systems occupy the third position in the Nikkei Computer Customer Satisfaction rating (fig. 7-25).

Hardware and Software Satisfaction Trends

			Percent Satisfied		
	1985	1986	1987	1988	1989
Hardware					
S/36	XX	XX	XX	XX	XX
Comp A	XX	XX	XX	XX	XX
Comp B	XX	XX	XX	XX	XXX
S/38	XX	XX	XX	XX	XX
Comp A	XX	XX	XX	XX	XX
Comp C	XX	XX	XX	XX	XX
AS/400					XX
Comp A					XX
Comp B					XX
Software					
S/36	XX	XX	XX	XX	XX
Comp A	XX	XX	XX	XX	XX
Comp B	XX	XX	XX	XX	XX
S/38	XX	XX	XX	XX	XX
Comp A	XX	XX	XX	XX	XX
Comp C	XX	XX	XX	XX	XX
AS/400					XX
Comp A					XX
Comp C					XX

Source: IBM M&S Customer Satisfaction Survey

Figure 7-22.   Satisfaction Trends Compared to Best-of-Breed Competition.

	AS/400 A	B	C	D	Avg.
Hardware service	9.2	8.0	8.0	8.2	7.6	8.2
Software support	7.6	5.9	6.7	6.6	6.1	6.6
System performance	8.8	8.2	7.5	7.4	7.2	7.7
Average	8.5	7.4	7.4	7.4	7.0	7.5

Scale: 10=Very satisfied; 1=Very dissatisfied
Source: Sierra Group

Figure 7-23.   1990 Sierra 5000 Research Results.

	Percent Satisfied					
	IBM	**A**	**B**	**C**	**D**	**Ind. Avg.**
Hardware	XX.X	XX.X	XX.X	XX.X	XX.X	XX
Hardware service	XX.X	XX.X	XX.X	XX.X	XX.X	XX
Software	XX.X	XX.X	XX.X	XX.X	XX.X	XX
Software service	XX.X	XX.X	XX.X	XX.X	XX.X	XX
Average	XX.X	XX.X	XX.X	XX.X	XX.X	XX

Source: 1989 IBM Europe Survey

Figure 7-24.   IBM Europe Competitive Survey Results—Assessment.

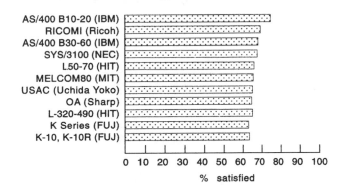

Figure 7-25.   Nikkei Computer Satisfaction Ratings. AS/400 satisfaction leads Japanese competitors in Japan.

Sierra Group and Nikkei Computer surveys put the AS/400 system in the lead of the customer satisfaction race. Our own research shows that AS/400 satisfaction continues to improve.

	Service Satisfaction			
	IBM	**A**	**B**	**C**
Dispatch & Arrival	X.X	X.X	X.X	X.X
Actual repair	X.X	X.X	X.X	X.X
Quality & Value	X.X	X.X	X.X	X.X
Service relationships	X.X	X.X	X.X	X.X
Administration	X.X	X.X	X.X	X.X
Knowledge of Rep	X.X	X.X	X.X	X.X

Scale: 1=Very dissatisfied; 4=Very satisfied
Source: Service Competitive Assessment

Figure 7-26.   Service Survey Results Compared to Competition.

Service Competitive Assessment: The service competitive assessment measures key service satisfaction features important to customers (fig. 7-26).

Rochester Hard Disk Drives: We commissioned a survey to measure our disk drives against our competitors'. Figure 7-27 demonstrates our leadership in this competitive market. We are the best-of-breed provider in low-end disk drives. The introduction of our 3.5″ 320MB disk drive was a breakthrough for us and the entire market.

	1988	1989
IBM	**X.X**	**X.X**
Comp A	X.X	X.X
Comp B	**X.X**	X.X
Comp C	X.X	X.X
Comp D	X.X	X.X
Comp E	X.X	N/A
Comp F	N/A	X.X
Comp G	N/A	X.X
Comp H	N/A	X.X
Scale: 1=Very satisfied, 5=Very dissatisfied		

Figure 7-27.   Hard Disk Satisfaction Survey Results.

7.8.b. Surveys and Other Recognition: Our System/3X products have consistently led the DataPro user satisfaction survey (fig. 7-28). The System/38 was top rated in overall satisfaction in 1986–1988. System/3X products were not rated in 1989. The DataPro survey is an industry-accepted survey published annually.

DataPro System Satisfaction Ratings for System/3X

	1985	1986	1987	1988
Overall satisfaction	4th	1st		
Operating system	7th	1st		
Compilers/assemblers	3rd	1st	2nd	1st
Ease of programming	6th	3rd	4th	1st
Reliability of system	2nd	1st	3rd	2nd
Ease of operation	7th			
Number of vendors rated (* tie)	16	14	18	11
Source: DataPro Survey				

Figure 7-28.   IBM Satisfaction Rating Comparison.

AS/400 customer satisfaction has improved significantly since the DataPro survey was conducted in 5/89. Recent software enhancements as a result of customer feedback (for example, installation and ease-of-use improvements) led to the improved satisfaction ratings. The average installed time for AS/400 users in the DataPro survey was only 4.5 months compared to competitive products with an average installed time that was three to six times longer. Our customers were still on a *learning curve* and adjusting to their AS/400 system when the survey was taken.

Figure 7-29 relates the timing of independent surveys to the improvements we measured using the AS/400 Customer Satisfaction Survey.

A survey of 20,000 Japanese engineers published in 1989 by Nihone Kogyo Shinbun, a Japanese industrial journal, rated the technology image of top enterprises in Japan. IBM ranked first in midrange systems in the areas of: total performance, hardware, software, originality, and innovative technology. Survey comments credited the favorable results to the AS/400 system. The 1989 Nikkei Computer Survey (fig. 7-25) supports the excellent worldwide acceptance of the AS/400 system.

The AS/400 system was selected as the preferred midrange departmental processor in a 1989 Yankee Group survey of four top industry markets—wholesale and retail, financial services, manufacturing, and government.

Sierra 5000 Research (2/90)

	AS/400	A	B	C	D
Hardware service	9.2	8.0	8.0	8.2	7.6
Software support	7.6	5.9	6.7	6.6	6.1
System performance	8.8	8.2	7.5	7.4	7.2
Average	8.5	7.4	7.4	7.4	7.0

Scale: 10 = Excellent   Competitors

1989 Datapro Survey (5/89)

Vendor	Overall satisfaction	Average install time (mo.)
HP	9.0	26.5
DEC	8.7	14.8
AS/400	8.4	4.5
Wang	8.4	18.5
NCR	8.2	23.0
Unisys	8.0	19.1

Scale: 10 = Excellent

Date of survey   4/89   8/89   3/90

AS/400 Customer Satisfaction Surveys (% satisfied)

				Trend
Overall satisfaction	XX	XX	XX	↑
Recommend system	XX	XX	XX	↑
Sales	XX	XX	XX	↑
Systems engineer	XX	XX	XX	↑
Hardware quality	XX	XX	XX	↑
Hardware service	XX	XX	XX	—
Software quality	XX	XX	XX	↑
Software service	XX	XX	XX	—

Figure 7-29. *AS/400 Customer Satisfaction.* Internal and independent surveys demonstrate rapidly improving AS/400 user satisfaction.

"IBM Goes to the Head of 3.5 Inch Class," said *Computer Systems News* in referring to our 3.5 inch hard disk file announcement in April 1989. InfoCorp, a Gartner Group industry research firm, said in a March 2, 1990, Update Report, "IBM is again leading the world in developing and commercializing innovative, high capacity disk drive technology. . . ."

IBM Rochester won the Best Site award in the 1989 IBM US Quality Award Competition. IBM's National Service Division recognized Rochester's Level-2 Software Support Group with their 1989 Award for Excellence.

7.8.c. Trends in Gaining and Losing Customers: The installed base of the combined System/3X and AS/400 system grew to over 400,000 in 1989 (fig. 7-30), with 60% outside the U.S. More than 100,000 AS/400 and AS/Entry systems have been installed in the last 18 months.

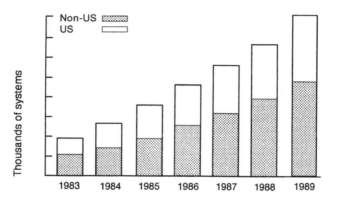

Figure 7-30.   Rochester Worldwide Installed Systems.

In a special study of marketplace participation, we analyzed an independent database of 94,000 computer installations. Our study showed (fig. 7-31) that:

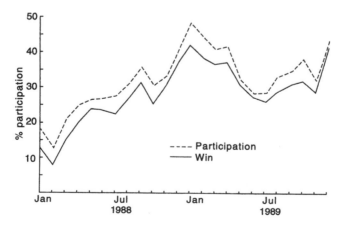

Figure 7-31.   AS/400 System Competitive Success. AS/400 system wins 85% of the time it is proposed.

- Eighty-five percent of the time we submit a bid, we win the business.
- Our frequency of submitting bids is increasing.

Our quarterly tracking survey shows where AS/400 systems are going and why. Figure 7-32 shows customer groups that are buying our computers compared to our original forecasts. The AS/400 system is doing very well in new and additional accounts and re-placing competitors' equipment (item 7.2.g.).

	1988	1989	4Q89	Forecast
Migrate	XX%	XX%	XX%	XX%
Competitive replace	X%	XX%	XX%	XX%
New/Additional	XX%	XX%	XX%	XX%
Enterprise end-user	XX%	XX%	XX%	XX%
Source: Market Tracking Survey				

Figure 7-32.   Installations by Customer Group.

The AS/400 system continues to be popular in the traditional System/3X markets. Figure 7-33 shows placement trends in several traditional System/3X industry segments.

	3/X Inventory	AS/400 System		
		1988	1989	4Q89
General & Public Sectors				
Health	X%	X%	X%	X%
State & Local Gov't	X%	X%	X%	X%
Computer related	X%	XX%	X%	XX%
Services				
Distribution	X%	X%	X%	X%
Finance	X%	X%	X%	X%
Industrial				
Manufacturing Process	XX%	XX%	XX%	XX%
Others (11)	XX%	XX%	XX%	XX%
Source: Market Tracking Survey				

Figure 7-33.   AS/400 Population by Industry Class.

The top three reasons given by customers (from our AS/400 tracking surveys) for select-ing the AS/400 system are application availability, software compatibility, and service and support. Each of these had been identified early in development of the AS/400 system as a critical success factor, and specific quality features and actions were put in place to en-sure success.

7.8.d. Trends in Market Share Gains and Losses: Dramatic reductions in cycle time from quality improvement initiatives have enabled us to deliver superior product functions and features at a rapid pace, giving us a competitive advantage. Improvements in product quality through new tools and technology and market-driven process improvements are directed to customer needs for quality product and service features, and customer satis-faction. These improvements have resulted in worldwide industry leading market share results as follows:

- We are the only one of six leading competitors to grow faster than the industry average in 1988 and 1989.
- Our revenue growth was more than double the industry growth rate in 1989, and double digit in each of the major geographic units.
- We gained one percent market share in each of the last two years.

Figure 7-34 shows our revenue growth compared to the industry average.

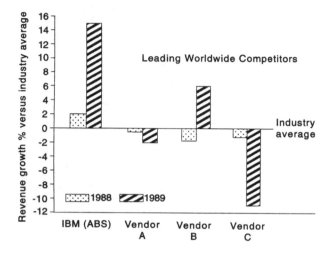

Figure 7-34. *Trends in Revenue Growth.* Our revenue growth has outpaced the competitors.

A March 1990 report published by Fuji-Keizai, a market research and consulting firm in Japan, stated ". . . growth of IBM Japan is noteworthy. Their outstanding growth is attributed to the introduction of a new line of System 38/36, called AS/400, which emphasized the expandability, in 1988. This company commands the highest growth rate" (fig. 7-35).

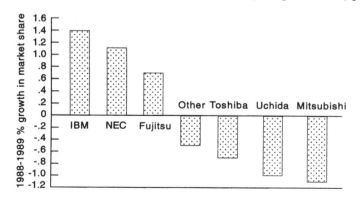

Figure 7-35. *Market Share in Japan.*

Delighted Customers

"How do you know if you have quality? How do you know if you have excellence? There is only one measure, and that is delighted customers. If the other fellow has more delighted customers than we do, we're not excellent. If the customer thinks our service is average, or if we get a 'C,' that's not excellent. Everybody who works in a laboratory or a manufacturing facility or a sales, service, or support organization should ask: 'How am I doing?' " . . . John F. Akers, interviewed in *THINK,* February 1989.

APPENDIX B

1991, 1992, and 1993 Criteria: Malcolm Baldrige National Quality Award

Each year since 1988, the criteria for the Malcolm Baldrige National Quality Award have been revised. In earlier chapters of this book, we included the criteria for the years 1988 through 1990. In this appendix, we are reprinting the Baldrige criteria for 1991, 1992, and 1993. For future versions of the criteria or to obtain an application for the Malcolm Baldrige National Quality Award, we encourage our readers to write or phone the National Institute of Standards and Technology at the following address:

Malcolm Baldrige National Quality Award
National Institute of Standards and Technology
Route 270 and Quince Orchard Road
Administration Building, Room A537
Gaithersburg, MD 20899
Telephone: (301) 975-2036
Telefax: (301) 948-3716

Individual copies of the award criteria and application forms and instructions are free of charge.

1991 EXAMINATION CATEGORIES/SUBCATEGORIES
Malcolm Baldrige National Quality Award

MAXIMUM
POINTS

1.0	**LEADERSHIP**		**100**
	1.1 Senior Executive Leadership	40	
	1.2 Quality Values	15	
	1.3 Management for Quality	25	
	1.4 Public Responsibility	20	

2.0	**INFORMATION AND ANALYSIS**		**70**
	2.1 Scope and Management of Quality Data and Information	20	
	2.2 Competitive Comparisons and Benchmarks	30	
	2.3 Analysis and Quality Data and Information	20	

3.0	**STRATEGIC QUALITY PLANNING**		**60**
	3.1 Strategic Quality Planning Process	35	
	3.2 Quality Goals and Plans	25	

4.0	**HUMAN RESOURCE UTILIZATION**		**150**
	4.1 Human Resource Management	20	
	4.2 Employee Involvement	40	
	4.3 Quality Education and Training	40	
	4.4 Employee Recognition and Performance Measurement	25	
	4.5 Employee Well-Being and Morale	25	

5.0	**QUALITY ASSURANCE OF PRODUCTS AND SERVICES**		**140**
	5.1 Design and Introduction of Quality Products and Services	35	
	5.2 Process Quality Control	20	
	5.3 Continuous Improvement of Processes	20	
	5.4 Quality Assessment	15	
	5.5 Documentation	10	
	5.6 Business Process and Support Service Quality	20	
	5.7 Supplier Quality	20	

6.0	**QUALITY RESULTS**		**180**
	6.1 Product and Service Quality Results	90	
	6.2 Business Process, Operational and Support Service Quality Results	50	
	6.3 Supplier Quality Results	40	

7.0 CUSTOMER SATISFACTION	300

7.1	Determining Customer Requirements and Expectations	30
7.2	Customer Relationship Management	50
7.3	Customer Service Standards	20
7.4	Commitment to Customers	15
7.5	Complaint Resolution for Quality Improvement	25
7.6	Determining Customer Satisfaction	20
7.7	Customer Satisfaction Results	70
7.8	Customer Satisfaction Comparison	70

TOTAL POINTS   **1000**

1992 EXAMINATION CATEGORIES/SUBCATEGORIES
Malcolm Baldrige National Quality Award

MAXIMUM
POINTS

1.0 LEADERSHIP	90

1.1	Senior Executive Leadership	45
1.2	Management for Quality	25
1.3	Public Responsibility	20

2.0 INFORMATION AND ANALYSIS	80

2.1	Scope and Management of Quality and Performance Data and Information	15
2.2	Competitive Comparisons and Benchmarks	25
2.3	Analysis and Uses of Company-Level Data	40

3.0 STRATEGIC QUALITY PLANNING	60

| 3.1 | Strategic Quality and Company Performance Planning Process | 35 |
| 3.2 | Quality and Performance Plans | 25 |

4.0 HUMAN RESOURCE DEVELOPMENT AND MANAGEMENT	150

4.1	Human Resource Management	20
4.2	Employee Involvement	40
4.3	Quality Education and Training	40
4.4	Employee Performance and Recognition	25
4.5	Employee Well-Being and Morale	25

5.0 MANAGEMENT OF PROCESS QUALITY	140

5.1	Design and Introduction of Quality Products and Services	40
5.2	Process Management—Product and Service Production and Delivery Processes	35
5.3	Process Management—Business Processes and Support Services	30
5.4	Supplier Quality	20
5.5	Quality Assessment	15

6.0 QUALITY AND OPERATIONAL RESULTS	180
6.1 Product and Service Quality Results	75
6.2 Company Operational Results	45
6.3 Business Process and Support Service Results	25
6.4 Supplier Quality Results	35

7.0 CUSTOMER FOCUS AND SATISFACTION	300
7.1 Customer Relationship Management	65
7.2 Commitment to Customers	15
7.3 Customer Satisfaction Determination	35
7.4 Customer Satisfaction Results	75
7.5 Customer Satisfaction Comparison	75
7.6 Future Requirements and Expectations of Customers	35

TOTAL POINTS 1000

1993 EXAMINATION CATEGORIES/SUBCATEGORIES
Malcolm Baldrige National Quality Award

MAXIMUM
POINTS

1.0 LEADERSHIP	95
1.1 Senior Executive Leadership	45
1.2 Management for Quality	25
1.3 Public Responsibility and Corporate Citizenship	25

2.0 INFORMATION AND ANALYSIS	75
2.1 Scope and Management of Quality and Performance Data and Information	15
2.2 Competitive Comparisons and Benchmarking	20
2.3 Analysis and Uses of Company-level Data	40

3.0 STRATEGIC QUALITY PLANNING	60
3.1 Strategic Quality and Company Performance Planning Process	35
3.2 Quality and Performance Plans	25

4.0 HUMAN RESOURCE DEVELOPMENT AND MANAGEMENT	150
4.1 Human Resource Planning and Management	20
4.2 Employee Involvement	40
4.3 Employee Education and Training	40
4.4 Employee Performance and Recognition	25
4.5 Employee Well-Being and Satisfaction	25

5.0	**MANAGEMENT OF PROCESS QUALITY**	**140**

5.1	Design and Introduction of Quality Products and Services	40
5.2	Process Management: Product and Service Production and Delivery Processes	35
5.3	Process Management: Business Processes and Support Services	30
5.4	Supplier Quality	20
5.5	Quality Assessment	15

6.0	**QUALITY AND OPERATIONAL RESULTS**	**180**

6.1	Product and Service Quality Results	70
6.2	Company Operational Results	50
6.3	Business Process and Support Service Results	25
6.4	Supplier Quality Results	35

7.0	**CUSTOMER FOCUS AND SATISFACTION**	**300**

7.1	Customer Expectations: Current and Future	35
7.2	Customer Relationship Management	65
7.3	Commitment to Customers	15
7.4	Customer Satisfaction Determination	30
7.5	Customer Satisfaction Results	85
7.6	Customer Satisfaction Comparison	70

TOTAL POINTS   **1000**

342

INDEX